Ethics in Real Estate

RESEARCH ISSUES IN REAL ESTATE

Sponsored by
The American Real Estate Society

Volume I

APPRAISAL, MARKET ANALYSIS, AND
PUBLIC POLICY IN REAL ESTATE
edited by
James R. DeLisle and J. Sa-Aadu

Volume II

ALTERNATIVE IDEAS IN
REAL ESTATE INVESTMENT
edited by
Arthur L. Schwartz, Jr. and
Stephen D. Kapplin

Volume III

MEGATRENDS IN RETAIL REAL ESTATE
edited by
John D. Benjamin

Volume IV

SENIORS HOUSING
edited by
Michael A. Anikeef and
Glenn R. Mueller

Volume V

ETHICS IN REAL ESTATE
edited by
Stephen E. Roulac

Ethics in Real Estate

edited by
Stephen E. Roulac

Kluwer Academic Publishers
Boston/Dordrecht/London

Distributors for North, Central, and South America:
Kluwer Academic Publishers
101 Philip Drive
Assinippi Park
Norwell, Massachusetts 02061, USA

Distributors for all other countries:
Kluwer Academic Publishers
Distribution Centre
Post Office Box 322
3300 AH Dordrecht, THE NETHERLANDS

Ethics in real estate / edited by Stephen E. Roulac.
    P. Cm. ~ (Research issues in real estate : v. 5)
    Includes bibliographical references and index.
    ISBN 0-7923-8228-5
    1. Real estate agents ~ Professional ethics. 2. Real estate business ~ Moral and ethical aspects. 3. Business ethics.
I. Roulac, Stephen E. II. Series.
HD1382.E88 1999
174'.933—dc21   99-12831
                                                            CIP

Printed on acid-free paper.

Printed in the United States of America

1998 AMERICAN REAL ESTATE SOCIETY

Officers

1998 President	Glenn R. Mueller, Legg Mason Wood Walker
President Elect	Karl L. Guntermann Arizona State University
Vice President and Program Chairman	G. Donald Jud University of North Carolina at Greensboro
Executive Director	James R. Webb* Cleveland State University
Secretary/Treasurer	Theron R. Nelson* University of North Dakota
Editor, JRER	G. Donald Jud University of North Carolina at Greensboro
Co-Editors, JREL	James B. Kau University of Georgia C. F. Sirmans University of Connecticut
Editor, JREPM	Willard McIntosh* Prudential Real Estate Investors
Editor, JREPE	Donald R. Epley* Washington State University
Editor, ARES Newsletter	Stephen A. Pyhrr, SynerMark Investments
Associate Executive Director	Roy T. Black Georgia State University
Ombudsperson	Larry E. Wofford* C&L Systems

Board of Directors

Michael A. Anikeeff (1998–00)
John Hopkins University
Jean Hutchinson (1998–02)
Appraisal Institute
James Carr (1997–01)
Fannie Mal Foundation
Deborah Jo Cunningham (1997–01)
Citicorp Real Estate
Geoffrey Dohrmann (1997–99)
Institutional Real Estate, Inc.
Terry V. Grissom (1997–00)
Georgia State University
Jacques Gordon (1997–00)
LaSalle Advisors
Steven D. Kapplin* (1996–98)
University of South Florida
Karen E. Lahey (1996–98)
University of Akron

Joseph Lipscomb (1996–98)
Texas Christian University
Christopher A. Manning (1997–99)
Loyola Marymount University
Willard McIntosh* (1998–02)
Prudential Real Estate Investors
Norman G. Miller (1997–00)
University of Cincinnati
Stephen E. Roulac* (1997–01)
The Roulac Group
Elaine M. Worzala (1998–00)
Colorado State University
Gordon Wyllie (1996–98)
NACORE International
John Williams (1997–99)
Morehouse College
Michael S. Young (1997–01)
The RREEF Funds

*Past President

1998 Fellows of the American Real Estate Society

Joseph D. Albert,
James Madison University
Michael A. Anikeeff,
Johns Hopkins University
Paul K. Asabere,
Temple University
John S. Baen,
University of North Texas
Stan Banton,
Banton Roach & Beasley
John D. Benjamin,
American University
Roy T. Black,
Georgia State University
Donald H. Bleich,
California State University at Northridge
Waldo L. Born,
Eastern Illinois University
Susanne E. Cannon,
DePaul University
James Carr,
FNMA Foundation
James R. Cooper,
Georgia State University
Glenn E. Crellin,
Washington State University
Deborah Jo Cunningham,
Citicorp Real Estate
John A. Dalkowski, III
Phoenix Real Estate Advisors
Charles G. Dannis,
Crosson Dannis, Inc.
James R. DeLisle,
ERE-Yarmouth
Gene Dilmore,
Realty Researchers
Mark G. Dotzour,
Texas A&M University
John T. Emery,
Louisiana Tech University
Donald R. Epley,
Washington State University
S. Michael Giliberto,
J. P. Morgan Investment Management
John L. Glascock,
University of Connecticut
Richard B. Gold,
Boston Financial Group
William C. Goolsby,
University of Arkansas at Little Rock
Jacques Gordon,
LaSalle Partners Limited
G. Hayden Green,
University of Alaska at Anchorage
D. Wylie Grieg,
The RREEF Funds

Terry V. Grissom,
Georgia State University
Karl L. Guntermann,
Arizona State University
Jun Han,
John Hancock Real Estate Investments Group
Richard L. Haney,
Texas A&M University
William G. Hardin III
Morehouse College
Chao-I Hsieh,
National Taipei University
William Hughes,
MIG Realty Advisors
Jerome R. Jakubovitz,
MAI
Linda L. Johnson,
Miller & Johnson
G. Donald Jud,
University of North Carolina at Greensboro
Steven D. Kapplin,
University of South Florida
George R. Karvel,
University of Saint Thomas
James B. Kau,
University of Georgia
William N. Kinnard, Jr.,
Real Estate Counseling Group of Connecticut
Karen E. Lahey,
University of Akron
Paul D. Lapides,
Kennesaw State University
Youguo Liang,
Prudential Real Estate Investors
Joseph B. Lipscomb,
Texas Christian University
Marc A. Louargand,
Cornerstone Realty Advisors
Christopher A. Manning,
Loyola Marymount University
Willard McIntosh,
Prudential Real Estate Investors
Issac Megbolugbe,
Price Waterhouse
Ivan J. Miestchovich, Jr.,
University of New Orleans
Norman G. Miller,
University of Cincinnati
Philip S. Mitchell,
Mitchell & Associates
Glenn R. Mueller,
Legg Mason Wood Walker
William Mundy,
Mundy Jarvis & Associates
F. C. Neil Myer,
Cleveland State University

Theron R. Nelson,
University of North Dakota
George A. Overstreet, Jr.,
University of Virginia
Joseph L. Pagliari, Jr.,
Citadel Realty
Thomas D. Pearson,
The Thomas D. Pearson Company
Stephen A. Pyhrr,
SynerMark Investments
Stephen E. Roulac,
The Roulac Group
Ronald C. Rutherford,
University of Texas at San Antonio
Karl-Werner Schulte,
European Business School
Arthur L. Schwartz, Jr.,
University of South Florida
M. Atef Sharkawy,
Texas A&M University
Robert Simons
Cleveland State University
C. F. Sirmans,
University of Connecticut
Petros Sivitanides
Westmark Realty Advisors
Almon R. "Bud" Smith,
National Association of Realtors
C. Ray Smith,
University of Virginia
Halbert C. Smith,
University of Florida
Rocky Tarantello,
Tarantello & Company
Stephen F. Thode,
Lehigh University
Ko Wang,
Chinese University of Hong Kong
James R. Webb,
Cleveland State University
John E. Williams,
Morehouse College
Larry E. Wofford,
C&L Systems Corporation
Andrew Wood,
ERE-Yarmouth
Elaine M. Worzala,
Colorado State University
Charles H. Wurtzebach,
Heitman Capital Management
Tyler Yang,
Price Waterhouse
Michael S. Young,
The RREEF Funds
Alan J. Ziobrowski,
Lander University

Contents

About the Editor

Stephen E. Roulac works with people to address the ongoing changes in how society relates to place and space. He supports people in making decisions about the places and spaces they interact with in ways that promote and enhance their experiences as well as the effectiveness of their roles, goals, and values, of society, and of the natural and built environments. He does this by leading a consulting firm that advises on high-stakes, complex real estate decisions as well as by engaging in primary academic research, writing, and professional speaking.

Stephen is CEO of The Roulac Group, Inc., a strategy and financial economics, consulting firm with offices in San Francisco and Hong Kong. His firm's work is characterized by a singular historic perspective on forces that define contemporary real estate markets and their implications, keen insights into future directions, rigorous analysis, conceptual innovation, pragmatic problem solving, and sensitivity to ethical and public policy concerns. He has had extensive experience as the primary advisor of major decision makers in all facets of the real estate business, research, deposition and courtroom testimony as an expert witness on damages, valuation, economics, due process, and fiduciary investing standards in approximately 100 matters involving complex, high-stakes litigation.

Kiplinger's Personal Finance Magazine described him as "perhaps the country's most influential real estate analyst." *California Business* described Stephen E. Roulac and his firm as "Real Estate's 'Rolls Royce' of consultants," and a profile in the *Professional Services Review* observed that "based on his business success, his unmatched academic foundation, and his ground-breaking contributions to the direction of the industry, in a sense, you could say Stephen E. Roulac invented the strategic side of the real estate business as we know it today."

Stephen is a leading academic and is presently a visiting professor of Global Strategy at the University of Ulster in Belfast. He has seryed as adjunct professor at the Texas Real Estate Research Center at Texas A & M University and lecturer at the Graduate School of Management of University of California, Los Angeles. He served on the faculty of the Stanford Graduate School of Business for ten years and concurrently held a joint appointment in the Department of Architecture, College of Environmental Design, and the Schools of Business Administration at the University of California, Berkeley. He was also an adjunct professor at Hastings College of Law.

Acknowledged as a leading author on real estate topics, Stephen has written over 350 articles and authored or edited a dozen books. His *Modern Real Estate Investment: An Institutional Approach* has been recognized as the authoritative treatise on contemporary real estate investment practice. He is writing a series of books on the renaissance of place and space. He has written the Property Strategy column for *Forbes* and hosts a weekly national talk radio show, the *Stephen Roulac Property Conversation.*

Much in demand as a professional speaker, Stephen has made presentations and speeches to some 500 organizations and has been the keynote speaker or featured instructor at many significant professional forums throughout the country an abroad.

His academic credentials include a B.A. from Pomona College; on M.B.A., from Harvard Business School; a J.D. from University of California, Berkeley; a Ph.D. in strategy and finance from Stanford University; as well as the AICP, CPA, and CMC professional designations. He is affiliated with numerous professional associations concerning strategy, economics, finance, and real estate, as well as nontraditional sources of knowledge. He is a past president of the American Real Estate Society and, as chair of the Strategic Management task force, is a member of the ARES Executive Committee.

Stephen's role in championing more effective and responsible decisions has been widely recognized. In addition to having received numerous awards for his published writing and research, in 1997 the American Real Estate Society awarded him the James A. Graaskamp Award, recognizing iconoclastic thinking that advances real estate paradigms in ways that transform theory and practice. In 1998 he was honored with the Werner Bloomberg award for continued conceptual thinking by the Bloomberg Committee on Excellence in Future Studies in Higher Education.

Forword

Greg Jones
Vice President and Division Controller
The Howard Hughes Corporation
Las Vegas, Nevada

Growing national attention has been focused on the ethical conduct of our political leaders and the business community that lobbies them. Seemingly at every turn, we are confronted with ethical dilemmas in modern life. One recent national survey found that 80 percent of America's high school students not only admit to cheating in school, but directly attribute their misconduct to the poor examples set for them by their political and business role models. Those of us in the real estate industry must take note of these national trends and attitudes, and we must respond with increased attention to ethics in our profession.

The Howard Hughes Corporation is pleased to sponsor this volume on ethics in real estate in conjunction with the American Real Estate Society (ARES). As southern Nevada's leading developer of quality residential and commercial environments, our company has a long tradition of being sensitive to, and accepting responsibility for, the effects of its activities. As a trendsetter in the national real estate industry through its affiliation with The Rouse Company of Columbia, Maryland, the Hughes organization also accepts a broader responsibility for setting the ethical bar as high as possible.

We hope this publication will serve as a reference tool for your day-to-day activities. But, more important, we hope it will foster healthy debate among you and your colleagues. Ethics is not a static science one can study and then set aside. Rather, it is a living and ever-changing art form we must each embrace with a sense of responsibility.

In 1962 Earl Warren, Chief Justice of the United States Supreme Court, told a *New York Times* reporter: "In civilized life, law floats in a sea of ethics." Certainly our industry is bound by the formal constraints of law in national, state, and local jurisdictions. What this volume reminds us, however, is that those laws are only as good as the personal "sea of ethics" in which each of us operates.

THE ETHICS OF PROPERTY INVOLVEMENTS

Stephen E. Roulac
The Roulac Group
San Rafael, California
and
Visiting Professor
University of Ulster

Ethical considerations are a dominant theme in the management literature. As "Ethics and ethical issues surround our liver, . . . ethics has become one of the most rapidly growing areas of management research, with over 800 articles and 1,400 books appearing since 1990" (Schminke, Ambrose, and Miles, 1998). Compared to business and business management, however, the research and writing on real estate in an ethics context is in the very early stages of development.

The lack of a developed literature on ethics in real estate is reflected in the response by one highly placed executive to my solicitation for funding to support the publication of this volume: "I didn't know there *were* any ethics in real estate!" Fortunately, the Summa Corporation and the American Real Estate Society believe in the importance of ethics in real estate, for their cosponsorship has made possible this special monograph on the subject of *Ethics in Real Estate*. The support of the Summa Corporation and the American Real Estate Society of this pioneering volume is warmly and appreciatively acknowledged.

The objective of this volume is to begin to fill that void and to encourage a dialogue about a subject that is inherently a dialogue. We anticipate a lively dialogue, since *Ethics in Real Estate* will receive a significant readership. In addition to reaching the thought leaders of the real estate discipline who comprise the membership of the American Real Estate Society, this volume is being distributed to deans of professional schools, libraries, and important public officials throughout the world.

Given the financial magnitude (most real estate transactions are the largest of any household's or company's financial involvement) and nonfinancial significance (real estate transactions are rated as among life's most stressful experiences), ethical connotations loom large. Issues of land policy have extraordinary ethical content. Yet there has been a paucity of overt recognition, let alone explicit writing, on the subject. Although ethical topics in real estate have been touched on at various times in literature, such as the subject of a *Harvard Business Review* article ("Is Bobbitt Dead?"), the subject of *Ethics in Real Estate* is in need of more thoughtful and thought-provoking treatment.

Contributors were encouraged to think broadly and widely on ethics issues in a real estate context and also to employ a multidisciplinary view of ethics embracing philosophic, physical, political, societal, economic, legal, and regulatory considerations—in addition to such fundamental real estate issues as dual-agency representation, seller disclosure obligations, rent control, fair housing policy, plant closings, track-record disclosure, presentation of probable future performance, analytic methodology, fiduciary responsibilities, and the like.

The preparation of a research volume such as *Ethics in Real Estate* depends not just on selfless contributions of the authors but also on the encouragement, high standards, and constructively critical reviews of the hard-working editorial review board. Members of the review board for *Ethics in Real Estate* included John D. Benjamin, Waldo L. Born, Peter R. Colwell, Julian Diaz III, Mark Dotzour, Jack P. Friedman, Terry, V. Grissom, Richard L. Haney, Jr., Linda Johnson, G. Donald Jud, Karen E. Lahey, Joseph Lipscomb, Emil Malizia, ChristoPher A. Manning, Dowell Meyers, Norman G. Miller, Stephen A. Pyhrr, Ronald L. Racster, John Renesch, Ronald C. Rutherford, J. Sa-Aadu, Layla Smith, James R. Webb, John E. Williams, and Larry E. Wofford. These hard-working and sensitive reviewers have done much to advance the thought leadership of the real estate discipline and to promote the conversations about ethics in real estate. The diligent, caring, and responsible contributions of each of these individuals are warmly and appreciatively acknowledged.

Reasons one would expect extensive and lively literature on issues concerning ethics in real estate include the following:

- Social import, as captured by Winston Churchill's classic dictum, "We first design our structures, then they design our lives";
- Business importance, since for most enterprises property expenditures are the second-largest expense category after the payroll;
- Economic significance, with real estate representing 28 percent of GNP and as much as 46 percent when secondary and tertiary effects are included (Roulac and Volk, 1989);

- Wealth importance, with real estate representing as much as one-half of the world wealth portfolio (Ibbotson, Siegel, and Love, 1985).

Despite these factors there has been very little writing on ethical issues concerning real estate involvements.

While the ethical aspects of land use have been explored in various settings, the little writing that has emerged about real estate ethics has been primarily concerned with issues of professionalism in the context of brokerage or appraisal. *Professionalism* is often perceived and used as a code word for *integrity*. Such writing is often more about preferred professional practice than about ethics issues. The one most visible exception to the lack of an academic and professional literature on real estate ethics was the American Society of Real Estate Counselors' December 1994 edition of *Real Estate Issues*, which was devoted to an inquiry into ethics in real estate. Another visible statement was the 1995 BOMI Institute monograph, whose point of view is reflected in its title, *Ethics Is Good Business* (BOMI, 1995).

The fifteen chapters that comprise this *Ethics in Real Estate volume* are organized into five primary sections, embracing policy issues, industry practice, environmental issues, ethical issues in the context of transactions, and tenants and ethics. This collection of papers on ethics in real estate combines conceptual and empirical work. Many of the chapters are challenging, provocative, even disturbing to established practice. Their twelve authors are drawn from five countries, many diverse disciplines, and the academy, as well as professional practice.

Collectively and individually, these chapters encourage an ongoing conversation about ethics. No thoughtful professional can read them without being prompted to reexamine her or his own property involvements in the context of ethical considerations. Many enterprises with property involvements and especially professional associations serving property professionals may choose, at a minimum, to reassess their own posture toward ethics, if not alter their fundamental approach to doing what they are chartered to do. Although these fifteen chapters were prepared separately and independently, collectively they offer complementary challenges to the reader.

Part I: Policy Issues

The first four chapters, which comprise the *policy issues* section, draw less heavily from the real estate literature than they do from such disciplines as cognitive science, medieval history, religion, philosophy, psychology, jurisprudence, strategic management, and organization theory. Collectively, these chapters frame the exploration of conceptual and applied approaches to ethics in real estate.

In Chapter 1, Stephen E. Roulac proposes that ethics in real estate is more a conversation about than absolute codification of conduct. The topics that comprise the conversation concerning ethics in real estate can be usefully explored from the perspectives of three of the practices from the Buddhist eightfold path to enlightenment: right speech, right action, and right livelihood. Operationalizing these concepts in the context of ethics in real estate, right speech involves disclosure and honesty; right action embraces competence, fiduciary responsibility, decision processes, and trust; and right livelihood encompasses both one's worldview and paradigms employed to implement that worldview. The application of right livelihood to property involvements leads to a worldview that honors the land and respects all sentient beings in their experiences of environments in all forms, across all cultures, and unbounded by time. An individual whose aspiration is to have ethics sensitivity reflected in her real estate involvements may find guidance by considering how congruent her actions are with her values as well as the relationship of those actions to concepts of right speech, right action, and right livelihood.

Larry E. Wofford in Chapter 2 explores real estate ethics from the perspective of rational choice theory through a synthesis of economics, psychology, sociology, and related disciplines to advance a view that combines both science and philosophy. He proposes a framework of multiple elements and ideas, to serve "as a starting point and catalyst for additional development" and research into real estate ethics. His chapter is challenging in the sweep of its scope and ambitious in its objective to harness philosophy and science in an integrated assessment of real estate ethics.

Ric Small advances in Chapter 3 a future vision of real estate professionalism through an engaging assessment of the present and the past. He reviews contemporary property development practices to highlight issues concerning professional quality and then proceeds to explore the role of ethics in medieval guilds and the subsequent deprofessionalization following the demise of medieval feudalism.

In the policy issues section's concluding essay (Chapter 4), Marvin L. Wolverton and Mimi Wolverton go beyond rule ethics and end-point ethics to examine the persistence of perceived unethical behavior that ignores stipulated standards of professional conduct. They seek a dialogue concerning the creation of professional real estate organizations that champion integrity and overcome habitual self-interested behavior.

Part II: Industry Practice

The four chapters that comprise the *industry practice* section represent a rich commentary from the diverse cultural context of the Netherlands, West Germany, the United Sates of America, and England. Jeroen Broeders and Jacco Hakfoort explore corruption in real estate in Chapter 5. Their paper combines anecdotal evidence of the principal-agent relationship and then explores corruption from its different levels, its pervasiveness, and economic models. They then advance a means to fight corruption.

In Chapter 6, Klaus Homann examines the German real estate industry and concludes that an application of the classic prisoner's dilemma model leads to shortfalls in ethical behavior. He proposes a code of conduct involving a binding system of rules and regulations that builds on and draws from existing codes of conduct from Germany and Great Britain.

Norman G. (Chapter 7) Miller asserts that the relative ethical behavior of industry professionals is influenced by economic circumstances. The results of preliminary testing of this theory support this proposition, since suspensions of real estate licenses increase as sales decrease. Noting the need for many further tests, Miller offers illuminating insights concerning the interdependency of economic events and ethical behavior.

The actions and decisions surrounding real estate development projects can often create considerable controversy, a truism that is compellingly and controversially captured in the title chosen by Michael Benfield for his essay on ethics and modern property development—"War Is When They Kill Your Children" (Chapter 8). Through the empirical assessment of thirty-two decision processes involving major European development projects—two in the Czech Republic, eleven in England, five in France, two in Germany, two in Hungary, five in Italy, and five in the Netherlands— Benfield criticizes the propensity to emphasize short-term financial objectives and political goals at the expense of longer-term and broader scale considerations. Benfield passionately champions the consideration of multiple forms of capital to embrace social, welfare, community, cultural, and environmental resources, and advocates a higher natural justice involving the setting of new agendas respectful of the Earth's geophysiology.

Part III: Environmental Issues

Environmental issues are explored through two chapters concerning the Superfund and brownfields. In Chapter 9, Ellen Weisbord asserts that environmental laws encourage unethical behaviors such as hiding the problem, the waste, and the cleanup. By imposing inequitable burdens on those who lack the resources to fund compliance, a standardized and centralized system of enforcement encourages unethical and illegal behavior. To correct these problems, she proposes a voluntary environmental compliance system.

Robert L. Shedlarz and Karen Eilers Lahey (Chapter 10) suggest that state-certified "brownfields" may be a reasonable and ethical compromise to those environmental sites for which "greenfield" status is unattainable and "deadfield" status is unacceptable. Recognizing that a "brownfields" scheme is laden with ethical issues, the authors suggest that such an approach is better than the alternative and, in an unperfect world, can deliver the "greatest good to the greatest number."

Part IV: Ethical Issues in the Context of Transactions

Ethical issues arise not infrequently in the context of real estate transactions. In Chapter 11, Chris Manning explores the challenges of buyers and sellers of real estate who must choose between what is ethical and what is unethical behavior. While acknowledging that responsibility to protect the financial interests of someone on the other side of the deal is contrary to the premise of a competitive market, he does identify certain principles that provide guidance as to what constitutes ethical and unethical behavior. Beyond advancing a conceptual framework for ethical behavior in real estate transactions, Manning advances certain *good business* reasons for being trustworthy and compassionate, since in some instances there in fact is a market for a reputation for compassion and honesty.

Norman G. Miller in Chapter 12 examines the twenty-three articles of the Professional Code of Conduct of the National Association of Realtors to classify their intention and their relative internal orientation as opposed to an external one. While fourteen articles have an outer orientation to the general public, six are concerned solely with internal industry behavior, and three have dual internal and external orientation. Miller concludes that ethics are not very complicated and further that most ethics codes can be presented much more succinctly, without sacrificing their core essence or intentions.

A. Ason Okoruwa and A. Frank Thompson (Chapter 13) provide an empirical assessment of real estate brokerage practices as they relate to both the National Association of Realtors' Code of Ethics and Standards of Practice and the legislative standards of practice for the state of Iowa. Their study provides a baseline for comprehending real estate agents' perspectives concerning the timing to present disclosure statements, disclosing information about the listing, how and when to present buyers' offers, and related factors.

Part V: Tenants and Ethics

Highly sensitive ethics issues can be associated with tenants, especially when the legal consequences of human behavior are involved. In Chapter 14, Robert J. Aalberts and Terrence M. Clauretie explore the ethical and legal issues surrounding sexual harassment of tenants in rental housing. Just as sexual harassment is an issue of great concern in the workplace, so also is it in housing. A fundamental problem with employing a *reasonable person standard* to address sexual harassment in housing is widely varying differences of perception of sexual behavior. One proposed resolution is adopting a *reasonable victim standard*, which operationally would be a woman's standard. Such a standard would be more demanding and less accommodating than a gender-neutral reasonable person standard.

Craig P. Dunn and A. Quang Do (Chapter 15) explore the ethical aspects of rent regulation. Dunn and Do observe that while rent control has been extensively studied, the ethical aspects of rent regulations have been relatively unexplored. Their exploration of rent regulation ethics employs general ethics frameworks of concern for various rights, overall welfare, and fairness. In contrast to much of the literature of rent control that addresses economic considerations to determine appropriate rent levels, Dunn and Do examine rent regulations from a variety of ethical points of view to determine how and under which conditions a "just price" for rental housing might be established.

These fifteen essays on ethics in real estate represent a lively, provocative, and diverse collection of viewpoints. Some are coolly analytic and empirical, while others are passionate and polemic in style. Some writings proceed from the premise of the priority of the market as an efficient allocation mechanism, while others start from and end with social justice and environmental equity.

These chapters are not consistent and uniform in their point of view and style and do not reflect a consensus as to what *ethics in real estate* should or should not embrace. What these fifteen essays have in common, most important, is that each is a point of departure for conversation. Each chapter advances thoughts and ideas, some challenging, some controversial. Although readers may take exception with parts or even much of what a particular author advances, no reader can come away from any of these essays without some new information, insights, and perspectives that can be employed to join in the conversation concerning ethics in real estate.

The authors and reviewers of *Ethics in Real Estate* have done their job well. Now it is up to you, the reader, to do yours: to read, reflect, and join in the conversation about *Ethics in Real Estate*. Contact the authors directly, write papers that extend their concepts and challenge their findings, and post your comments on the ARES web page at www.aresnet.org.

References

BOMI Institute. (1995). *Ethics Is Good Business*. BOMI Institute.

Burns, L.S., (1967). "Is Babbitt Dead?" *Harvard Business Review* (September–October).

Ibbotson, Roger G., Laurence B. Siegel, and Kathryn S. Love. (1985) "World Wealth: Market Values and Returns." *Journal of Portfolio Management* (Fall).

Roulac, Stephen E., and Loren D. Volk. (1989). "Deal-Marking Strategies in the New Era." *Real Estate Finance* (Winter).

Schminke, Marshall, Maureen Ambrose, and Jeffrey A. Miles. (1998). "Ethical Frameworks: An Examination of Sex Differences, Setting and Accuracy Perceptions." Paper prepared to be presented to the Academy of Management.

Ethics in Real Estate

POLICY ISSUES

1 BEING RIGHT—IN SPEECH, ACTION, AND LIVELIHOOD—IN PROPERTY INVOLVEMENTS

Stephen E. Roulac

The Roulac Group
San Rafael, California

Abstract

Ultimately, all aspects of contemporary society, its politics, its economy, its culture and its social relationships, occur on the land. The notions of right speech, right action and right livelihood may offer an illuminating approach to addressing the appropriate property involvements. Right speech, right action and right livelihood provide the means by which ethical factors can be incorporated into property involvements and real estate decision-making, which can integrate dynamism with responsiveness to changing conditions and simultaneously reflect the continuity as well as permanence. Relationships to the land follow from one's world view and paradigms and are implemented by speech and action in the context of one's livelihood. The implementation of right speech, right action and right livelihood in property involvements follows from one's world view, for that world view is the foundational thinking from which the paradigms, institutions, strategies, decision models, and decision criteria follow. These collectively give shape to individuals', organizations', and societies' relationship to the land, other sentient beings, environments in many forms, different cultures and times.

Introduction

A worldview that treats land as a commodity to be exploited, used, and discarded leads to very different strategies and outcomes for property involvements than does a worldview that perceives land as a precious, vulnerable resource that must be sustained, protected, and honored. These divergent approaches were eloquently captured by Aldo Leopold, who observed, "We abuse land because we regard it as a commodity belonging to us. When we see land as a community to which we belong, we may begin to use it with love and respect" (Leopold, 1949).

Ishmael, an engaging, elegant novel, illustrates the differences exceedingly well (Quinn, 1992). In *Ishmael*, two strategies of being are advanced: the strategy of *Leavers* emphasizes honoring the land and respecting all sentient beings across time, and that of *Takers* emphasizes dominating every thing and every being they encounter, without consideration of the past or the future. This story poses a simple and yet profound challenge concerning humankind's destiny in relationship to the physical environment and all sentient beings.

Property involvements that are informed by a *Leavers'* worldview will necessarily take a very different form than those that follow from a *Takers'* point of view. Property involvement objectives that one would emphasize, functions that one might seek to maximize, and relationships one might seek to optimize, diverge and vary sharply depending on whether one applies a *Leavers'* or *Takers'* philosophy (Quinn, 1992).

The Takers' strategy is reflected by rapidly increasing population requiring intensive production of food and leading to destruction of basic, irreplaceable resources and the disappearance of species in numbers that grow in each year (Quinn, 1992). The Takers' strategy and its consequences are what Thomas Robert Malthus warned of: population increasing more rapidly than the ability of the earth's capacity leads for profoundly negative consequences. The Takers' worldview is limited in scope and perspective.

The *Leavers/Takers* dichotomy is the story of sustainability, which ultimately depends on society's perceptions toward and relationships to land and *the* land. The *Leavers'* worldview is unbounded by time and culture, respects all sentient beings and environments in all forms, and honors the land. The essence of a *Leavers* worldview, and the community perspective that Aldo Leopold (1949) advocates, could be captured in the idea—familiar to all who are professionally involved in property matters—that *under all is the land*. While the National Association of Realtors' maxim is "Under all is the land," popular perception and experience of interactions with members of that organization lead most to divergent rather than congruent experiences of the application of that maxim. Ultimately, all aspects of contemporary society—its politics, its economy, its culture, its social relationship—occur on *the land*.

If the interplay of politics, economics, culture, and social relationships with the land is neither sustainable nor nourishing, then those institutions, as a consequence of the behaviors they influence, inevitably, necessarily, and unavoidably are compromised, if not destined for severe disappointment or even overt disaster. Relationships to the land follow from one's worldview and paradigms and are implemented by speech and action in the context of one's livelihood, as depicted in Figure 1.1. Consideration of right speech, right action, and right livelihood for property involvements necessarily follows from the worldview employed.

The perspectives of three practices from the Buddhist eightfold path to enlightenment—right speech, right action, and right livelihood—can illuminate consideration of property involvements. Right speech involves disclosure and honesty, and right action embraces competence, fiduciary responsibility, decision processes, and trust. Applying right livelihood to property involvement leads to property involvements that honor the land, respect all sentient beings, and respect their experiences of environments in all forms, across all cultures, and unbounded by time.

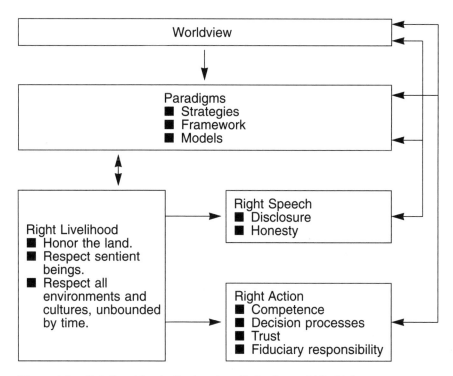

Figure 1.1.   Relationships to the Land as Reflections of Worldview

Worldview

Implementing right speech, right action, and right livelihood in property involvements follows from one's worldview, which is the foundational thinking that leads for paradigms, institutions, strategies, decision models, and decision criteria. These collectively shape individuals', organizations', and society's relationships to the land, other sentient beings, and environments—in many forms, different cultures, and times.

Central to considering worldview is interpreting an enterprise's primary responsibility and the decisions it makes in implementing that responsibility. In practice, this public policy issue turns on several perceptionsts— priorities for surviving in a dynamic, rapidly changing, highly competitive global economy; employee rights and entitlements; community interests; and the distribution of the burdens and rewards of implementing decisions concerning these issues among multiple parties, including shareholders, senior executives, workers, and the communities in which such businesses are located.

For the corporation, the priority is "to press for the protection of its economic interests so it can remain viable over the long haul. The issue is what kind of balance to strike among a company's stakeholders as you do it," observes Peter Feuille, director of the Institute of Labor and Industrial Relations at the University of Illinois. This priority reflects that "the first and most important responsibility of any corporation is to be economically viable, because if it's not it will eventually die," observes Feuille (Stevenson, 1996).

One worldview of the corporation's role holds that emphasizing community objectives is both the right thing to do and good for business. At the other end of the spectrum, tactics such as plant closings and worker layoffs are perceived as a necessary arsenal to ensure company viability, preserve jobs within the company, and indeed protect overall industries from the loss of business to more cost-effective competitors (which may be located in different countries) (Stevenson, 1996). Collectively, difficult decisions made to enhance productivity are intended to be reflected in tangible benefits to workers in the form of a surge in job creation that leads to low unemployment and to shareholders through generation of higher profits that enable more capital to be available to fund investment, new jobs, improved equipment, and new ventures (Stevenson, 1996).

Central to considering a relevant contemporary worldview is the struggle to balance two themes—spirituality and technology, serenity and advances. Plato described one of these orders of reality as timeless—mystical perfection—and the other as dynamic—material, economic, social, and political change (Nisbet, 1980). The dichotomy of these dual emphases is eloquently captured in Nicholas Sparks's (1996, pp. 105–106) poignant novel *The Notebook*. Set in North Carolina in 1946, the book has its female protagonist reflect on the attributes of the life she observes and the life she is drawn to:

> This was a worker's world, not a poet's, and people would have a hard time understanding Noah. America was in full swing now, all the papers said so, and people were rushing forward, leaving behind the horrors of war. She understood the reasons, but they were rushing, like Lon, toward long hours and profits, neglecting the things that brought beauty to the world.
>
> Who did she know in Raleigh who took time off to fix a house? Or read Whitman or Eliot, finding images in the mind, thoughts of the spirit? Or hunted dawn from the bow of a canoe? These weren't the things that drove society but she felt they shouldn't be treated as unimportant. They made living worthwhile.

While a worldview is implicit in every significant work of political philosophy, political economy, and management, seldom is that worldview made explicit. However, it is useful to address explicitly certain articulations of a worldview to facilitate the conversation concerning right speech, right action, and right livelihood property involvements. An explicit worldview is important because most involved in property are more task-focused than conceptual and strategic in their approach. Without a broad perspective, disproportionate numbers of property professionals may be trained to approach their craft in a manner similar to accountants who are not broadly educated, do not read widely, do not think in conceptual terms, and emphasize the what rather than why (Hall, 1987).

The worldview one elects and the paradigms one champions in implementing that worldview give form to the right speech, right action, and right livelihood perspective. A worldview that leads to a strategy emphasizing the narrow economic priority of "a continuing search for rent" (Bowman, 1974) leads to a very different emphasis than an objective of "species solidarity" would. The latter would emphasize the harmonious balance of individual freedom and social consciousness (Reich, 1971) and the intertwining of the individual's desired outcomes with those of society (Bowie, 1991).

Paradigms

The real estate discipline currently lacks coherence and consensus about the essence of real estate and the operative paradigms for comprehending and making order of the discipline. Multiple paradigms have been proposed for property involvements:

- Traditional: legal or descriptive (Harwood and Jacobus, 1990)
- Traditional: balanced (Dasso and Ring, 1989)

- Consumer transaction (Epley and Rabianski, 1986)
- Financial (Kau and Sirmans, 1985)
- Modern multidisciplinary (Smith and Corgel, 1992)
- Entrepreneurial (Eldred, 1987)
- Managerial administrative (Bloom, Weimer, and Fischer, 1982)
- Corporate (Nourse, 1990)
- Property rights (Jaffe, 1996)
- Game with winners and losers (Dasso and Ring, 1989; Wofford and Clauretie, 1992; Wurtzebach and Miles, 1991)
- Engineering or science (Diaz, 1994)
- Solvency (Graaskamp 1976b)
- Value (Grissom and Liu, 1994)
- Spatial market structure (Grissom and Liu, 1994)
- Land-use succession (Grissom and Liu, 1994)
- Urban structure (Grissom and Liu, 1994)
- Real estate process (Graaskamp, 1976b; Grissom and Liu, 1994)
- Risk management (Graaskamp 1976a)
- Highest and best use (Grissom and Liu, 1994)
- Most fitting use and most probable use (Grissom and Liu, 1994)
- Strategic management (Roulac, 1993)

Real estate is not the only discipline characterized by multiple paradigms and approaches, for "Management is a combination of science, art, philosophy, social sciences, psychology, and industrial psychology. . . . this conglomeration of disciplines undoubtedly contributes to the fullness and complexity of management theory, as well as conflicts over the theories" (Pindur, 1995).

One perspective (Taylor, 1992, p. 32) with direct applicability to property involvements is that the 1980s were a period of big ideas that revolutionized corporate finance through

> the democratization of capital and the creation of financial structures so fluid and flexible that companies could adjust effortlessly to the vagaries of the business cycle. More than anything, the 1980s testify to the power of those ideas—as well as to the dangerous tendency of even the soundest ideas, in a world of global capital flows and financial transactions measured in nanoseconds, to overheat, overshoot, and, eventually, be distorted beyond recognition.

What applies today and follows tomorrow is a function of yesterday's ideas.

Just as finance has assumed a more dominant role in contemporary business, so also has finance assumed a more dominant role in property. Today, the majority of academics teaching real estate do so from appointments in finance departments. Not surprisingly, there are those who assert that the financial paradigm is the dominant and most valid lens through which one might view property involvements (Jaffe, 1995). Just as there are those who challenge the relevance of management of corporate enterprise being dominated by new finance (Lowenstein, 1991), so also are those who advocate a perspective other than the finance paradigm dominating property involvements (Roulac, 1996).

Today, two competing strands influence real estate decision making. A financial paradigm of real estate, reflecting the influence of financial engineering (Jaffe, 1995) and the securitization of real estate interests, competes with a paradigm that acknowledges larger social concerns, reflecting a deemphasis of materialism, an integration of spirituality in business, and greater interest generally in including concepts of culture and higher purpose in business.

Considering ethics in real estate decision making reflects this modern spirituality orientation. Those who would make a real estate decision relying primarily on a financial paradigm model are at least implicitly, if not explicitly, addressing considerations that embrace ethics concerns. The conflict between these two competing interests (the profit-optimizing thesis of the financial school and the social concerns of the values school) resonate with the dialectical theories of change articulated by German philosopher Friedrich Hegel.

Right Speech, Right Action, and Right Livelihood

The topics that comprise the conversation concerning ethics in real estate can be usefully explored using the notions of *right speech*, *right action*, and *right livelihood* from the Buddhist eightfold path to enlightenment. An individual whose aspiration is to have ethical sensitivity reflected in her real estate involvements may develop personal guidelines by considering how congruent her actions are with her values and how those actions relate to notions of right speech, right action, and right livelihood. Similarly, a community or industry that aspires for having ethical sensitivity reflected in their involvements may consider the relationship of industry behavior to notions of right speech, right action, and right livelihood.

In real estate, these notions provide a powerful means of bridging the institutionalized approach to ethics to explore broader concepts of behavior. They serve as an excellent point of departure for a communitywide conversation by facilitating an enlightened consideration of the ethical appropriateness of action with real estate involvements and consequences.

In the context of ethics in real estate, *right speech* encompasses the notions of *disclosure* and *honesty*. Right speech in the property context is served by disclosure and honesty. Disclosure is important since it enables informed and balanced decisions. Honesty and trust are important because they are the bedrock of all of society's intrapersonal, interpersonal, intra-organizational and interorganizational communications.

In the context of ethics in real estate, the notion of right action encompasses the notions of *competence, decision processes, trust,* and *fiduciary responsibility.* Right action in the property context is served by competence, decision processes, trust, and fiduciary responsibility. Action is the expression and activating of speech, so right action necessarily incorporates the honesty of right speech. Competence is important because decisions with as much significance as those that characterize real estate must, if society is to function effectively, efficiently, and efficaciously, involve reliance on the expertise of professionals who are entrusted with important responsibilities.

Since decision processes involve the action of selection among alternatives, problem solving, and implementation to achieve desired objectives, effective decision processes are crucial to right action. Trust is important to the implicit expectation that the professional in her or his conduct is truly being professional (that is, competent) and that the professional's action is consistent and congruent with the honesty that is inherent in right speech.

In the context of ethics in real estate, the notion of *right livelihood* encompasses the notions of honoring the land and of respecting all sentient beings in their experiences of environments in all forms, across all cultures, and unbounded by time. Right livelihood includes those factors that influence how one makes a living, specifically the particular work pursued and the consequences of that work generally and how it is pursued specifically. Right livelihood in the property context is served by respecting sentient beings, all environments, and all cultures and by honoring the land, with such honor and respect being unbounded by time. In a sense, right livelihood can be viewed as the guiding framework for right action and right speech.

In the context of real estate, the essence of ethics in real estate can be viewed in the framework of right speech, right action, and right livelihood. Virtually every ethical issue one might confront can be ultimately subsumed within the notions of right speech, action, and livelihood.

Right Speech

Disclosure

Fundamental to right speech in property involvements is the responsibility and reliability of information disclosure. In an economy dominated by information (Castells, 1996), the role of information becomes ever more important for property involvements, for "superior insights will be derived more from a superior explicit information strategy than the implicit information premises dominant at other times" (Roulac, Lynford, and Castle, 1990).

Those who would gain access to capital are obligated under federal securities laws to make a full and fair disclosure of all information that might influence the prospective outcome of the contemplated investment. The cumulative traditions of disclosure in public and private transactions have raised the bar of expectations of what information might be reasonably made available on one side of the transaction and what might reasonably be expected to be received from the other side of the transaction. As the responsibility to provide information and the reliability of the information provided assume ever-greater importance, the implications of the values that underpin the disclosure of information become ever more significant.

The responsibility for the reliability of information on which decisions are based is a highly sensitive issue. The traditional practice for those involved in real estate transactions has been to present an investment offering in terms of information concerning the property's attributes and past and proposed performance. Most such presentations of information concerning the property's attributes and performance are presented in a deterministic rather than probabilistic format. Deterministic single-point outcomes are too often presented as the equivalent to a certainty of expected outcome, when in fact they are but representations along a spectrum of possibilities. Most presentations of a property's future investment performance lack the explicit consideration of probabilities, ranges of and expected outcomes, risk premiums, and discounts.

Representations concerning a property's future performance and the relative responsibilities of buyers and sellers to investigate the premises of those representations are fraught with potential problems. One real estate entrepreneur, who sold a troubled retail shopping center based on assumptions of future performance that were not realized, ended up paying approximately one-third of the transaction proceeds to the seller in order to settle litigation in which fraud was claimed (Doe, 1991). Significantly, crucial to this dispute was a probing cross-examination in which plaintiff's counsel, in a series of carefully crafted questions, established that the defendant held the CCIM designation, which implied a level of professional competence equivalent to that of "a highly educated specialist who has mastered the theories and the practical applications of those theories in commercial real estate" (Doe, 1991, p. 10). The attorney then effectively forced the defendant into a position where he had to settle the case, through asking him, "If, as a knowledgeable professional, you prepared a series of cash flow projections on which my client properly relied, and the actual performance of the center is not even close to those projections, then you are stupid (which you clearly are not), or you consciously created a scenario intended to defraud my client. Is that correct?" (Doe, 1991, p. 10).

The representation of information about an enterprise and an investment carries with it *truth and consequences* for the reliability of what is disclosed. When truth is lacking, the consequences can be extreme. The disclosure responsibility embraces, in practice, not just the reliability of what is disclosed but also the responsibility to disclose what a party who has an interest in that situation or circumstance would want to know. As M. Scott Peck so cogently observes, integrity involves not just the accuracy of what is said but also what is not said, especially if the other party would have an interest in, would be influenced by, or would like to know what was not said (Peck, 1980).

In a probing *Baron's* story that presaged "Chainsaw" Al Dunlap's demise as Sunbeam CEO, the following word picture aptly captures a dark disclosure philosophy, one that is not infrequently applied to reflect property performance (Laing, 1998, p. 17):

> Sunbeam's financials under Dunlap looked like an exercise in high-energy physics, in which time and space seemed to fuse and bend. They are a veritable cloud chamber. Income and costs move almost imperceptibly back and forth between the income statement and balance sheet like charged ions, whose vapor trail has long since dissipated by the end of any quarter, when results are reported. There are also some signs of other accounting shenanigans and puffery, including sales and related profits booked in periods before the goods were actually shipped or payment received.

Dunlap, who shortly after this article was published was forced to resign in disgrace, observed, albeit with a very different intended meaning, "We had an amazing year" (Laing, 1998, p. 17).

Another highly visible incident of disclosure controversy concerns the $2 billion cost overrun and sixteen-month delay in the opening of the Denver International Airport. The Securities and Exchange Commission enforcement action was described in a *New York Times* investigative article (Wane, 1996, p. 17) as

> focusing on showing that all parties knew full well in 1991 and 1992 that the proposed baggage system—so crucial to the airport's opening—was an unproven technology that would fail and could not be built on time, if ever.
>
> This would mean that the October 1993 opening date promised to investors— the date when the airport would start generating revenues to repay bonds—was known to be impossible when it appeared in the bonds' prospectus.

Significantly, while an October 1990 report from Brieier Neidle Patrone and Associates contained the statement that "with regards to the single bag DCV, considering the prototype stage, we strongly feel it is not capable of being implemented within the project schedule" (Wane, 1996, p. 17), an April 1, 1991, bond offering document did not mention the baggage system's reliable and timely functioning as one of eleven possible risks. Although a subsequent February 1, 1992, bond offering added the line, "any significant delay with regard to the automated baggage system could delay the Date of Beneficial Occupancy of the New Airport" (Wane, 1996, p. 17), the prospectus was silent concerning the challenges to and likelihood of the baggage system being operative within the scheduled timeframe. While the consequences of a delay in the baggage system delaying the opening was briefly addressed, what was not addressed was the likelihood of such an outcome.

Another sensitive disclosure issue centers around Rockefeller Center Properties, the troubled real estate investment trust whose conduct was described in a probing *Barron's* investigatory essay as the antithesis of the broad public perception of the Rockefeller name being "synonymous with public service and trustworthiness" (Stein, 1996, p. 18). Six weeks after shareholders of the cash-constrained Rockefeller Center Properties agreed to a buy out, NBC announced that it would acquire its space at 30 Rockefeller Plaza for $440 million. The shareholder approval came just one week after "Rockefeller Center Properties issued a press release saying that 'its cash resources would be exhausted by the end of April 1996' unless someone took over the company" (Stein, 1996, p. 18). Yet nearly a year earlier, in May 1995, NBC executives had considered buying their space in 30 Rockefeller Plaza. Significantly, on February 18, 1996, one month prior to the fateful press release, "an investment group that eventually would acquire Rockefeller Center Properties, holder of a mortgage on 12 Rock Center buildings, says in a filing that it would be capitalized 'with equity of $440 million'" (Stein, 1996, p. 18).

In describing the "sad story of Rockefeller Center Properties," the *Barron's* investigative article observes (Stein, 1996, p. 18):

> The tale has been one of gullible investors failing to grasp the structure of the company and the huge risk facing the New York City market for office space when the REIT was formed in 1985. It has also been a tale of a management that compounded inflated prospects for the commercial real estate market with misjudgments and wrong guesses and interest rates.
>
> Though that picture is accurate, it is sadly incomplete. Today, following the demise of Rockefeller Center Properties as a publicly owned entity, fresh questions are surfacing about the recently announced sale of office space in the complex to the parent of broadcast giant NBC. Specifically, if shareholders had

known about the possible sale of the space for $440 million, which would have provided desperately needed liquidity, would they have voted to be bought out for $8 a share this past spring by an investment group that included David Rockefeller?

Insufficient disclosure can create legal liability, yet too much could have the consequences of critically compromising the company's competitive position, actions that could themselves be the source of liability.

Disclosure requirements can mandate companies to disclose information that is of very definite interest to investors and that concurrently can enable competitors to gain access to information that was previously unavailable. The AICPA SOP 94–6, "disclosure of certain significant risks and uncertainties," requires public and private companies alike to disclose information about the enterprise's products, services, and principal markets; the degree to which estimates have been employed in meeting reporting requirements; the vulnerability of making those estimates within the next twelve months; and if a company could be adversely affected as a consequence of a change in any concentration of its business on a certain customer, supplier, product or market, geographic location, or product and service. The SOP 94–6 disclosure requirement can create the financial equivalent of the choice between "a rock and a hard place." Much of this information is perceived by strategists as being the essence of the source of competitive advantage, especially if such information is not widely known and not readily duplicated.

The general expectation of disclosure of relevant information to support an investment decision may be overtly contrary to the prospective implications of such disclosure, as captured so cogently in the observation by John Maynard Keynes that few investors (or entrepreneurs, for that matter) would likely proceed with many ventures if they really knew what they were embarking on. More specifically, Keynes observed that no one would commit capital to an entrepreneurial venture if a true, careful, and comprehensive analysis of its risks and rewards were in fact performed in advance of such capital being committed (Keynes, 1936).

Honesty

Much of right speech is about telling the truth. The ninth commandment states, "Thou shalt not bear false witness." Nonetheless, honesty has widely been perceived as a missing ingredient in real estate transactions (Inman, 1996). As real estate investment commentator Jack Reed observes, "Lying is epidemic in modern life and in real estate. Prospective tenants lie about where they've lived. Prospective mortgage borrowers lie about income and net worth. Appraisers make 'made-as-instructed' appraisals" (Inman, 1996).

Honesty and its antonym, perjury, are the subject of recent renewed emphasis. Over time there has been an evolution toward higher expectations concerning honesty. Significantly, only relatively recently have defendants in a court proceeding been held to the standard of not committing perjury. Not widely recognized is that any statement to a federal official that is false, fictitious, or fraudulent is a violation of the False Statements Act (Rosen 1998).

Noted moral philosopher Sissela Bok observes that it is "worse to lie to those with a right to truthful information than others" and " worse to lie to those who have entrusted you with their confidence about matters important to them than to your enemies" (Bok, 1989). The application of these concepts to matters concerning property turns on the question of the rights of other parties to truthful information, generally, and for fiduciary responsibilities specifically.

Right Action

Right speech is important because words are given form in action, but the implementation of right action is crucial. Ultimately, what is done is much more powerful than what is said, for as Mitroff observes, "Something becomes true only through its implementation or to the extent that it is implemented" (Mitroff, 1998, p. 68).

In application, the Buddhist precept of right action is closely linked to and defined by the honesty element of right speech, for as noted philosopher William James cogently observed, an idea becomes true and is made true by events (James, 1991). Extending James's assertion that an idea is made true by events, noted management philosopher Ian Mitroff proclaims that "No paper ought to published unless it has an implementation plan" (Mitroff, 1998, p. 68). Mitroff goes on to advance the dual theses that "With few exceptions, none of the major schools of ethics is concerned with implementation" and that "Most schools of ethics commit the fallacy of assuming that ethical propositions are self-implementing" (Mitroff, 1998, p. 68). The worldview advanced by Mitroff would hold that the truth of something is in its implementation.

Right action is reflected by the *rightness* of choices made. Actions that lead to outcomes that are congruent with right action are ethical per se. At the same time, it is important not to interpret ethics in terms of outcomes per se, since what could be considered a very desirable outcome may be the result of what might be perceived as highly unethical behavior. And conversely, a most undesirable outcome could follow from what might be considered highly ethical behavior. In a stochastic world characterized by variability of outcome that could cause even the most ethical a priori judgment to be deemed unethical as a consequence of unfortunate results, the primacy of right action mandates an emphasis on process and intention. Keith Darcy, president of the Foundation of Leadership Quality and Ethical Practice, expresses it this way: "Ethics is how we choose, how we respond to, everyday situations. We choose by our actions and our inactions" (Darcy, 1992).

Psychoanalyst Jean Shinoda Bolen concludes the chronicle of her journey of spiritual self-discovery with the observation, "Over and over again, it seems to me, life comes along and says, Choose! The small and large moments of truth that shape what goes into or is left out of a book, find parallels in the small and large moments of truth that go into the choices we make in life about what to add or delete. These are the decisions that shape our lives, which ultimately are soul journeys" (Bolen, 1994).

Competence

Competence is fundamental to right action and therefore ethical property involvements. If the broad public cannot rely on the competence of those who represent themselves as competent in their chosen field of professional endeavor, an extraordinary burden of due diligence investigation, verification, and validation is placed on the users of goods and services. Individually and collectively, incrementally and cumulatively, such burdens not only compromise the prospects of the efficient and effective functioning of society and markets but also do violence to realization of values-based institutions, strategies, decisions, processes, and outcomes.

The competent professional is expected to possess knowledge and skills that are not possessed by the layperson. Ethicists assert "that codes of professional conduct will have rules that instruct the professional to use her expert knowledge for the benefits of those who have a right to it" (Jamal and Bowie, 1995). In most instances, there is asymmetry between the knowledge of the professional and that of the client. But even when a client's knowledge parallels that of the professional, such as in an instance where one professional retains another, the client relies on the professional retained to perform at a highly professional level. More specifically, the client should not have to take on personal responsibility to ensure that the professional competently implements his professional responsibilities.

In a society characterized by burgeoning complexity, those who are entrusted with the responsibility for significant decisions increasingly seek expert assistance in evaluating, implementing, and managing those decisions. In the instance of institutional investing, pension trustees and staff have fiduciary responsibilities to represent the interests of pension beneficiaries. Further, the investment managers and professional advisors that pension trustees and staff retained to assist them in implementing their tasks are, by extension, fiduciaries.

Fiduciaries are held to this prudent investing standard, being expected to exercise due diligence in managing their investments in a manner similar to what a prudent person would do in similar circumstances. A prudent person in managing investments either possesses or retains the requisite expertise and capability because in highly complex endeavors the knowledge and skill of the expert are preferred over the unfamiliarity and limited ability of the neophyte.

Because expertise is integral to the effective functioning of institutional real estate investment markets, institutional investors seek to retain managers and advisors who are experts. It is important that investors and those they retain know the reasonable expectations of expertise by those managers and advisors who serve institutional investors.

If a prudent person would retain an expert, what level of competence would the prudent person expect that expert to possess? Answering this question of the competence expectations of an expert involves considering who, in fact, is an expert. An individual is regarded as an *expert* both for his or her recognized expertise and also by representations made concerning his or her professional role. Individuals representing themselves to be experts with respect to business decisions, in which role they advise others for compensation, are considered by the public to be experts.

The public reasonably relies on individuals who represent themselves as performing a specified professional function to be, in fact, experts in that function. Under the *shingle theory*, by holding oneself out to the public as engaging in a particular profession, the public rightly relies on that person or firm as being an expert in performing that profession. The public reasonably expects the expert to have the requisite *knowledge* and *skill* for the professional tasks in which the expert engages and then to employ appropriate *due care* in applying that knowledge and skill.

The *shingle theory* is articulated in section 3372(b)(1) of the California Corporation Code (emphasis added):

A person represents that such person is an "expert" within the meaning of this section if such person represents that he or she is a "financial planner," "financial adviser," "financial counselor," "financial consultant" or an "investment adviser," "investment counselor" or "investment consultant" or that such person renders "financial planning services," "financial advisory services," "financial counseling services," "financial consulting services" or "investment advisory services," "investment counseling services" or "investment consulting services" *or makes substantially equivalent representations with respect to such person's business or qualifications.*

Consideration of synonyms for the word *expert* illuminates the level of competence the public reasonably expects from an expert. In the martial arts, a practitioner who wears *black belt*—a status that is widely recognized as requiring sustained discipline and practice and that connotes the highest level of achievement—is known as an expert. Other synonyms of expert include *specialist, authority, master, maven, maestro,* and *virtuoso.* Adjectives that relate to expert include *proficient, adept, practice, experience, skillful, knowledgeable, learned, well-versed,* and *well-informed* (Rodale, 1978).

When retaining a financial consultant or adviser, the public should expect a high standard of skill and competency, as well as care in applying that skill to the financial matter on which the expert consults. The dictionary definitions of *expertise* embrace concepts of a "high degree of skill in or knowledge of" a certain subject. The *Oxford English Dictionary* definition of *expert* embraces experience, training, skill, and special knowledge that "causes him to be regarded as an authority, a specialist."

The responsibility of an expert and the reasonable expectations of the public in engaging the service of an expert are articulated in the California Civil Code section 3372(a) (emphasis added):

Any person *engaged in the business of advising others for compensation* as to the advisability of purchasing, holding or selling property for investment and who *represents himself or herself to be an expert with respect to investment decisions in such property, or any class of such property,* shall be liable to any person to whom such advisory services are furnished for compensation and who is damaged by reason of such person's compensation and for such damages, unless the person rendering such services proves that *such services were performed with the due care and skill reasonably to be expected of a person who is such an expert.*

The expectations of a client who retains an expert include three critical elements:

- Anyone representing himself or herself to the public to perform professional functions is expected to be an expert.

- An expert is expected to have the requisite knowledge and skill for the professional tasks in which the expert engages.
- The expert is expected to employ appropriate due diligence in applying that knowledge and skill.

Whereas in times past certain firms and individuals have trafficked casually in the terminology of *consultant*, *advisor*, and even *expert*, such representations to the public that one provides certain services carry the substantial responsibility to have both a high degree of competence in those services and a high degree of responsibility in implementing those services. Institutional investors should reasonably expect their professional advisers to be both competent and conscientious in applying that competence.

Today it is no longer enough merely to be a technical specialist. At the very time that professionals are expected to "master an ever-increasing body of knowledge" (Evers and Rush, 1996, p. 275) and technical expertise, a professional is expected to master certain managerial competencies, including mobilizing innovation and change, managing people and tasks, communicating, and managing self (Evers and Rush, 1996). These requisite managerial competencies can be considered as crucial capabilities in maintaining professional currency and relevance and also in communicating and delivering professional services. These managerial competencies enable the professional to maintain overall technical competence, as well as to communicate with clients and deliver professional services effectively. Indeed, a professional who lacks facility in applying his knowledge and in communicating clearly to clients could, arguably, be functionally as incompetent as a person who lacks the knowledge. Thus, the crucial managerial competencies not only balance, complement, and enhance professional competence but are integral to the application of the professional's specific expertise.

The expectations of competency increase over time (Ordway, 1996). While knowledge workers (a group that includes real estate professionals as a subgroup) generally commence their careers at a competency level above minimum competency requirements, over time, unless competency is both expanded and kept current, competency diminishes to a level below perceived competency at entry (Dalton and Thompson, 1991). Thus, absent a conscious and conscientious effort to enhance competency over time, the original modest competency surplus deteriorates to a substantial competency deficit. The inevitable competency deficit creates a significant need for continual competency enhancement.

An approach to property involvements that is informed by considerations of right speech, right action, and right livelihood goes beyond competence concerning particular tasks per se to consider the relationship of that task to the worldview and the paradigms that give voice to that worldview. This perspective has application to and implication for those involved with and exercising leadership concerning property involvements.

Decision Processes

Since the means by which a decision is made is increasingly as important as the decision itself, the decision process assumes itself greater import. Fair process is concerned with not just the outcome but with how the outcome was achieved to combine procedural justice with distributive justice. While distributive justice emphasizes satisfaction with the outcome, procedural justice stresses a process of involvement, explanation, and clarity that reflects trust and commitment (Kim and Mauborgne, 1997).

When the fairness of the processes that produce the outcomes are viewed as at least as important as the outcomes themselves, the economic assumption of utility maximization focused solely on outcome may be incomplete. If insufficient consideration is given to the processes that lead to outcomes, people may feel frustrated and deeply unhappy, even though the outcome itself is what they desire (Kim and Mauborgne, 1997). Thus, an investment manager who delivers results that meet performance expectations but is cavalier in communicating appropriate information and providing reports to investors may be perceived to fall short of the process expected of an investment manager by institutional investors. Outcome alone does not equate with competence.

The decision processes employed to implement right action concerning property involvements reflect worldviews. One worldview reflects dominance by a central authority as contrasted to another worldview that emphasizes entrepreneurial-motivated self-initiative. The command-and-control managerial style follows from the principles of scientific management promulgated by Frederick Taylor in the early years of the twentieth Century. Taylor's scientific management philosophy reflects such core concepts as "management thinks and employees do," "management and employees operate with conflicts of interest," "employees are costs to be minimized," and "management's role is to control and direct employees" (Koch, 1998).

According to an alternative worldview of right action, decision processes follow from employee involvement, leadership, and alignment of interests with management and shareholders. The philosophic underpinnings of what is described as market-based management, credited by Charles Koch for the growth in annual sales of Koch Industries from $177 million to $30 billion in three decades, is the Austrian school of economics, particularly the work of Ludwig von Mises and Friedrich von Hayek (Koch, 1998). The market process school of economics proceeds from the premise of a spontaneous internal dynamic operating without direction by central authority and control. This approach applies to a company Hayek's thesis that centralized control for an economy is a "fatal conceit" (Koch, 1998).

A core property issue is the prevalence, or lack thereof, of discrimination concerning access to classes of property, generally, and particular properties, specifically. The spectrum of private property to public property involves gradients of perceived property access that are less than clear cut. As captured by the saying "a man's home is his castle," it is understood that save for addressing certain instances of health and safety, both generally and for particular inhabitants within a structure, a family's property is their own domain, not to be visited or violated by anyone who is not invited. In application, this concept is made murky in instances where the residence is rented, rather than owned, as well as in those instances where the residence is in an ownership regime that has common participatory interests, such as a condominium, cooperative, planned unit development, or neighborhood whose homeowner's association imposes certain covenants, codes, restrictions, rules, and regulations.

Discrimination concerning access to housing and more recently to membership in certain private clubs has been at the core of public policy debate and legal activism over the last half century. In practice, discrimination operates in the realms of housing choice and also in the realm of gaining access to the resources in order to implement a housing purchase. With certain exceptions involving housing affordability and rent control, discrimination is generally presumed to be acceptable if it is based on the economic factor of price. All other forms of discrimination are legally prohibited.

Right action decision processes applied to housing access involve housing choice, mortgage eligibility, and, significantly so, the research on which policies are formulated and business practices implemented concerning housing choice and mortgage access. Consequently, the very research on which property decision processes are based involves significant right action responsibilities. Over the last decade, alleged racial discrimination resulting from differential assessment of mortgage applications, depending on the applicant's race, has been the subject of an ongoing debate. The 1989 amendments to the Home Mortgage HMD&A Act require banks to maintain certain detailed information concerning rejected mortgage applicants. Studies of the data concerning discrimination in lending have been vigorously debated in such publications as the *American Economic Review* and The *Wall Street Journal*, resulting in assertions that research concerning racial discrimination in mortgage lending is defective in its methodology, tainted by ideological preconceptions, motivated to mislead, and irresponsible in the data manipulation (Passell, 1996).

One model of the real estate discipline is a problem-solving approach that recognizes that problems are situations that call for a decision that initiates action either directly by the involved party or indirectly by authorizing a third party to perform such action on behalf of the involved party. Real estate as a series of problems to be solved reflects parallels to the consideration of "life is a succession of problems" philosophy articulated by Sufi Master Inayat Khan.

The question, then, is what criteria and considerations should be employed in the problem-solving approach? And the answer to that question is influenced by the particular problem to be solved, the factors to be addressed, the interests to be considered, and the broader context of that problem. A multitude of factors influence the effective and responsible implementation of the due diligence responsibility for a particular real estate investment decision (Roulac, 1995). If careful consideration of the context of that decision is absent, the resulting decision may be a suboptimal and less than desirable outcome. An effective and responsible due diligence investigation considers the multiple stakeholders, including investors, owners, managers, public and private service providers, space users and their guests and customers, the interests of adjacent property owners, members of the community, and such enterprises and institutions that may be affected by the property activity, such as retail stores, schools, and theaters. Consideration of context should involve consideration of right livelihood from the perspective of the operative and relevant worldview. Further, a compelling case can be made that sensitivity to ecology is congruent not just with right action and right livelihood but also with self-interest (Roulac, 1999).

Implementing self-initiated right action is no easy undertaking. Institutional forces seem to presume many are less than inclined to right action, for "in modern society an enormous apparatus of law and enforcement makes the temptation to cheat resistible. But how can reciprocal altruism work in the absence of those authoritarian institutions so despised by Kropotkin's anarchists?" (Nowack, May, and Sigmund, 1995, p. 76).

The application of decision processes to property involvements links an interpretive application of right action and right livelihood to determine the guiding principle for decisions. Contrary to the premise of many—that real estate transactions inherently involve conflict, with resolution only from a win-lose perspective—a win-win outlook can be effective in achieving superior results, especially on a risk-adjusted basis. This thinking is contrary to popular perception, however. In real estate transactions, it is often perceived that one party's gain is the other's loss. Those favoring such a perception assert that it reflects the basic biological principle, identified by Charles Darwin, of survival of the fittest (Darwin, 18).

But Darwin himself championed the role of cooperation in human evolution, highlighting social qualities involving giving and receiving as more than counterbalancing man's small strength and speed (Darwin, 1871). Cooperation, rather than exploitation, may in fact be the dominant enduring value (Nowack, May, and Sigmund, 1995), for within the family a good turn is its own reward. But a good turn to an unrelated fellow being has to be returned in order to pay off. Reciprocal aid—the trading of altruistic acts whose benefit exceeds cost—is essential to economic exchange. Significantly, cooperation is viewed as essential to the evolution of competitive markets became it is instrumental to the emergence of complex structures (Nowack, May, and Sigmund, 1995).

Behavior that is not motivated primarily by self-interest may be perceived as alien to the approaches employed by many in their property involvements. Many perceive real estate as inherently exploitative became property rights have been claimed and preserved through group force—in ancient times, in the Middle Ages through a feudal landlord system, and most recently through military aggression aided by contemporary weapons technology. While a short-term advantage is achieved through exploitative behavior, can that advantage be sustained over the long term? Stephen Covey asks whether a cooperative strategy emphasizing collaboration might yield a higher payoff (Covey, 1989). If exploitation can be viewed as a win-lose approach, with one party prevailing only at the expense of the other, then cooperation can be considered a win-win approach to negotiation (Covey, 1989).

In the short term, the real estate operative may prevail through aggressive practices that lead to an advantageous acquisition of a particular property. How will that approach affect the experience of tenants in that property and the patrons of those tenants? Will the best tenants, who recognize that they have multiple options as to where they might locate, be drawn to a property owner who is known to engage in very aggressive, sharp practices? Is a high quality of physical structure, maintenance, and service compatible with very aggressive, sharp practice? If the environment lacks these attributes, will it be as appealing as facilities that possess them? Will consumers and customers want to patronize the latter or the former type of facility? Will tenants who experience a lower level of business because of reduced patronage by consumers and customers be motivated to pay higher rents? How do sharp aggressive business practices at the commencement of a real estate transaction ultimately affect the overall value and successful outcome of that transaction?

Rather than the simplistic dominance of exploitation, simulations of game theory applications with classic *prisoner's dilemma* choice conflicts lead to "dynamics of dazzling complexity . . . that . . . are intrinsically unpredictable and chaotic" (Nowack, May, and Sigmund, 1995, p. 76). Such models "illustrate how cooperation might arise and be maintained in real biological systems. Sophisticated creatures may be drawn to follow strategies that encourage cooperation because of repeated interactions among individuals who can recognize and remember one another. But in simpler organisms, cooperation persists, perhaps by virtue of self-organized spatial structures generated by interactions with immediate neighbors in some fixed spatial array" (Nowack, May, and Sigmund, 1995, p. 76).

Intriguingly, collections of tangible real property interests that convey a sense of community are more appealing and therefore possess greater long-term value than those that reflect disparate, distancing attitudes resulting from feelings of exploitation and noncooperation. Properties located in communities that reflect the attributes of the new urbanism and traditional neighborhood development sell at a premium over equivalent properties located in sprawling suburbs, where disproportionate land is devoted to roads and cars, connection is frustrated, and the urban form is singular and isolating rather than mixed and integrating.

Ethical considerations embrace not just outcomes but the means employed to achieve those outcomes. The application of right action in decision making considers the decision processes employed to achieve outcomes, the degree to which decisions are reached by concentrated command-and-control styles as contrasted to a market-based management process, and the degree to which decisions reflect third-party-imposed direction as contrasted to individually initiated self-knowing. These three themes of decision processes are interdependent and share many common philosophic premises.

Trust

Right action is premised on and incorporates trust. Central to trust are the concepts of predictability—pervasively and consistently applied in business matters (Stevenson and Cruikshank, 1997)—and the confidence that one can proceed to participate in property involvements without the fear that one's exchange partner might act opportunistically (Bradach and Eccles, 1989). Francis Fukiyama has advanced the motivational rationale for ethical conduct through the economic self-interest of the thesis that high-trust nations are more prosperous than low-trust nations (Fukiyama, 1996).

Trust is crucial to real estate involvements in multiple realms:

- The client *trusts* that the real estate professional is competent.
- The client *trusts* that the real estate professional will exercise competence in her or his work.
- The client *trusts* that the real estate professional will conduct herself or himself in a way that is objective and independent.
- A party to a real estate transaction *trusts* that the other party will honor representations made.

Central to trust is the concept of *moral hazard*, which covers actions—such as agency problems and conflicts of interest—by professionals that fail to represent their clients' interests.

The premise of trust in property involvements is operationalized through the *real estate trust chain* concept. Explicitly, trust is more likely to prevail if it is expected than if property involvements proceed from the expectation that trust will be violated, for "contracts that assume the other cannot be trusted in the present are unlikely to lead to trust in the future" (Mahoney, Huff, and Huff, 1994, p. 153). At the same time, in a Buddhist context, the emphasis is more on being trustworthy than assessing the trustworthiness of another. This orientation of taking the initiative to be trustworthy would tend to motivate approaches to contracting that presume the presence of trustworthiness rather than the lack of trustworthiness.

Fiduciary Responsibility

As a consequence of assuming the role of a fiduciary in a business or investment venture generally and for property involvements specifically, the individual and/or enterprise taking on such a role undertakes to act primarily for the benefit of those for whom he or she serves as a fiduciary. Many insufficiently perceive the breadth and depth of the responsibilities associated with the fiduciary role.

The fiduciary obligation implies a high standard of conduct. More than a century and a half ago the court established that the general rule of the fiduciary "stands upon our great moral obligation to refrain from placing ourselves in relations which ordinarily excite a conflict between self-interest and integrity" (*Michoud v. Girod*, 1846). As Justice Cardozo observed, where fiduciaries are involved, the standards they must meet are "not the morals of the marketplace but the punctilio of an honor the most sensitive" (*Meinhard v. Salmon*, 1928). Harfield concluded that "a fiduciary owes to his beneficiary a duty of perfect loyalty, such that no departure from it will be condoned, and to the extent possible, the beneficiary will be placed always in the same position as if the duty of perfect loyalty had been perfectly discharged" (Harfield, 1971).

Integral to right action is not just the awareness of the implications of the fiduciary responsibility but the direct incorporation in action of the fiduciary standard. In addition to the competence of the expert in effective decision processes, trust and fiduciary responsibility are two concepts that are closely intertwined, and fundamental to right action. The competent professional making effective technical decisions could, lacking appropriate sensitivity to trust and fiduciary responsibility, engage in conduct that might fall short of what represents *right action*.

Ultimately, trust and fiduciary responsibility in practice are about integrity.

Right Livelihood

Right livelihood embraces the expectation that good work is being done and will be done. Operationalizing good work in the real estate context, this means that an individual engages in livelihood work having processes, outcomes, and consequences that are both internally consistent and also congruent with that individual's values. Similar right livelihood concerns apply to enterprises that invest capital, use space, provide services, develop and build properties, own and manage properties, and represent the public interest. Right livelihood is given explicit form by operative paradigms, strategic frameworks, industry structure, the balance and reconciliation of technology and sustainability in the economy, land tenure and ownership systems, models of urban form and development patterns, and decision criteria.

Various forces and trends are arrayed against a right livelihood approach to business generally and property involvements specifically. The publishing aspirations of academics lead researchers to advocate narrower paradigms and employ narrower disciplinary definitions "that are more tractable for empirical research and theoretical modeling" than are the broader strategic management perspectives that encompass multiple considerations (Mahoney, Huff, and Huff, 1994, p. 153), explicitly those concerning "the kind of economic and human organization (the company) is or intends to be, and the nature of the economic and noneconomic contributions it intends to make to its shareholders, employees, customers and communities" (Andrews, 1980).

An explicit articulation by Kenneth Andrews of the Harvard school of strategic management emphasizes consideration of the nature of anticipated contributions by the organization to shareholders, employees, customers, and communities, reflected in both economic and noneconomic terms (Andrews, 1980). Such an emphasis necessarily leads to consideration of the degree to which the company's fundamental premises and approaches to business, which are given form in the action of the company, are congruent with right livelihood. Right livelihood informed by spirituality necessarily presumes a multiplicity of stakeholders being treated with caring, concern, and dignity.

Whether an enterprise's business reflects right livelihood—from the perspectives of the individuals that comprise that enterprise, those who interact with it as suppliers or customers, and the society of which it is a part—is seldom addressed. For one, the very process of posing the question could lead to severe realignments of roles and priorities within the organization, an outcome that may be less than desired by at least some of the most powerful individuals in the organization, if not others. And further, determining the appropriate context for assessing this question is certainly daunting. If the Buddhist precepts of compassion and loving kindness are applied to a consideration of this issue, they lead to the conclusions of selecting and engaging in work that honors the land and respects all sentient beings in their experiences of environments in all forms, across all cultures, and unbounded by time.

Right livelihood, as applied to real estate, involves bigger ideas that transcend the right action competence expected for particular tasks to consider the very appropriateness of that task, not just in the present but especially in the future and beyond. Consideration of right livelihood in a real estate investing context involves addressing not merely such issues as investment analysis, property management, and financial reporting but such bigger questions (Roulac, 1996b) as the following:

- For any proposed real estate venture, what are the assumptions about why people choose to spend their time and resources at that space?
- What motivates people to be at this space and place?
- Why would people want to spend their resources at this space rather than other spaces?
- How many people are presumed to live, work, shop, and play at this space?

- What alternatives to this space would these people have?
- How much money is it presumed that customers will spend in this space?
- Are such expenditures consistent with their motivation and resources?
- Why do people choose to live where they do?
- How do our values influence the design of the structures in which we live, work, shop, and play?
- How does the design of the structures in which we live and work influence our values?
- How do our values influence the place where we choose to live?
- How do the places where we choose to live, work, and visit affect our values and our experience of life?
- What is the appropriate strategy for providing access to those who are not from a special place, while preserving that special place so it is not despoiled by those who come?
- What are the implications of these choices on the place and the people?

Ultimately, the degree to which a property involvement reflects *right livelihood* can be considered in terms of whether that real estate involvement reflects, reinforces, and is congruent with a certain view of the world and the physical environment.

Honor the Land

In his study of the ethics of land use, Thomas Beatley suggests that a proposed development—which would involve filling wetlands are recognized as having significant environmental importance, to convert the land to a shopping center—raises ethical obligations relative to these wetlands and society (Beatley, 1994). The interpretation of these ethical obligations turns on the definition of the relevant moral community. As Beatley (1994) observes:

> Perhaps we have obligations to migratory waterfowl or other forms of life that depend on the wetlands for survival. Perhaps we have obligations to prevent the creation of harm to other people that will result from filling the wetlands. . . . perhaps we have obligations to future generations to protect these wetlands as part of our natural heritage; for example, as ecological treasures to be viewed, contemplated, and enjoyed by our descendants.

One worldview would lead to a very different outcome than might an alternative worldview. As Beatley (1994) observes:

> Other people, using different processes of moral reasoning and different ethical standards, can arrive at different conclusions about the case at hand. For those who believe that no moral obligations exist to other forms of life, or to future generations, or to the land itself, there may, in fact, be no ethical obligation on their part to protect or avoid the wetlands.

Beatley (1994) goes on to recognize that:

> Others may conclude that there is indeed an ethical obligation to *develop* the wetlands. If one believes, for instance, that the jobs and economic benefits to be generated by the mall are substantial, and important locally in terms of relieving unemployment and expanding the local tax base, this might argue for such a project almost regardless of the environmental impacts.

The field of ecopsychology has as a central tenet the futility of endeavoring to "help people lead 'happier' lives while the world they lived in was deteriorating," according to Allen Kanner, psychologist in private practice in Berkeley ("Ten Innovative Therapists," 1997, p. 57). According to Kanner, "Therapists collude with the culturalwide denial of environmental problems by reinforcing the notion that all that matters are our interactions with others" ("Ten Innorative Therapists," 1997, p. 57). Ecopsychology emphasizes the interdependency of the individual psyche, family systems, technology, and the physical environment (Kanner, Gomes, and Roszak, 1995).

Experiences of Environments

Individual properties are the physical building blocks of communities. The form of those properties and their relationship to other properties exert a powerful influence on the degree of *civic engagement* that characterize communities. While Alexis de Tocqueville highlighted voluntary associations as a defining cultural attribute of the United States of America, in recent years civic participation has declined, as the bond between individuals and their communities weakened and civic engagement less and less characterizes life in this country (Lang and Hornburg, 1998). Decisions concerning the physical design of communities, particularly the attributes of individual properties and their relationships to other properties, can have major influences on social connectedness and civic engagement, and thereby enhance the stability, vitality, and overall well-being of a community (Langdon, 1997).

Overall, as eloquently documented in the work of William Whyte (1980), James Vance (1977), Oscar Newman (1972), Jane Jacobs (1961), and Kevin Lynch (1960), space matters, since physical design ultimately is social design (Bothwell, Gindroz, and Lang, 1998). A study of the revitalization of Diggs Town, a public housing project located in Norfolk, Virginia, concludes that the application of traditional neighborhood development design principles "transformed a socially alienated and distressed neighborhood into a socially integrated and functional one . . . by facilitating the social exchanges it creates social capital" (Bothwell, Gindroz, and Lang, 1998, p. 89).

Consideration of property involvements from the context of right livelihood embraces and integrates individual, family, organizational, and societal concerns. A right livelihood approach to property involvements recognizes the interconnectedness and interdependency of all experiences of property—that one person's housing problem is everyone's housing problem and that someone else's housing problem is their housing problem.

The interdependency and pervasiveness of the housing problem was eloquently described by the late Donald Terner (1994, p. 390):

> The housing problem affects all of us in another way, because as people seek decent, affordable housing, they are moving further and further toward the periphery of the metropolis. They are commuting horrendous distances, through stall and crawl traffic for sometimes an hour or two, and polluting all the way. They come to work tired, cranky, and then put in an eight-hour day behind a cash register or a computer or a lathe or a service desk. When the five o'clock whistle blows, they head home through that same commute, get home, see their spouse and kids, and they're not fit. They're not fit, and they don't feel fit, to give the patience, attention, and love that they have to in order to have a functional family.

Central to right livelihood is the philosophic underpinning of those charged with teaching the disciplines concerned with the physical design of urban environments, specifically architecture and planning. The crux of the problem is that architects too often employ hyperindividualistic styles, concentrating on single buildings, and "are not trained to be practical managers of space" (Marshall, 1997, p. 35). The new urbanism movement, according to Shelley Poticha, is "challenging some of the core values of the traditional architectural establishment: that single buildings aren't the most important things to focus on. That the place and the fabric are important, and that the architecture should contribute to the place" (Marshall, 1997, p. 35). Today, too many graduates of planning schools can enter professional practice largely innocent of architectural education, just as many architects can graduate without schooling on the discipline of planning (Marshall, 1997). The centrality of right livelihood is reflected in the debate now underway concerning such value-laden issues as the mission of architectural education and the role of design in society (Schmidt, 1997b).

Unbounded by Time

The crucial premise of right livelihood extends beyond the relative temporal concentration on short-term profit optimization to emphasize the optimization of multiple interests at a particular point in time and deference to a longer-term view of time.

Arguing that "Spirituality is an integral part, if not the very essence, of management," Mitroff asserts that "spirituality follows a different set of laws" than does conventional, current economic thinking (Mitroff, 1998, p. 68). Specifically, conventional economics discounts the future as "future earnings and, much more seriously, future generations are less valuable to us measured in current dollars" (Mitroff, 1998, p. 68). From a spiritual perspective, such a proposition is not just specious but evil, for "There is no discount function that applies to caring, granting dignity to another human being, and loving other human beings" (Mitroff, 1998, p. 68).

Whereas Native Americans lived with reverence for the land, the European colonists that came to the Americas in the fifteenth and subsequent centuries viewed nature as something to be confronted, subdued, and dominated. In the New World, land was plentiful, and ownership was offered in exchange for its development to encourage opportunity and liberty. Perceptions of superabundance led to virtual depletion of animals and forests and to the degradation of topsoil through irreverent and irresponsible mining, energy extraction, and farming. More recently, urban development patterns have reflected a continuation of the destruction of land resources (Boyce, 1997). While the pattern of destruction of land resources occurs virtually everywhere that population grows, destruction of land resources has been a particularly pronounced North American or New World phenomenon.

Conclusion

The perspectives of three of the practices from the Buddhist eightfold path to enlightenment—right speech, right action, and right livelihood—can illuminate consideration of property involvements. Right speech involves disclosure and honesty; right action embraces competence, fiduciary responsibility, decision processes, and trust. The application of right livelihood to property involvements leads to property involvements that honor the land and respect all sentient beings in their experiences of environments in all forms, across all cultures, and unbounded by time. An individual whose aspiration is to have ethics sensitivity reflected in her real estate involvements may find guidance by considering how congruent her actions are with her values as well as the relationship of those actions to concepts of right speech, right action, and right livelihood.

What constitutes right speech, right action, right livelihood in the context of real estate is the essence of *ethics in real estate*. Virtually every, if not every, ethical issue one might confront is ultimately subsumed within the consideration of the rightness of speech, action, and livelihood. Right speech as it is applied in the property context encompasses disclosure and honesty. Honesty and trust are important because they are the bedrock of intrapersonal, interpersonal, intraorganizational, interorganizational, and all of society's communications. Disclosure is important since it enables informed and balanced decisions.

Although one may not necessarily encounter an extended discourse in Buddhist tracts on the question of competence, implicit in right action is the presumption of competence. For how can one engage in right action if that action is characterized by incompetence? Although the application of competence in the context of right action is addressed here from the perspective of property involvements, many students of Buddhism would concur that right action is essentially synonymous with competence.

Consideration of what amounts to right speech, right action, and right livelihood in property involvement turns on one's worldview. Ultimately, perceptions concerning humankind's relationship to nature define the worldview that determines property involvements. One's worldview is largely influenced by ideas and specifically what one's definitions are for "good" and "right." As important as this issue might be, relatively few address it explicitly. Although legions of psychoanalysts tend to discourage philosophizing and overintellectualizing and are disinclined to address explicitly issues of good and right, a growing number of individuals are offering philosophical counseling to enable people to use philosophy as a lens through which to see the world (Wexler, 1997).

Certain elements of the model of right speech, right action, and right livelihood advanced here are reflected in what is expected of architects. The rules of conduct for the National Council of Architectural Registration Boards address the five issues of competence, conflicts of interest, full disclosure, compliance with laws, and professional conduct, with the objective of protecting the public rather than advancing the interests of the architecture profession (Schmidt, 1997a). Recognizing that the topics that ethical codes seek to address are both subtle and complex, the new Code of Ethics of the American Institute of Architects is articulated in terms of three levels, including canons (broad principles of conduct), ethical standards (goals toward which to aspire), and mandatory rules of conduct (Schmidt, 1997a).

The notions of right speech, right action, and right livelihood may offer an illuminating approach to addressing appropriate property involvements. Right speech, right action, and right livelihood provide means by which ethical factors can be incorporated into property involvements and real estate decision making, can integrate dynamism with responsiveness to changing conditions, and can reflect both continuity as well as permanence.

By balancing virtue and profit, considering there multiple interests through compassionate pragmatism and pragmatic compassion may reconcile what have been perceived of as the competing objectives of altruism championed by moral philosophers and self-interested profit maximization of capitalists. As divergent as the perspectives of self-interest and property as a covenant may appear to be, ultimately they are reconcilable. Those who pursue self-interest from core values of their culture, family, and heritage will inevitably arrive at perspectives congruent with the concept of property as a covenant. And those who advocate an approach reflecting property as a covenant do so from self-interest.

Table of Cases

Meinhard v. Salmon, 249 N.Y. 458, 164 N.E. 545 (1928).
Michoud v. Girod, 4 How. 503 (1846).

References

Andrews, Kenneth R. (1980). *The Concept of Corporate Strategy*. Homewood, IL: Irwin.

Beatley. (1994). *Ethical Land Use: Principles of Policy and Planning*. Baltimore: John Hopkins University Press.

Bloom, George F., Arthur M. Weimer, and Jeffrey D. Fischer. (1982). *Real Estate* (8th ed.). New York: Wiley.

Bok, Sissela. (1989). *Lying*. New York: Vintage Books.

Bolen, Jean Shinoda. (1994). *Crossing to Avalon: A Woman's Midlife Pilgrimage*. San Francisco: Harper.

Bothwell, Stephanie E., Raymond Gindroz, and Robert E. Lang. (1998). "Restoring Community Through Traditional Neighborhood Design: A Case Study of Diggs Town Public Housing." *Housing Policy Debate* 9(1): 89.

Bowie, N.E. (1991). "The Firm as a Moral Community." In R.M. Coughlin (ed.), *Morality, Rationality and Efficiency: New Perspectives on Socio-Economics.* Armonk, NY: Sharpe.

Bowman, E.H. (1974). "The Epistemology, Corporate Strategy and Academe." *Sloan Management Review* 15: 35–50.

Boyce, Mark W. (1997). "A Land Ethic: The Vital Foundation for Sustainable Community Development." Unpublished paper.

Bradach, J.L., and R.G. Eccles. (1987). "Price, Authority and Trust." *Annual Review of Sociology* 15: 97–118.

Brand, Stewart. (1998). "In Dyson's Brain." *Wired* (February): 131.

Castells, Manuel. (1996). *The Information Age: Economy, Society and Culture—The Rise of the Networked Society* (Vol. 1). Oxford: Blackwell.

Covey, Stephen R. (1989). *The Seven Habits of Highly Effective People.* New York: Simon & Schuster.

Dalton, Gene W., and Paul H. Thompson. (1991). *Novations: The Four Stages of Careers and Organizations.* Provo, UT: Novations Group.

Darcy, Keith T. (1992). "Letters: Ethical Questions." *Fortune* (May 18).

Darwin, Charles. (1871/19   ). *The Descent of Man, and Selection in Relation to Sex.* New York: Appleton.

Darwin, Charles. (1860/19   ). *The Origin of Species: By Means of Natural Selection or the Preservation of Favoured Races in the Struggle for Life.* New York: Appleton.

Dasso, Jerome, and Alfred A. Ring. (1989). *Real Estate Principles and Practice* (11th ed.). Englewood Cliffs, NJ: Prentice-Hall.

Diaz, Julian. (1994). *Journal of Real Estate Literature.*

Doe, John. (1991). "The Dark Side of 'Professionalism.' " *Commercial Investment Real Estate Journal* (Spring): 10.

Eldred, Gary. (1987). *Real Estate Analysis and Strategy.* New York: Harper & Row.

Epley, Donald R., and Joseph Rabianski. (1986). *Principles of Real Estate Decisions.* Englewood Cliffs, NJ: Prentice-Hall.

Evers, Frederick T., and James C. Rush. (1996). "The Bases of Competence: Skill Development During the Transition from University to Work." *Management Learning* 275.

Graaskamp, James A. (1976a). "An Approach to Real Estate Finance Education by Analogy to Risk Management Principles." *Recent Perspectives in Urban Land Economics.* Vancouver, BC: University of British Columbia.

Graaskamp, James A. (1976b) "Redefining the Role of University Education and Real Estate and Urban Land Economics." *Real Estate Appraiser* (March–April): 23.

Grissom, Terry V., and Crocker H. Kiu. (1994). "The Search for Discipline: The Philosophy and the Paradigms." In James R. DeLisle and J. Sa-Aadu (eds.),

Appraisal, Market Analysis and Public Policy in Real Estate: Essays in Honor of James A. Graaskamp. Boston: Kluwer.

Hall, William D. (1987). *Accounting and Auditing: Thoughts on Forty Years in Practice and Education*. Chicago: Arthur Andersen.

Harfield. (1971). "The Nature of the Fiduciary Obligation in Today's Environment." *New York State Business Journal* 394 (October).

Harwood, Bruce, and Charles J. Jacobus. (1990). *Real Estate Principles* (5th ed.). Englewood Cliffs, NJ: Prentice-Hall.

Inman, Brad. (1996). "High Tech Eliminates Guesswork from Real Estate." *San Francisco Sunday Examiner and Chronicle*, September 15, p. E-3.

Jacobs, Jane. (1961). *The Death and Life of Great American Cities*. New York: Vintage.

Jaffe, Austin. (1995). Pages Presented to the European Real Estate Society, Stockholm, June.

Jaffe, Austin. (1996). Presidential address to American Real Estate and Urban Economics Association meeting, San Francisco, January.

Jamal, Karim, and Norman E. Bowie. (1995). "Theoretical Considerations for a Meaningful Code of Professional Ethics." *Journal of Business Ethics* 14: 703–714.

James, William. (1991). *Pragmatism*. Buffalo, NY: Prometheus.

Kanner, Allen D., Mary Gomes, and Theodore Roszak. (1995). *Ecopsychology: Restoring the Earth, Healing the Mind*.: Sierra Club Books.

Kau, James B., and C.F. Sirmans. (1985) *Real Estate*. New York: McGraw-Hill.

Keynes, John Maynard. (1936). *The General Theory of Employment, Interest and Money*. New York: Harcourt, Brace & World.

Kim, W. Chan, and Reneé Mauborgne. (1997). "Fair Process: Managing in the Knowledge Economy." *Harvard Business Review* (July–August): 65.

Koch, Charles G. (1998). "Empowering the Entrepreneur Within." *Chief Executive* (March): 46.

Laing, Jonathan R. (1998). "Dangerous Games." *Barron's* (June 8): 17.

Lang, Robert E., and Steven P. Hornburg. (1998) "What Is Social Capital and Why Is It Important to Public Policy?" *Housing Policy Debate* 9(1): 1.

Langdon, Philip. (1997). "Can Design Make Community?" *Responsive Community* 7(2): 25.

Leopold, Aldo. (1949). *A Sand County Almanac and Sketches Here and There*. New York: Oxford University Press.

Lowenstein, Louis. (1991). *Sense and Nonsense in Corporate Finance*. Reading, MA: Addison-Wesley.

Lynch, Kevin. (1960) *The Image of the City*. Cambridge, MA: Harvard University Press.

Mahoney, Joseph T., Anne S. Huff, and James O. Huff. (1994). "Toward a New Social Contract Theory in Organization Science." *Journal of Management Inquiry* (June): 153.

Marshall, Alex. (1997). "Teaching New Urbanism." *Metropolis* (October): 35.

Mitroff, Ian I. (1998). "On the Fundamental Importance of Ethical Management: Why Management Is the Most Important of All Human Activities." *Journal of Management Inquiry* (March 1998): 68.

Newman, Oscar. (1972). *Defensible Space: Crime Prevention Through Urban Design.* New York: MacMillan.

Nisbet, Robert. (1980). *History of the Idea of Progress.* New York: Basic Books.

Nourse, Hugh O. (1990). *Managerial Real Estate: Corporate Real Estate Asset Management.* Englewood Cliffs, NJ: Prentice-Hall.

Nowack, Martin A., Robert M. May, and Carl Sigmund. (1995). "The Arithmetic of Mutual Help." *Scientific American* (July): 76.

Ordway, Nicholas, Cynthia L.M. Yee, and Will McIntosh. (1996). "The Diminishing Competency Curve and the Need for Continuing Education." Paper presented to the American Real Estate Society Annual Meeting.

Passell, Peter. (1996). "Race, Mortgages and Statistics." *New York Times*, May 10, p. C-1.

Peck, M. Scott. (1980). *The Road Less Traveled.* New York: Simon & Schuster.

Quinn, Daniel. (1992). *Ishmael.* New York: Bantam.

Reich, Charles A. (1971). *The Greening of America.* New York: Bantam.

Rodale, J.R. (1978). *The Synonym Finder.* Emmaus, PA: Rodale Press.

Rosen, Jeffrey. (1998). "The Perjury Trap." *The New Yorker* (August 10): 28.

Roulac, Stephen E. (1993). "Toward a Proposed Real Estate Body of Knowledge and Strategic Framework." Paper presented at American Real Estate Society Meeting, Key West, FL, April.

Roulac, Stephen E. (1995). "Due Diligence in Real Estate Transactions." In Joseph Pagliari (ed.), *Handbook of Real Estate Portfolio Management* (pp. 729–772). Boston: Irwin.

Roulac, Stephen E. (1996a). "The State of the Discipline: Malaise or Renaissance." *Journal of Real Estate Research* (special issue commemorating the tenth anniversary of the American Real Estate Society) 12(2): 111–121.

Roulac, Stephen E. (1996b). "Whose Ideas Are Represented in Your Portfolio?" *Institutional Real Estate Letter* (June): 25–26.

Roulac, Stephen E. (1999). *Geostrategy: The Strategy of Place and Space.* Forthcoming.

Roulac, Stephen E., Lloyd Lynford, and Gilbert H. Castle III. (1990). "Real Estate Decision Making in an Information Era." *Real Estate Finance Journal* (Summer): 8.

Roulac, Stephen E., and Scott R. Muldavin. (1994). "Toward the New Strategic Paradigm: The Conceptual Framework for the Body of Knowledge." Paper presented at the meeting of the American Real Estate Society, Santa Barbara, CA, April 13–16.

Schmidt, Elizabeth. (1997a). "Codifying Ethics: The Long Route to Architecture's Codes of Ethical Conduct." *Metropolis* (October): 73.

Schmidt, Elizabeth. (1997b). "Teaching Ethics." *Metropolis* (October): 72.

Smith, Halbert C., and John B. Corgel. (1992). *Real Estate Perspectives: An Introduction to Real Estate* (2nd ed.). Homewood, Ill: Irwin.

Sparks, Nicholas. (1996). *The Notebook* New York: Warner Books.

Stein, Benjamin J. (1996). "A Family Business." *Barron's* (June 24): 18.

Stevenson, Howard H., and Jeffrey L. Cruikshank. (1997). *Do Lunch or Be Lunch: The Power of Predictability in Creating Your Future*. Boston: Harvard Business School Press.

Stevenson, Richard W. (1996). "Do People and Profits Go Hand-In-Hand?" *New York Times*, May 9, p. C-1.

Taylor, William. (1992). "Crime? Greed? Big Ideas? What Were the eighties About?" *Harvard Business Review* (January–February): 32.

"Ten Innovative Therapists Who Do More Than Just Talk." (1997). *Utne Reader* (January–February): 57.

Terner, Donald. (1994). "Affordable Housing: An Impossible Dream?" *The Commonwealth* (June 27): 390.

Vance, James E. (1977). *This Scene of Man: The Role and Structures of the City and the Geography of Western Civilization*. New York: Harpers College Press.

Wane, Leslie. (1996). "Socked in by the S.E.C." *New York Times*, May 11, p. 17.

Wexler, Laura. (1997). "Thinking, Not Shrinking." *Utne Reader* (January–February): 50.

Whyte, William H. (1980). *The Social Life of Small Spaces*. Washington, DC: Conservation Foundation.

Wofford, Larry E., and Terence M. Clauretie. (1992). *Real Estate* (3rd ed.). New York: Wiley.

Wurtzebach, Charles H., and Mike E. Miles. (1991). *Modern Real Estate* (4th ed.). New York: Wiley.

2 ETHICAL CHOICE IN REAL ESTATE: SELECTED PERSPECTIVES FROM ECONOMICS, PSYCHOLOGY, AND SOCIOLOGY

Larry E. Wofford

C & L Systems Corporation
Tulsa, Oklahoma

Abstract

This chapter considers real estate ethics from the perspective of choice, or decision making, under uncertainty. The emphasis is on initiating a synthesis between economics, psychology, and sociology in order to broaden the scope of explorations of choice in real estate ethics. Starting with the generally accepted normative decision-making framework provided by rational choice theory, the study explores findings in psychology and sociology that describe how humans make decisions in the real world. Some of these findings may be useful in adding to the understanding of decision making provided by rational choice theory. It is suggested that a multidisciplinary framework, combining philosophy and science, is essential for significant progress in real estate ethics. Possible preliminary elements of such a framework are presented in the appendix.

Introduction

Real estate ethics is about making choices. In particular, real estate ethics is about making choices under uncertainty, a condition real estate ethics shares with real estate decision making in general. Real estate ethics also shares with the rest of real estate decision making a generally accepted normative framework for making choices under uncertainty, rational choice theory (RCT). The linchpins of RCT are rationality and expected utility (EU), sometimes referred to as subjective expected utility (SEU). While almost universally accepted as a guide to how choices *should* be made, RCT is not immune to criticism.

The primary criticism of RCT is that it may be an excellent normative model but is a poor representation of how humans actually make decisions. It is argued that sometimes humans simply are not as rational and logical in practice as RCT posits they should be. It is not suggested that humans are *always* irrational but that from time to time they depart from the particular type of rationality defined by RCT in consequential and systematic ways. RCT utilizes *instrumental rationality* in which ends or goals are considered exogenous and choice and rationality are limited to choosing the best means to satisfy given ends. Critics contend that selecting ends, the very goals an individual seeks to achieve, is a fundamental component of human choice (Schmidtz, 1995). Further, they contend that such ends may be influenced materially by many factors, with an important factor being social context. These arguments do not suggest that RCT is without merit but rather that a purely economic framework may be too lean to describe actual human decision making, including decisions involving ethics. Thus, this study emphasizes *supplementing* RCT by incorporating considerations of how humans think and the impact of social considerations and does not recommend supplanting RCT with these concepts.

Objectives

This study explores problem solving and decision making in real estate and their relationship to real estate ethics. The emphasis is on initiating a synthesis between economics, psychology, sociology, and other disciplines in order to broaden the scope of explorations of choice in real estate ethics. The study also proposes a view of real estate ethics that involves philosophy *and* science.

The possible considerations in a study dealing with real estate ethics are limitless, but this chapter's objectives are limited to examining selected aspects of how real humans make decisions in the real world. Many excellent summaries of the philosophical foundations of general and business ethics exist in which deontological, utilitarian, social choice, and a myriad of other theories are considered in varying levels of detail.[1] Consequently, this philosophical foundation is not discussed here. This omission is not intended to denigrate the value of the philosophical foundations of ethics in any manner. In this study it is assumed that philosophy and science can inform each other. This study also does not differentiate between prescriptive and descriptive ethics but, rather, examines ethics in an applied context.

Throughout the study it is assumed that moral philosophy benefits from an understanding of human possibilities and limitations and that scientific research related to ethics needs the compass provided by moral philosophy.

Why Bother to Study Real Estate Ethics?

At this point, it is reasonable to consider why we should bother to study real estate ethics. Implicit throughout this study is the assumption that the examination of real estate ethics, meant here to include research and teaching, has the potential to improve ethical decision making in real estate. If, ultimately, results that improve applied real estate ethics are not forthcoming, then it may be argued that time and effort may be spent more productively elsewhere. Rest and Narvaez (1994, p. x) outline the assumptions that underlie the development and teaching of ethics courses if they are to be worthwhile:

> If courses in ethics are worth curricular space and student time, then at least three assumptions must be true:
>
> 1. Some ways of deciding what is right (making ethical decisions) are more justifiable than others. Given some moral problem, we do not assume that every conceivable action or reason is as good as every other.
> 2. There must be some agreement among "experts" on what the more justifiable ethical positions are. Although there might not be complete agreement on one unique line of action, nevertheless, presumably fair-minded people familiar with the facts must agree that some positions are defensible but that others are less so. Defensibility cannot be completely idiosyncratic.
> 3. Ethics courses influence students in some positive way. The way students will live their lives as professionals is constructively influenced by ethics courses.
>
> If any of these three assumptions is not true, then there is not much point in having applied ethics courses.

These assumptions also must hold for research into real estate ethics to be worthwhile. If useful, research findings influence ethics systems, including codes of ethics, various supporting materials, and real estate ethics courses. If combined research and teaching efforts do not improve applied real estate ethics, then there is little use in continuing to utilize resources pursuing them. However, until significant efforts are expended on real estate ethics research and education and appropriate techniques for empirically evaluating the effectiveness of these efforts are developed and implemented, these assumptions must represent the foundation arguments for pursuing ethics research and education efforts.[2]

Decision Making, Uncertainty, and Real Estate Ethics

Having choices, often difficult ones, is the crux of ethical concerns. In the absence of choice, ethical considerations generally disappear as an individual is seldom held accountable for situations in which there are no degrees of freedom and no choice is possible. However, an individual with the freedom to choose a course of action, sometimes even from very narrow choice sets, will generally be held accountable. Thus, the freedom to choose is a precondition to responsibility, including choices involving real estate ethics. However, choice is not the only precondition to ethical responsibility.

Dawes (1988) posits that uncertainty is also a precondition to ethical choice and the resultant responsibility. If certainty exists, then decisions can be fully evaluated, including all primary, secondary, and tertiary effects on ourselves *and* others. In such a situation, all decisions automatically incorporate ethical considerations. Thus, if all options are known and for each option *all* of the effects on the decision maker and others can be identified, then the preferred option, with all ethical considerations included, can be selected. Under certainty, a real estate decision maker can evaluate over any relevant time period whether he or she is better off making one decision or the other. For example, a developer is able to determine whether the ill will generated over today's project will produce greater or lower total profits over his or her lifetime discounted to today and then choose a course of action accordingly.

However, certainty is not a situation real estate decision makers need consider with vigor, except perhaps as a simplifying but unrealistic ideal. In real estate, as in most decision-making environments, uncertainty generally prevails. As noted by Hansson (1996, p. 369),

> In practice, all decision making takes place under conditions of uncertainty. Decision making under *certainty* is an idealized limiting case found only in textbooks. In that case, it is known for sure what the options are, what the outcome is if one chooses each of these options, and what the value is of each of these outcomes. In textbooks, by decision making under *uncertainty* is meant a situation in which it is still known what the options are and what the values are of the various possible outcomes. However, at least some option can be followed by more than one outcome, and the exact probabilities of the outcomes, given different options, are not known.

In real estate, decision makers frequently do not know all the options and the related possible outcomes. While a distinction sometimes is made between risk and uncertainty, such a distinction is not germane to this study, and uncertainty is used to identify any condition other than certainty.

Uncertainty in real estate ethics often assumes especially pernicious forms that make it difficult to solve such problems and choose an appropriate course of action. Many real estate problems are not fully specified in the sense that all variables may not be known or the relationships between them may not be clearly identified. Such problems may be labeled "ambiguous," and along with an overall resistance to solution, even *attempting* to solve ambiguous problems may generate second- and third-order problems over time (Hart, 1986). For especially messy ambiguous problems the goal may become simply to make the second- and third-order problems created by attempting a solution less severe than the original problem.

Hansson (1996) develops the concept of *great uncertainty* to describe problems particularly resistant to solution. He identifies four types of uncertainty, one or more of which commonly are found in problems classified as exhibiting great uncertainty (Hansson, 1996):

- *Uncertainty of demarcation* It is not well determined what the options are;
- *Uncertainty of consequences* It is not known what the consequences of the options are;
- *Uncertainty of reliance* It is not clear whether information from others (such as experts) can be relied on; and
- *Uncertainty of values* The values of decision makers or of relevant others are not well determined.

It is not difficult to envision real estate ethics problems frequently exhibiting one or more of the uncertainties detailed by Hansson and, therefore, characterized by great uncertainty. For example, simply recognizing whether a real estate problem involves ethical issues is frequently an uncertain business. Likewise, in solving an ethics problem or making a decision involving ethics, all options may not be known, the consequences of each option may not be known, and the "correct ethical values" to apply to the problem in order to develop an ethically acceptable solution or decision may not be known. In some situations the question is not whether one wants to be ethical but which set of relevant ethical values, among many possible ones, is to be used. For now, the notion that real estate ethics involves problem solving and decision making under uncertainty and that ethical problems may be quite difficult to resolve are the germane concepts.

Under certainty, all outcomes are known at the time the decision is made. This situation is in stark contrast to conditions of uncertainty in which outcomes, and, hence, the ethical consequences are not known until *after the fact*—sometimes well after the fact. This mismatch in time between decision and outcome contributes to the difficulty of ethics problems. It also contributes to the difficulties associated with learning from experience.

Under uncertainty a decision maker may face an incomplete array of possible outcomes—some ethically desirable, some not. A decision maker must choose now based on known possible outcomes and their related probabilities. A decision ultimately will produce a single outcome which may or not have been desired, or even considered, by the decision maker. An *ex post* evaluation of the outcome of the decision may find it either ethically desirable or undesirable. Of critical importance is the notion that the outcome is evaluated after the fact and may or may not represent what the decision maker expected or even contemplated. Further, the outcome may be evaluated using different measures and different ethical standards than were relevant when the decision was made.

This situation leads to an important rule: *Given uncertainty, the outcome of a decision cannot be used to evaluate the decision itself* (Dawes, 1988). In an uncertain world, decisions must be evaluated in light of the information and circumstances extant when the decision is made. The same is true for evaluations of the ethical nature of decisions; they are best judged using the information and ethical standards available at the time the decision was made and not by examining outcomes and imputing ethical or unethical intent. Just because a decision produces an outcome that is ethically undesirable does not mean that the decision was unethical. Along the same lines, just because an outcome is perceived to be ethical does not guarantee that the decision was ethical. This relationship between uncertainty and ethics is critical because the motivation for a decision frequently is inferred from its outcome, a questionable exercise (Dawes, 1988). The relationship between uncertainty and real estate ethics is a direct and important one.

An Overview of Rational Choice Theory

Given the important relationship between decision making under uncertainty and real estate ethics, it is useful to develop a clear understanding of how the accepted normative framework of RCT deals with uncertainty. As discussed earlier, the critical components of RCT are rationality and EU. Both are defined very carefully and used in particular ways in RCT. Thus, rationality and EU provide a foundation for discussing possible limitations, objections, and alternatives to RCT. What follows is intended as an overview, not as a detailed review.

Rationality in RCT

Because the word *rational* has many connotations, it is important to define its meaning in RCT. A decision is *rational* in RCT if it best serves the achievement of the objectives of the decision maker. It does not matter what the objectives are, but the decision must be the best one available to achieve them (Baumol and Blinder, 1982). Rationality that assumes a set of objectives and identifies an action as rational because it is the one most likely to satisfy those objectives is called *instrumental rationality* (Hargreaves Heap et al., 1992).[3] In instrumental rationality the relationship between action and objectives is direct and clear. A decision maker is assumed to be capable of developing preferences among the various options and choosing the one providing the best chance of achieving specified objectives.

Instrumental rationality characterizes economic man, also known as *homo economicus*.[4] *Homo economicus* is assumed to be in relentless pursuit of ends with preferences predicated on selecting the means with the greatest likelihood of achieving those ends. Because constraints, usually in the form of resource limitations, often exist on choices, *homo economicus* must satisfy preferences subject to limited room to maneuver. Thus, complete freedom does not exist for *homo economicus* (Hargreaves Heap et al., 1992).

Dawes (1988) more precisely defines *rationality* using three criteria that a decision must meet in order to be considered rational:

- It is based on the decision maker's *current* assets. Assets include not only money but physiological state, psychological capacities, social relationships, and feelings.
- It is based on the possible consequences of the choice.
- When these consequences are uncertain, their likelihood is evaluated without violating the basic rules of probability theory.

These criteria, if followed, prevent contradictory choices. Conversely, violations of any of them may result in contradictory (irrational) choices such as when a person simultaneously prefers choice A over choice B, choice B over choice C, and choice C over choice A. Rationality, and the concept of rational behavior, determines what *cannot* be concluded and not what can or should. Rationality, then, provides a mechanism for avoiding contradictions and not for guiding one to particular conclusions.

Expected Utility

The notions that people are capable of evaluating the satisfaction, or utility, associated with various opportunities and that they seek to maximize that utility date back at least to the eighteenth century. For events that are certain, it was assumed for many years that individuals could directly estimate utility. Estimating utility for uncertain events had to wait for an approach that was initially developed, appropriately enough, for gambling. Bernoulli extended the idea that individuals are capable of estimating the utility of certain outcomes to the notion that individuals could incorporate uncertainty into the utility calculus. He contended that people seek to maximize expected utility, the mean of the utilities of the possible outcomes weighted by the probability of each outcome. This concept is based on the mathematical expectation of a distribution and represents what should eventuate over the long term (Payne, 1985). Uncertainty, as used in this context, implies that probability distributions of outcomes exist and may be specified or estimated by the decision maker.

The concept of individuals directly estimating utilities and then making choices was troublesome to many. In 1944, many of the objections to the idea that individuals can and do assign numerical utility values to possible outcomes were overcome by von Neumann and Morgenstern (1944/1972). In place of the direct estimation of utility, they developed a set of mathematical axioms based on preferences and demonstrated that preferences and preference orderings satisfying their axioms can be used to develop a utility function. The utility function developed by von Neumann and Morgenstern describes the preference ordering "as if" the decision maker had used it to develop the original ordering. Rationality comes into play in that it is a necessary condition for following the rules developed by von Neumann and Morgenstern. Accordingly, the three requirements for rationality discussed earlier are preconditions for the development of expected utility theory.

The axioms developed by von Neumann and Morgenstern deal with the *consistency* of choices. While detailed discussions of the axioms are available in the original work; Maital (1982, p. 194) provides a concise summary:

- For any pair of objects or events, people have "a clear intuition of preferences. . . . [their] system of preferences is all-embracing and complete."

- People's preferences are consistent and do not embody internal contradictions.
- Consider two events, A and B. Suppose a certain A is preferred to a certain B. This implies that a one-in-a-thousand chance of A is better than a one-in-a-thousand chance of B. (For one-in-a-thousand you can substitute any probability between zero and one.)
- Suppose A is preferred to B and B to C. No matter how desirable A itself is, its influence can be made as weak as desired by attaching a sufficiently small chance to it.
- The way a choice is packaged, or expressed, makes no difference. If a bet is broken into two parts or combined as one part, the choice should be the same. This is the anti–Proctor & Gamble axiom of gambles. It essentially means no pleasure derives from the act of gambling itself or the way the gamble is marketed.

These axioms and the utility framework they support provide the foundation for the *instrumental rationality* that economists assume that humans practice (Hargreaves Heap et al., 1992).

Criticism of Rational Choice Theory

Rational choice theory is not without critics, with the primary criticism being that RCT is a good normative model but a poor description of how humans actually make decisions. Rationality is viewed as one of the resource limitations faced by humans making decisions, including those involving ethics. Because humans must deal with enormous quantities of data with limited cognitive resources, they may not be as rational and logical in all situations as *homo economicus* is in theory. In a nutshell, critics contend that *homo economicus* perhaps knows what should be done but has difficulty putting the normative framework into practice.

The argument is not that humans are always irrational but that they depart from rationality from time to time. If the departures from rationality were inconsequential or random, they would not be very interesting. However, it is contended that these deviations are consequential and systematic, making them much more interesting. Likewise, if markets are efficient enough to cause rapid and complete corrections of erroneous choices, then there may be little cause for concern; however, the efficiency of real estate markets remains an empirical question.

Thus, rational models have an important normative role to play, but a better understanding of how humans actually make decisions may be helpful in avoiding or reducing the problems associated with what generally is called irrationality. Thaler (1991) summarizes the situation in what he describes as two false statements:

- Statement 1: All decisions are rational.
- Statement 2: All rational models are useless.

Simply recognizing that both of these statements are false eliminates a great deal of unnecessary debate. If the statements are accepted as false, attention can turn to how humans think and make decisions, especially to identifying any systematic cognitive elements that may provide practical assistance to problem solving and decision making.

Cognitive Psychology and Human Decision Making

The study of how people think, including how they make decisions, is the domain of psychology—more specifically, cognitive psychology. Cognitive psychology is part of a larger enterprise labeled cognitive science.[5] But it is cognitive psychology that is of primary interest here because within its somewhat loosely defined boundaries exists a large and growing body of research on human cognition and rationality developed over the last four decades. Cognitive psychology research efforts have focused on how humans gather, process, and use information, including how they solve problems. Explicitly considering mental processes is a departure from the black box approach to cognition often assumed in economics.

Cognitive psychology research has generally concluded that human cognitive abilities are not equal to the normative abilities assumed in RCT (Simon et al., 1992, p. 33–34):

> What chiefly distinguishes the empirical research on decision making and problem solving from the prescriptive approaches derived from SEU theory is the attention the former gives to the limits on human rationality. These limits are imposed by the complexity of the world in which we live, the incompleteness and inadequacy of human knowledge, the inconsistencies of individual preference and belief, the conflicts of value among people and groups of people, and the inadequacy of the computations we can carry out, even with the aid of the most powerful computers.

Evans (1989, p. 2) summarizes the systematic nature of the inevitable difficulties created by the inherent limits on human cognition:

> A massive amount of psychological research into human thinking, reasoning and judgment has been conducted, especially in the past 20 years or so. Although

there are difficulties in defining criteria for correct performance on such tasks—which I shall discuss later—these studies have resulted in widespread reporting of a host of systematic errors, or *biases* as they are usually called.

The root cause of these deviations is the limited human ability to process the virtually unlimited flow of data. These cognitive limitations were recognized by Miller (1956) when he contended that human ability to perform critical mental processes is limited to roughly seven discrete "chunks" of information at one time.

Simon (1978) subsumes cognitive limitations under the heading of *bounded rationality*.[6] In light of the difficulty of the real-world problems to be solved, including many of those involving real estate ethics, and the enormous amount of information to be processed with limited cognitive abilities, it is not surprising that humans utilize simplifying strategies and heuristics in order to cope. It also is not surprising that, as noted by Evans (1989), these significant data-reduction efforts lead to systematic biases in human cognition.[7]

Working generally, but not exclusively, within the basic framework of limited cognitive capabilities and the resulting biases, research in cognitive psychology has generated many findings of interest to real estate decision making in general and decision making involving real estate ethics in particular.[8] The findings in Table 2.1 are only a sample of research results, but they have a broad range of applicability for applied real estate ethics. In considering the applicability of cognitive psychology research results for real estate ethics decision making, it may be helpful to consider Rest's (1994) four-component model in Table 2.2, which categorizes the psychological activity associated with moral behavior into four categories or components—moral sensitivity, moral judgment, moral motivation, and moral character. These components are similar to the familiar problem-solving strategy of identifying the problem, generating and selecting options, relating options to goals and making a choice, and implementing the solution. In order to behave ethically, one must be able to identify situations involving ethics issues, judge which action(s) are right and wrong, determine that being ethical is the appropriate course of action, and have the courage, skill, and perseverance to pursue the ethical course. Because ethics is often viewed in the negative—that is, in terms of failure—the four-components in Table 2.2 also may be viewed as four sources of moral failure in the sense that an individual may not behave ethically because of a failure in any of these four components. It is not difficult to see that the cognitive psychology findings in Table 2.1 have applicability to these four components and represent areas of potentially fruitful research in applied real estate

Table 2.1. Selected cognitive psychology research findings

1. *The earlier stages of problem solving—such as framing problems, fixing agendas, setting goals, and identifying courses of action—have received less attention than the later stage of decision making.* The earlier stages involving framing problems, agenda fixing, setting goals, and identifying options are more open-ended and less amenable to research and experimentation. Work in operations research and other quantitative solution techniques has caused many problems to be reshaped in the early stages of problem solving to fit the available tools, even when the reshaping creates only an approximate fit at best. This "tool in search of a use" or "solution in a box" approach may produce precise numerical answers, but these answers are often inappropriate in the sense that they solve a reconstituted problem representation and not the base problem. Given that many real estate problems are ill structured and open ended and, therefore, not readily solvable by standard techniques, the development of a problem representation, or structure, is critical to solving them. Likewise, additional research into setting goals and objectives and identifying options may be beneficial to real estate problem solving, including ethics problems.

2. *Limited cognitive capacity necessitates large-scale data reduction efforts that lead to many of the systematic biases observed in human cognition and the extensive use of heuristics to solve problems.* It is ironic that in an age characterized as the "information age" humans, perhaps more than ever, are incapable of processing all the information available to them. As a result, humans must reduce the amount of information with which they deal in order to avoid being overwhelmed. Such data reduction is accomplished using mental shortcuts or rules of thumb, called *heuristics*. As with any data-reduction effort, heuristics may introduce bias and the resulting inaccurate assessments of situations and responses. Such biases are not just a possibility; they are an *inevitable* result of using heuristics (Evans, 1989).

3. *Human cognition is a highly contingent activity, being affected by even small changes in context.* Human cognition is highly sensitive to environment, wording, and other contextual factors. The mind reconstructs events from a skeletal outline containing only essential information with details being recreated each time the event is recalled. If access to memory is affected by heuristics, which, in turn, are affected by a number of contextual factors, overall memory is context sensitive. The contingent nature of cognition and memory is an important finding for real estate problem solving and ethics.

4. *Learning from experience is difficult.* Selectivity in cognition and its related strategies make it difficult to learn from experience (Dawes, 1988). The use of samples and grouping mechanisms to avoid exhaustive searches may lead to bias because one's paradigm, or worldview, systematically determines what information is perceived or retrieved. Thus, humans may fail to pay attention to relevant information about a problem because it was filtered out.[a] Compounding this problem is the uncertain and probabilistic nature of the world and the problems of interpreting events in such an environment. Experience generally is not the best teacher.

Table 2.1. (continued)

5. *Risk management is a process, not a discrete event, and explicit consideration of risk-taking behavior may be useful in real estate problem solving.* According to comprehensive research by MacCrimmon and Wehrung (1986) involving 509 top-level executives, risk is not perceived as a discrete event, but rather as a process. The process includes steps ranging from risk recognition to tracking the results of choices. Humans manage risk by modifying situations or delaying rather than simply accepting an initial risk state. MacCrimmon and Wehrung's findings also indicate that risk preferences can be formally assessed. These assessments may be useful in making preferences explicit for the problem solver and for communicating such information between the parties involved in solving a problem or making a decision.

6. *Prospect theory is a potentially useful descriptive theory of human decision making.* The anomalies associated with RCT and EU beg the question of whether an alternative theory may provide a better description of human decision making. Prospect theory, developed by Kahneman and Tversky (1979), provides such an alternative. In prospect theory the utility function is replaced by a "value" function reflecting risk aversion for gains and risk seeking for losses. As a theory that incorporates findings from cognitive psychology, prospect theory may provide insights into real estate ethics problem solving and decision making.

7. *The study of error has made inroads into how and why humans make errors.* Related to cognitive psychology, human factors, and other disciplines, research into how humans err has made progress in identifying types of errors and their causes. Reason (1990) has developed a generic error-modeling system in which errors are classified using a number of dimensions. He identifies three basic error types: skill-based slips and lapses, rule-based mistakes, and knowledge-based mistakes. In the same vein, Dorner (1996) examines the "logic of failure" and provides a detailed account of mental processes underlying errors and failure. He posits that it is the accumulation of small mental errors that often leads to disaster, ethical or otherwise. He then provides insight into how these errors can be minimized. Focusing on human error and engineering ways to reduce such error represent potentially fruitful areas of cognitive research. Whether ethics decisions can be engineered raises interesting philosophical and practical issues.

8. *Techniques have been developed for improving decision making capabilities and avoiding mistakes.* There are numerous approaches to understanding and reducing some of the problems created by cognitive limitations. Awareness of the inevitability of such problems is a necessary first step. Other general approaches include replacing the human problem solver with a formalized procedure, improving education and training, changing the task environment, and developing and using interactive decision aids. Attention should also be given to building positive attitudes toward problem solving that overcome the passive nature of the mind. Creative problem solving is an active process requiring a view of problems as challenges, not sources of frustration.

Table 2.1.   (continued)

Making risk preferences explicit may provide an avenue for improving problem solving and decision making.

9. *A theory of the development of moral reasoning and its measurement has been developed by Kohlberg.* Kohlberg (1981, 1984) proposes a psychological theory of moral development in which he asserts that an individual develops moral reasoning capabilities in a series of six invariant stages. In this theory, stages move from simple to more complex, with each new stage being an elaboration of the previous one. Kohlberg thought that few individuals attain stage six moral reasoning, with individuals achieving varied levels of development in the course of their lifetimes. Philosophically, Kohlberg sought to settle the argument between deontologists and teleologists by asserting that stage five characterized utilitarian approaches, while stage six characterized the deontologists. Stages were determined using the open-ended moral judgment interview, the scoring of which is described in a manual containing over 800 pages. Subsequently, a multiple-choice approach, the defining issues test, has been developed for assessing principled moral thinking (Rest, 1994). Numerous studies of moral reasoning using Kohlberg's ideas have been performed in accounting, urban planning, nursing, and many other areas, but little work has been forthcoming in real estate with the exception of Long (1995) and Izzo (1998).[b]

10. *Time and stress affect decision making.* Time constraints produce pressure on decision making, including decisions involving ethics. A lack of time limits the range and scope of information that is considered and thereby increases the likelihood of bias and irrationality. Time constraints also create stress, another factor affecting cognitive performance. Research indicates that low to moderate levels of stress may actually improve cognitive performance, while higher levels of stress impair cognitive performance. Perhaps the realization that cognitive resources are not infinite suggests that our assessment of rationality and rational behavior should always include a consideration of time constraints (Gardner, 1985). Once again, context is critical in cognition.

---

a. The interaction of one's paradigm of the world with incoming information, often called *filtering*, is the opposite of what may be commonly thought. According to Neisser (1976), one's paradigm determines which stimuli are recognized rather than which are rejected. In this regard, cognitive filters operate much like the human eye, which does not filter out ultraviolet radiation but is simply not equipped to recognize and process it. Filtering is a positive process of recognizing the expected, not actively rejecting the unexpected. Adopting this perspective drastically reduces the amount of mental activity and time humans require to simply receive information. The role and importance of filtering in real estate decision making has been considered by Wofford (1985).

b. Rest (1994) provides an excellent summary of Kohlberg. Baron (1993) also provides a summary of Kohlberg's work along with an excellent summary of criticism. Izzo (1998) provides a detailed application of Kohlberg's principles to real estate brokerage.

Table 2.2.   Four psychological components determining moral behavior

1.	*Moral sensitivity*	Interpreting the situation
2.	*Moral judgment*	Judging which action is morally right or wrong
3.	*Moral motivation*	Prioritizing moral values relative to other values
4.	*Moral character*	Having courage, persisting, overcoming distractions, implementing skills

Source: Rest (1994).

ethics. Some of the findings may apply primarily to one of Rest's components, while others may apply to two or more of them.

The four component model provides a foundation for procedural model approaches to applied real estate ethics. A decision maker may develop basic questions, detailed flowcharts, or checklists relating to each of the four components as guides to making decisions involving ethics. For example, the first component, moral sensitivity, may translate into defining the ethical problem and building a problem representation that includes identifying the issues and the parties affected by the decision.

Another set of questions, related to moral judgment, may deal with whether proposed solutions are ethical and so on for the other components in the model. This procedural model approach can be as simple or detailed as one chooses to make it, but however it is constructed, the intent is to guide a decision maker through the ethics decision-making process in an orderly and consistent manner.[9]

While procedural models are valuable in ensuring that important problem solving elements are not overlooked, experience with procedural models in other areas indicates they may not be *sufficient* to ensure ethical choices. Consider the procedural models outlined by Jaffe and Sirmans (1995) and Pyhrr et al. (1989) for performing real estate investment analysis. The Pyhrr et al. procedural model contains ten steps with each step having numerous components. Properly implementing each component of each step of these models requires skill, judgment, and knowledge. Unfortunately, some individuals simply do not possess these attributes in adequate quantities or do not have sufficient interest to care enough to competently use the procedural model. For example, an experienced real estate analyst may use the ten-step investment analysis model to make well reasoned, supportable investment decisions, while a less experienced analyst may use the same model to make poor decisions. Even the experienced analyst may occasionally produce poor results using the model because of distractions, time constraints, physical ailments, simple errors of judgment, and cognitive limitations outlined earlier. The same is true for procedural models in ethics: the models are only as good as the users. Essentially, different people using different values and approaches and with differing time constraints may use the same procedural model and develop entirely different answers. Cognitive psychology research results outline many reasons that, even when using good procedural models, ethics decision making may vary significantly from one situation to another for a given individual and between individuals.

In summary, psychology may have something to offer applied real estate ethics. Johnson (1996, p. 49) provides a succinct summary of its potential value:

> The answer to the question of why moral theory needs a robust moral psychology is this: our morality is a human morality, and it must thus be a morality directed to our human concerns, realizable by human creatures like ourselves, and applicable to the kinds of problematic situations we encounter in our lives. This means that we cannot do good moral theory without knowing a tremendous amount about human motivation, the nature of the self, the nature of human concepts, how our reason works, how we are socially constituted, and a host of other facts about who we are and how the mind operates. Moreover, we cannot know how best to act unless we know something about the details of mental activity, such as how concepts are formed, what their structure is, what constrains our inferences, what limits there are on how we understand a given situation, how we frame moral problems, and so forth. Without knowledge of this sort, we are condemned to either a fool's or a tyrant's morality.

Knowledge of psychology, whether labeled moral or cognitive, is a potentially valuable addition to the standard economics approach to real estate ethics problem solving and decision making. Put another way, *homo psychologicus* may have some relevant insights for *homo economicus*.[10]

Problem Solving and Decision Making Within the Context of Others

Neither *homo economicus* nor *homo psychologicus* lives in isolation. Rather, they both inhabit a world in which others exist with whom they must interact. From recognizing that others exist, it is a short step to the realization that one is affected by others and, in turn, that one's decisions and actions affect others. In short, problem solvers and decision makers live in a world of relationships. From these relationships a complex set of expectations about how people should behave in order to make life as enjoyable as possible for everyone develops. These expectations initiate a process that begins to limit one's freedom to do as he or she wishes.

Essentially, the process is straightforward. From social interaction *expectations* form about how things will be done and how interactions will occur. These expectations become the *norms* by which particular types of activities are conducted. Individuals participating in these activities find that norms establish *roles*. In summary, human interaction creates expectations about behavior that become norms which, in turn, create roles. *Homo economicus* finds the range of acceptable behavior and, hence, personal choice defined by others in a way that reduces individual freedom. The concept of maximizing expected utility subject to constraints has just had another set of considerations added to the list and *homo sociologicus* is born.[11]

Social norms have at least two significant consequences for decision makers. First, already limited individual freedom is diminished further or, in some instances, completely eliminated. Norms define acceptable behavior in terms of contributing implicitly or explicitly to agreed upon goals and objectives and thereby eliminate other options that may be more appealing to the individual on other dimensions. Second, norms cause individual preferences to be of diminishing importance in understanding behavior. In assessing the ethics of any decision, sociological norms must be part of the analysis.

Some norms find their way into common and codified law, violations of which may carry strong social sanctions in the form of monetary fines or imprisonment.[12] Certain other social norms for particular categories of activities are stated explicitly as codes of ethics with varying enforcement mechanisms and penalties, ranging from mild to severe. Many social norms are not codified as law or stated explicitly in a code of ethics and are simply implicit, part of being a member of a group, whether that group is humankind in general or real estate appraisers. Despite not being part of an enforcement system, many social norms are willingly followed by individuals, even when other actions may provide greater personal utility.

Of critical importance is the role relationships play in the lives of many humans, whether the relationships are professional or personal in nature. With relationships come expectations, which lead to norms, which lead to roles, which lead to voluntary reductions in personal freedom, which lead to socially acceptable behavior and acceptance in a given culture. The repeated reinforcement of norms and roles leads to recognizing certain behaviors as the "right thing to do" and, ultimately, the internalization of these behaviors. This internalization is an important element of socialization within a culture and reflects the impact of others on individual behavior and choices. It may also explain why much human behavior is *learned* rather than chosen.

Decision-Making Differences: Homo Economicus and Homo Sociologicus

It is not always clear as to whether in any given situation an individual should act as *homo economicus* making decisions and choices based on unfettered personal preference or as *homo sociologicus* making decisions and choices appropriate for the norms and roles associated with the relevant cultures. Using this perspective, unethical behavior may be viewed as a rational consideration of costs and benefits (*homo economicus*), as a deviation from expected norms and roles (*homo sociologicus*), or as some combination of both. For a given situation and decision, including those involving ethics, one may have to deal with ambiguous or conflicting guidance in determining the appropriate role to play (Hargreaves Heap et al., 1992).

Consider automobile speed limits as an example (Hargreaves Heap et al., 1992). *Homo economicus* faced with the problem of driving from point A to point B may analyze the situation from a cost-benefit perspective and decide that the expected utility of reaching point B by a certain time exceeds the cost, in terms of expected utility, of being caught speeding and paying the resulting fines. Faced with the same situation, *homo sociologicus* will not take a straight cost-benefit approach but also will consider the importance of the speed limit as an explicitly stated social norm and the importance of playing the expected role of a law-abiding citizen. For *homo sociologicus* the decision of whether to speed is constrained by the need to consider societal pressures associated with norms and roles. It is easy to see that *homo economicus* and *homo sociologicus* may make different driving speed decisions.

However, if instead of a speed limit, the state offered permits to exceed posted speed limits for a specified price, the removal of the social stigma and costs associated with speeding may make a cost-benefit calculation appropriate for both *homo economicus* and *homo sociologicus* and both may reach the same decision. Thus, differences in perspective have potentially important implications for ethics decision making because problem representation and solution are contingent upon one's point of view. This situation may also explain why studies indicate that humans tend to want explicit rules for their behavior as such rules may eliminate or reduce the stress created by the mental jousting between *homo economicus* and *homo sociologicus* (Fisk, 1982).

Elementary Forms of Social Relationships

Each individual relates to a number of cultures and each culture influences behavior. For example, in the work environment an individual has relationships with coworkers, customers, vendors, competitors, and other professionals. The same individual may also have relationships with professional organizations, which in real estate may be the Appraisal Institute, Institute of Real Estate Management, Counselors of Real Estate, Building Owners and Managers International, or others. Other relationships include friends, family, and social organizations. In each of these relationships, the individual encounters a different set of expectations, abides by different norms, and plays different roles. For example, the norms and roles within the firm are likely to be quite different from those of a professional organization. Thus, an individual confronts an array of norms and roles, some complementary and others contradictory. This array of cul-tures makes it difficult for researchers to identify and isolate the cultures influencing an individual's behavior at any point in time.

Social psychology research has distilled four basic models of relationships, or sociality, and the associated patterns of expectations, norms, and roles from the myriad of human relationships (Fiske, 1992). The four elementary social forms are communal sharing, authority ranking, equality matching, and market pricing. These *four elementary forms of sociality* capture the breadth of what virtually all cultures consider acceptable behavior (Fiske, 1992, p. 689):

> The theory postulates that people in all cultures use just four relational models to generate most kinds of social interaction, evaluation, and affect. People construct complex and varied social forms using combinations of these models implemented according to diverse cultural rules. People's chief social conceptions, concerns, and coordinating criteria, their primary purposes and their principles, are usually derived from the four models; they are the schemata people use to construct and construe relationships.

These social forms are labeled "elementary" because they represent the most fundamental social forms and all other social forms can be constructed from combinations of these four elementary social forms.

Elementary social forms differ with respect to resource allocation, sharing, authority, and other essential allocative and nonallocative processes.

In communal sharing all members of the group are considered to be equal, in authority ranking members are ranked in linear hierarchical order, in equality matching there is one-for-one balance and egalitarian distributive justice, and market-pricing relationships are based on proportionality and reduce all relevant components to a single value for qualitative and quantitative comparison of diverse factors. As examples, communal sharing may typify families, fraternal organizations, and other extremely close groups sharing some important common bond. Authority ranking may describe many work arrangements, the military, and other organizations in which rank is critical. Equality matching characterizes relationships such as car pools and dinner parties in which members expect a balance in what is given and what is received. Goldman (1993) also labels equality matching as "balanced reciprocity." Market pricing is the familiar social form in which bilateral exchange transactions occur and is the form commonly assumed in RCT.

Each culture establishes the relative importance of the elementary models in each relationship based on that culture's assessment of what constitutes fairness and equity. Individuals in a given culture, in turn, base their assessments of equity based on cultural norms. Of particular interest to real estate ethics is the fact that the market-pricing model generally assumed in many business situations is only one of four elementary models and most situations involve combinations of at least two models. Thus, decision makers may face roles that differ from the pure market pricing social form in many decisions involving real estate ethics. Equity theory, developed by Adams (1963), suggests that humans have a drive to be fair and, in turn, to be treated fairly. Thus, how a given culture chooses to define fairness in different situations and relationships is critical. Reaching agreement as to what constitutes appropriate behavior may be quite difficult.

Being in the Right Frame of Mind

Other people are an important, perhaps the most important, source of our feelings of right and wrong (Midgley, 1993). We are left with a situation in which we pursue effective means to our ends, in particular, ends related to our long-term self-interest, while at the same time doing what is right within a social context. It is not surprising that these two objectives may provide different behavioral cues. This difficult situation is summarized by Schmidtz (1995, p. 23):

> Prudential rationality counsels us to seek effective ways of serving our ends, and in particular our long-range self-interest. Morality counsels us to do what is right.

Each counsel seems incontestable on its own ground. From time to time, though, we need to choose. We can do what is in our best interest or what is right, but not both. It would be nice if we could settle which of the two—prudence or morality—has the stronger case, but the fact is that each has the stronger case on its own ground. Our only recourse is to explore the extent to which each, on its own ground, makes room for the other.

In Schmidtz's view, what is needed is balance. The existence of *homo economicus*, *homo psychologicus*, and *homo sociologicus* gives new meaning and importance to the concept of being "in the right frame of mind." Clearly, an individual switches between these frames of mind easily and frequently as situations in a dynamic environment demand. This is similar to the frequently cited difference between left-brain and right-brain thinking in which left-brain thinking is associated with analytical skills and right-brain thinking is associated with more creative, intuitive thinking. Being in the right ethics frame of mind is not a matter of being in one mind or the other but rather of establishing an appropriate weighting to give each frame of mind in any situation. In this sense, ethics is a portfolio problem of balancing the influences of *homo economicus* and *homo sociologicus* with proper attention paid to the complications introduced by *homo psychologicus*.

All three "minds" are necessary components of *homo ethicus*, a human being capable of acting as ethically as humanly possible in a real-world environment.[13] Flanagan (1991) developed the concept of *minimal psychological realism*, which maintains that for ethics, including real estate ethics, to be viable and authentic, ethical standards must be capable of being achieved by human beings. Of course, what is humanly possible in real estate ethics must be evaluated within the context of a challenging decision making environment characterized by uncertainty, multiple minds, multiple roles, conflicting ends, and ambiguous means.

Toward a Multidisciplinary Real Estate Ethics Framework Incorporating Philosophy and Science: A Means Ends Approach

The study of applied real estate ethics and the development of ethical systems requires a comprehensive approach bridging science and philosophy, theory and application, and incorporating an array of disciplines. Such an approach likely will not produce concrete answers to many ethical issues, questions, and dilemmas. Even approaches designed to assist the decision maker striving to become *homo ethicus* may be limited to bringing the ethical aspects of a decision into consciousness and to making the issues sharper, rather than providing precise evaluations of the ethics of specific solution options. But these improvements are quite valuable. However, little improvement in the study and development of applied real estate ethics systems is likely to occur without significant effort being expended and a promising approach to expending that effort is the development of a research framework to focus efforts, whether scientific, philosophical, theoretical, or empirical in nature. The same framework also can serve real estate ethics instruction.

It is tempting to suggest that what is needed is a theory of real estate ethics. Theoretical development in real estate ethics is necessary and desirable; however, it is unlikely that any single theory can adequately provide a definitive prescriptive and descriptive real estate ethics framework. A broader framework that embraces an interdisciplinary approach and multiple theories, along with a strong philosophical foundation, is needed. This framework may have several appropriate labels, one of which may be *paradigm* (Kuhn, 1970). Paradigms and the search for an appropriate paradigm for real estate have been discussed at length by Grissom and Liu (1994); Clapp, Goldberg, and Myers (1994); and Jaffe (1994). Diaz (1993) posits that real estate in general, not just in the area of ethics, has suffered slow knowledge growth because of the lack of a dominant paradigm to shape and guide research efforts. While a real estate ethics paradigm may be the ultimate goal, the development of such a paradigm is premature and must await significant work in real estate ethics.

Further, using the concept of paradigm may convey the message that only science is relevant and that, by implication, philosophy is of little or no importance in real estate ethics. In real estate ethics, moral philosophy provides rich thought on a wide variety of issues. It provides valuable guidance about the appropriate questions to ask and how to interpret research findings. Accordingly, the term *framework* is used here instead of *paradigm* to ensure an appropriate role for philosophy.

A means-ends approach to real estate ethics research, with moral philosophy providing the ends and science providing at least some of the means, may provide a reasonable model. Further, a feedback mechanism in which both areas constantly update and refine their efforts based on new findings adds a mechanism for progress. Care and attention must be given to ensure that ends and means are constantly reviewed and that scientism, the pursuit of science for its own sake, does not dominate or obscure either the contribution of philosophy or the selection of ends for ethical behavior.

Desirable ends for a real estate ethics research framework may include the following:

- *Real people In a real world*   While allowing for theorizing and the necessary abstractions, the framework should be firmly grounded in the actions of real people dealing with the real world. Without this grounding, a disconnect between theory and reality can significantly reduce the usefulness of the framework. Human capabilities are critical elements in ethics development as reflected in Flanagan's (1991) concept of minimal psychological realism.

- *Multidisciplinary nature*   It is doubtful that an area of inquiry as expansive as real estate ethics can be based adequately on a single discipline. A framework must draw from many relevant disciplines and support a research agenda with many facets in order to provide a comprehensive development platform.

- *Prescriptive and descriptive*   A framework must address "ought" as well as "is."

- *Theoretical and empirical*   Somewhat related to the immediately preceding goal, the real estate ethics framework should support both theoretical and empirical research. Even though the philosophical component is not subject to falsification, hypotheses and theories should be cast in terms that can be falsified through empirical tests when possible. Likewise, empirical work supporting inductive thinking should be encouraged.

- *Choice*   A framework must recognize that choice is the crux of ethics. Responsibility generally attaches to those with freedom of choice and does not attach to those without such freedom.

- *Uncertainty*   A framework must deal with the universal state of uncertainty in the real world. It must deal not only with standard forms of uncertainty but also with the ambiguity and great uncertainty that make many problems so resistant to solution.

- *Time*   Real estate ethics must consider time and the critical role it plays in ethics, including the mismatch of time between when a decision is made, an action taken, and the outcome eventuates and the notion that time is often a constraint on decision making involving ethics.

These goals, or ends, for a real estate ethics framework reduce the set of possible development paths considerably. Preliminary development of one such real estate ethics framework is summarized in the appendix. This framework is presented simply as a starting point and catalyst for additional development.

Prospects

A real estate ethics framework is a useful, perhaps necessary, starting point for research into real estate ethics. Both the development of the framework and subsequent progress require commitment and work. Gardner (1985, p. 392), writing about prospects for progress in cognitive science, makes a number of observations that are equally valid for real estate ethics:

> How much further cognitive science can proceed, and which of the competing visions it will choose to pursue, are issues that remain open. All who style ourselves as cognitive scientists are on the spot. If we heed the lessons entailed in our scientific history and lurking in our philosophical backgrounds, if we attend to but are not stymied by the reservations aired by shrewd skeptics, if we recognize the limitations of all inquiry but do not thereby encounter a failure of nerve, there are clear grounds for optimism.

Indeed, there are no promises of progress attached to the development of a real estate ethics framework. The only near certainty is that in the absence of such a framework research in real estate ethics will continue to be characterized by what Diaz (1993) labels *creative anarchy* and *slow knowledge growth*. Thus, we are free to choose between a relatively certain future with little to offer or a riskier one with the possibility for progress. This choice, too, may have profound ethical implications.

Appendix: Preliminary Real Estate Ethics Framework— Moving Toward a Paradigm[14]

Intellectual Antecedents

Description. General disciplines and areas providing ideas, views, metaphors, concepts, and theories to a scientist pursuing a paradigm

Elements
- Philosophy
- Economics
- Finance
- Psychology
- Sociology
- Cognitive Sciences
- Neurobiology

Pretheoretical Ideas

Description.   A set of core beliefs that characterize a paradigm.

Elements
- The defining act in ethics is choice, without which responsibility does not exist.
- Choice takes place in an environment characterized by uncertainty.
- Time is critical as a constraint on decision making and on assessing ethical consequences when decisions and outcomes are temporally separated.
- Humans generally seek to achieve the highest possible level of personal satisfaction subject to any constraints.
- Human information-processing capabilities are limited, while information supplied by the senses is limitless, causing humans to employ data-reduction techniques.
- Human choice behavior has rational and irrational components, with the irrationality resulting primarily from data-reduction efforts.
- Some human cognitive processes can be isolated.
- Human cognition is context sensitive.
- Humans are social animals and acquire at least some of their preferences from cultural norms and roles.

Subject Matter

Description.   Questions most relevant to understanding the system under study

Elements
- The essential ethical nature of humans and the sources and implications of that nature
- How the essential ethical nature of humans affects the ability to make ethical decisions and choices in a world characterized by uncertainty
- Human rationality and its relationship to ethical behavior
- Social impacts on ethics for individual and group decisions

Analogies

Description.   Casting lesser-known systems into more familiar and better understood systems

Elements
- Humans as information processing units with limited capabilities
- Humans as intuitive statisticians performing data-reduction duties

Concepts and Language

Description. Terminology and related concepts as used in the paradigm in order to have a standardized reference

Elements
- Rational choice theory, instrumental rationality, expected utility, and uncertainty are borrowed from economics and finance. From psychology, cognitive processes as measurable entities, biases, bounded rationality, representation, and prospect theory are borrowed. Sociology lends expectations, norms, roles, and social form. Along with these concepts and terms, the full complement of terminology is borrowed from philosophy. There are numerous other terms and concepts, but those listed provide a foundation and the flavor of the paradigm.

Methodology

Description. The approaches to research that are important to developing and testing the paradigm

Elements
- Survey research on ethical standards, compliance with standards, and other descriptive elements of real estate ethics
- Examination of cognitive processes such as bias and the use of heuristics using experimental isolation methodologies
- Empirical testing of procedures and aids to decision making
- Empirical testing of market valuation of ethical and unethical behavior
- Evaluation of the development of moral reasoning

Notes

1. For treatments of real estate ethics see BOMI (1995), Pivar (1979), Long (1995), and the special issue of *Real Estate Issues* devoted to real estate ethics (1994). General business

ethics are considered in Bear and Maldonado-Bear (1994), Boatwright (1993), and Vallance (1995). Sullivan (1995) considers ethics within the context of professions. Ethics and urban planning are considered in Hendler (1995), Howe (1994), and Solin (1997). For a comprehensive treatment of environmental ethics, see Beatley (1994). For general treatments of ethics, see Singer (1993), Solomon (1986), Sher (1987), and Carter (1996).

2. Real estate ethics articles and books are few in number compared to accounting, urban planning, and many other areas. For example, the detailed study of urban planning ethics prepared by Howe (1994) has no parallel in real estate. Long's (1995) book on real estate ethics and the BOMI (1995) review of real estate ethics are welcome additions to an otherwise sparse literature. The special issue of *Real Estate Issues* (1994) presents a collection of articles dealing with ethics, with articles by McCoy, White, and Tarantello being of special interest. Few principles of real estate textbooks have chapters on ethics. At least one principles textbook had a chapter on ethics in its first edition but removed it in subsequent editions because of comments from users and reviewers that little or no time was available to cover this material. Interestingly, in the Urban Land Institute's recent collection of classic articles on development, two of the three articles on ethics came from non–real estate sources. Within the *Journal of Real Estate Literature* there is not a freestanding category for real estate ethics.

3. For a detailed discussion of instrumental rationality in economics, see Stewart (1995).

4. The terms *homo economicus* and *economic man* are used to denote a purely economic approach to thinking and to contrast as clearly as possible this mode of thinking from other considerations to be presented later in this study. For examples of the use of *homo economicus*, see Hausman and McPherson (1996), Hargreaves Heap et al. (1992), Zey (1992), and Etzioni (1992).

5. For discussions of cognitive science see Gardner (1985) and Rabinowitz (1993).

6. For a discussion of bounded rationality, see Simon et al. (1992). For a discussion of bounded rationality in a real estate context, see de Bondt (1995).

7. Data reduction and mechanisms that were developed to achieve it introduced bias, but are not necessarily shortcomings. At the most primitive level, the goal of any organism is survival, and from a Darwinian perspective the demand made on humans has been to make quick decisions affecting immediate survival. Because of the need for instantaneous reactions and other relatively quick decisions simply to cope, contemplative logical reasoning has not been the dominant form of human thinking. In order to make time for contemplative thinking using scarce cognitive resources, cognitive efficiency is a necessity. Not surprisingly, humans became skilled at identifying the cognitive skills that help ensure that they are the fitter organism and species in the Darwinian sense. As Simon (1978) posits, "If one algorithm can compute the solution in an hour, while another takes two, it is worth pocketing the change." Thus, the selective processing of information in humans is not a weakness but a strength in the extremely long-term context of survival of the species and within the context of an individual who must make countless decisions on a timely basis in daily life and must do so efficiently.

8. For a detailed and readable account of human thinking and its development, see Calvin (1996).

9. See Tarantello (1994) for an example of an ethical check list and Vallance (1995) for an example of a procedural model for making decisions involving ethics.

10. The term *homo psychologicus* is used to differentiate a mode of thinking from that assumed in *homo economicus*.

11. The term *homo sociologicus* is used by Hargreaves Heap et al. (1992) to differentiate the sociological approach to decision making from the purely economic approach of *homo economicus*.

12. For discussions of law and morals, see Fuller (1964), Coase (1988), and Coleman (1988).

13. As earlier, the term *homo ethicus* is used to denote and differentiate a particular mode of thinking from other modes. It is used in the spirit of the generally accepted terms *homo economicus* and *homo sociologicus*. In reality, humans likely incorporate psychological and sociological considerations into their estimates of well being. This study seeks to make such considerations explicit.

14. The template for this framework is from Lachman, Lachman, and Butterfield (1979).

References

Adams, J. Stacy. (1963). "Toward an Understanding of Inequity." *Journal of Abnormal and Social Psychology* 67: 422–436.

Baron, Jonathan. (1993). *Morality and Rational Choice*. Dordrecht, The Netherlands: Kluwer.

Baumol, William J., and Alan S. Blinder. (1982). *Economics Principles and Policy* (2nd ed.). New York: Harcourt Brace Jovanovich.

Bear, Larry Alan, and Rita Maldonado-Bear. (1994). *Free Markets, Finance, Ethics, and Law*. Englewood Cliffs, NJ: Prentice-Hall.

Beatley, Timothy. (1994). *Ethical Land Use: Principles of Policy and Planning*. Baltimore: John Hopkins University Press.

Boatwright, John R. (1993). *Ethics and the Conduct of Business*. Englewood Cliffs, NJ: Prentice-Hall.

Building Owners and Managers International (BOMI). Institute. (1995). *Ethics Is Good Business*. Arnold, MD: BOMI Institute.

Calvin, William H. (1996). *How Brains Think*. New York: Basic Books.

Carter, Stephen L. (1996). *Integrity*. New York: Basic Books.

Clapp, John M., Michael A. Goldberg, and Dowell Myers. (1994). "Crisis in Methodology: Paradigms vs. Practice in Real Estate Research." In James R. DeLisle and J. Sa-Aadu (eds.), *Appraisal, Market Analysis, and Public Policy in Real Estate* (pp. 107–131). Boston: Kluwer.

Coase, R.H. (1988). *The Firm, the Market, and the Law*. Chicago: University of Chicago Press.

Coleman, Jules L. (1988). *Markets, Morals and the Law*. Cambridge: Cambridge University Press.

Dawes, Robyn M. (1988). *Rational Choice in an Uncertain World*. Fort Worth: Harcourt Brace.

de Bondt, Werner F.M. (1995). "Real Estate Cycles and Animal Spirits." In Joseph L. Pagliari, Jr. (ed.), *The Handbook of Real Estate Portfolio Management* (pp. 1153–1183). Chicago: Irwin.

Diaz III, Julian. (1993). "Science, Engineering and the Discipline of Real Estate." *Journal of Real Estate Literature* 1: 183–195.

Dorner, Dietrich. (1996). *The Logic of Failure*. New York: Metropolitan Books.

Etzioni, Amitai. (1992). "Normative-Affective Factors: Toward a New Decision-Making Model." In Mary Zey (ed.), *Decision Making: Alternatives to Rational Choice Models* (pp. 89–111). Newbury Park, CA: Sage.

Evans, Jonathan St. B.T. (1989). *Bias in Human Reasoning.* Hove, Eng.: Erlbaum.

Ferrell, O.C., and John Fraedrich. (1994). *Business Ethics: Ethical Decision Making and Cases* (2nd ed.). Boston: Houghton Mifflin.

Fisk, Raymond P. (1982). "Toward a Theoretical Framework for Marketing Ethics." In (ed.), *Marketing Theory: Philosophy of Science Perspectives.* Chicago: American Marketing Association.

Fiske, Alan Page. (1992). "The Four Elementary Forms of Sociality: Framework for a Unified Theory of Social Relations." *Psychological Review* 99: 689–723.

Flanagan, Owen. (1991). *The Science of the Mind* (2nd ed.). Cambridge, MA: MIT Press.

Fuller, Lon L. (1964). *The Morality of Law* (rev. ed.). New Haven: Yale University Press.

Gardner, Howard. (1985). *The Mind's New Science.* New York: Basic Books.

Goldman, Alvin I. (1993). *Philosophical Applications of Cognitive Science.* Boulder: Westview Press.

Grissom, Terry V., and Crocker H. Liu. (1994). "The Search for a Discipline: The Philosophy and the Paradigms." In James R. DeLisle and J. Sa-Aadu (eds.), *Appraisal, Market Analysis, and Public Policy in Real Estate* (pp. 65–106). Boston: Kluwer.

Hansson, Sven Ove. (1996). "Decision Making Under Great Uncertainty." *Philosophy of the Social Sciences* 26: 369–386.

Hargreaves Heap, Shaun, Martin Hollis, Bruce Lyons, Robert Sugden, and Albert Weale. (1992). *The Theory of Choice.* Oxford: Blackwell.

Hart, Stuart L. (1986). "Steering the Path Between Ambiguity and Overload: Planning as Strategic Social Process." In Milan J. Dluhy and Kan Chen (eds.), *Interdisciplinary Planning: A Perspective for the Future* (pp. 107–123). New Brunswick, NJ: Center for Urban Policy Research.

Hausman, Daniel M., and Michael S. McPherson. (1996). *Economic Analysis and Moral Philosophy.* Cambridge: Cambridge University Press.

Hendler, Sue. (1995). *Planning Ethics: A Reader in Planning Theory Practice and Education.* New Brunswick, NJ: Center for Urban Policy Research.

Howe, Elizabeth. (1994). *Acting on Ethics in City Planning.* New Brunswick, NJ: Center for Urban Policy Research.

Izzo, George. (1998). "Cognitive Moral Development and Real Estate Practitioners." Paper presented at the 1998 Annual Meetings of the American Real Estate Society, Monterey, CA.

Jaffe, Austin J. (1994). "Is There a Body of Knowledge in Real Estate? Some Mutterings About Mattering." In James R. DeLisle and J. Sa-Aadu (eds.), *Appraisal, Market Analysis, and Public Policy in Real Estate* (pp. 133–146). Boston: Kluwer.

Jaffe, Austin J., and C.F. Sirmans. (1995). *Fundamentals of Real Estate Investment* (3rd ed.). Englewood Cliffs, NJ: Prentice-Hall.

Johnson, Mark L. (1996). "How Moral Psychology Changes Moral Theory." In Larry May, Marilyn Friedman, and Andy Clark (eds.), *Mind and Morals* (pp. 45–68). Cambridge, MA: MIT Press.

Kahneman, Daniel, and Amos Tversky. (1979). "Prospect Theory: An Analysis of Decision Under Risk." *Econometrica* 47 (March): 263–291.

Kohlberg, Lawrence. (1981). *The Philosophy of Moral Development*. San Francisco: Harper & Row.

Kohlberg, Lawrence. (1984). *The Psychology of Moral Development*. San Francisco: Harper & Row.

Kuhn, Thomas S. (1970). *The Structure of Scientific Revolutions* (2nd ed.). Chicago: University of Chicago Press.

Lachman, Roy, Janet Lachman, and Earl C. Butterfield. (1979). *Cognitive Psychology and Information Processing: An Introduction*. Hillsdale, NJ: Erlbaum.

Long, Deborah H. (1995). *Doing the Right Thing*. Scottsdale, AZ: Gorsuch Scarisbrick.

MacCrimmon, Kenneth R., and Donald A. Wehrung. (1986). *Taking Risks*. New York: Free Press.

Maital, Shlomo. (1982). *Minds, Markets, and Money*. New York: Basic Books.

May, Larry, Marilyn Friedman, and Andy Clark (eds.). (1996). *Minds and Morals*. Cambridge, MA: MIT Press.

McCoy, Bowen H. "Buzz." (1994). "On Business Ethics." *Real Estate Issues* 19: 1–7.

Midgley, Mary. (1993). *Can't We Make Moral Judgments?* New York: St. Martin's Press.

Miller, G.A. (1956). "The Magical Number Seven, Plus or Minus Two: Some Limits on Our Capacity for Processing Information." *Psychological Review* 63: 81–97.

Neisser, Ulric. (1976). *Cognition and Reality: Principles and Implications of Cognitive Psychology*. New York: Freeman.

Ornstein, Robert. (1991). *The Evolution of Consciousness: The Origins of the Way We Think*. New York: Simon & Schuster.

Palmer, Donald. (1996). *Does the Center Hold? An Introduction to Western Philosophy* (2nd ed.). Mountain View, CA: Mayfield.

Payne, John W. (1985). "Psychology of Risky Decisions." In George Wright (ed.), *Behavioral Decision Making*. New York: Plenum Press.

Pivar, William H. (1979). *Real Estate Ethics*. Chicago: Real Estate Education Company.

Pojman, Louis P. (1995). *Ethical Theory* (2nd ed.). Belmont, CA: Wadsworth.

Pyhrr, Stephen A., James R. Cooper, Larry E. Wofford, Steven D. Kapplin, and Paul D. Lapides. (1989). *Real Estate Investment: Strategy, Analysis, Decisions* (2nd ed.). New York: Wiley.

Rabinowitz, Mitchell (ed.). (1993). *Cognitive Science Foundations of Instruction*. Hillsdale, NJ: Erlbaum.

Reason, James. (1990). *Human Error*. New York: Cambridge University Press.

Rest, James R. (1994). "Background: Theory and Research." In James R. Rest and Darcia Narvaez (eds.), *Moral Development in the Professions* (pp. 1–26). Hillsdale, NJ: Erlbaum.

Rest, James R., and Darcia Narvaez. (1994). *Moral Development in the Professions*. Hillsdale, NJ: Erlbaum.

Schmidtz, David. (1995). *Rational Choice and Moral Agency*. Princeton: Princeton University Press.

Sher, George. (1987). *Moral Philosophy*. San Diego: Harcourt Brace Jovanovich.

Simon, Herbert A. "On How to Decide What to Do." *Bell Journal of Economics* 9 (Autumn): 494–507.

Simon, Herbert A., et al. (1992). "Decision Making and Problem Solving." In Mary Zey (ed.), *Decision Making* (pp. 32–53). Newbury Park, CA: Sage.

Singer, Peter. (1993). *A Companion to Ethics*. Cambridge, MA: Blackwell.

Solin, Les. (1997). *Professional Practice Manual*. Washington, DC: American Planning Association.

Solomon, Robert. C. (1986). *The Big Questions* (2nd ed.). San Diego: Harcourt Brace Jovanovich.

Stewart, Hamish. (1995). "A Critique of Instrumental Reason in Economics." *Economics and Philosophy* 11: 57–83.

Sullivan, William M. (1995). *Work and Integrity: The Crisis and Promise of Professionalism in America*. New York: Harper Collins.

Tarantello, Rocky. (1994). "Expert v. Advocate: The Ethical Dilemma of Expert Testimony." *Real Estate Issues* 19: 8–11.

Thaler, Richard H. (1991). *Quasi Rational Economics*. New York: Sage.

Thaler, Richard H. (1993). *Advances in Behavioral Finance*. New York: Sage.

Vallance, Elizabeth. (1995). *Business Ethics at Work*. New York: Cambridge University Press.

Von Neumann, John, and Oskar Morgenstern. (1944/1972). *Theory of Games and Economic Behavior*. Princeton: Princeton University Press.

White, John R. (1994). "Lofty Expressions of Ethical Conduct Do Not Insure Adherence." *Real Estate Issues* 19: 26–33.

Wisudha, Ayleen D. (1985). "Design of Decision-Aiding Systems." In George Wright (ed.), *Behavioral Decision Making* (pp. 235–256). New York: Plenum Press.

Wofford, Larry E. (1985). "Cognitive Processes as Determinants of Real Estate Investment Decisions." *Appraisal Journal* 53 (July): 388–395.

Zey, Mary (ed.). (1992). *Decision Making*. Newbury Park, CA: Sage.

3 PROFESSIONALISM: THE MARKET FOR SERVICES AND REAL ESTATE

Garrick R. Small

Land Economics Program
University of Technology, Sydney

Abstract

Many of the attempts to reintroduce professional ethics in real estate reflect sincere and well intentioned efforts but are flawed by the absence of a systematic philosophical understanding of the relationships that exist between professionals and the community. This lack of understanding is due to both the state of moral philosophy in the twentieth century and the tensions between the professions and the community. The essence of professionalism lies in the specialized knowledge required in an occupation that is impractical for most members of a community to appropriate or evaluate. A professional uses specialized knowledge in a way that is trusted, but not understood, by the community, which gives rise to the necessity for professional associations, self-regulation, and specific codes of ethics and also accidental qualities that have come to be associated with professionalism, such as status and income.

Historically, the medieval guilds offer the prototype for professional associations, and their relationship to the community provides insights into professionalism today. These are reviewed and separated from the historical distortions of the intervening centuries that still heavily color our contemporary understanding.

Real estate is one of the several occupational areas that have appropriated the income and status associated with the professions. An analysis of the other necessary qualities of professionalism offers a test to establish how earnestly these occupations seek genuine professional status, especially in a world where many established professions are adopting practices that are not genuinely professional.

Current trends in professionalism are located as the product of philosophical systems underpinning social changes broadly known as postmodernism. The implications of postmodern professionalism for the real estate occupations are considered with the cautions they naturally generate.

Introduction

The real estate professions are relatively late starters among those occupations understood to be professions. To be located within the professions infers an understanding of exactly what a profession is, however defining professionalism, even pragmatically, proves to be a difficult task in our fast-changing world.

This chapter uses the history of occupations and the philosophic understanding of skilled work to develop an understanding of what is meant by the term *professional*. This exploration is closely tied to the ethical dimensions of working life and commerce itself. The close connections between ethics, commerce, and work yield important insights into the understanding of what it means to be a professional and the special issues for real estate practicioners.

The need for professional ethics is quite evident. Hurley has made a clear case for the necessity of ethics in the real estate professions and has signaled the difficulties extant in the industry, especially with respect to issues of trust (Hurley, 1996). To understand the ethical parameters of real estate practice, one needs to go beyond the general discourse on professional ethics and consider the additional issues that attend the practice of real estate itself (Small, 1997).

A final difficulty in developing an ethical definition of professionalism is the changing face of contemporary discourse, especially in terms of the emerging epistemologies sympathetic to the field of sociology of knowledge and postmodernism. These approaches to understanding must be addressed because of their strong relevance to the current behavior of society and pose a peculiar threat to those who would like to be known as professionals. An analysis of the developments in moral philosophy (ethics) is used to understand and respond to these issues.

Classical Roots

Plato used Socrates as a mouthpiece for argue from an understanding of professionalism in the *Republic* when he was considering justice. He was using the Greek notion of *techné*, which meant that attitude to skill or artful work that was carried on for its own sake, its own excellence. Plato was confident that his audience understood that the craftsman, if he were a true craftsman, sought excellence in his craft and that this pursuit of excellence was independent of his remuneration. Plato pointed out explicitly that the craftsman performed two functions simultaneously in performing his craft—one as craftsman, *techné*, and the other as laborer, earning a wage. Plato and his audience accepted this distinction as noncontentious.

The application of *techné* could be made to any art: plumbers, painters, engineers, and doctors all had the opportunity to display *techné*. To achieve *techné*, education and practice were typically required. This meant that while it may be possible for a prodigy to emerge who could work at an art excellently without any prior preparation, most commonly it was the result of dedicated effort. Necessarily, this meant that the craftsman had learnt specific skills that were not generally held. Rather than every person in a society exercising every craft, specialists emerged whose abilities in specific *techné* were considerably beyond what was possible for the average person. This was not the same as exclusionist trade union practices that limit numbers or gnostic secret initiations, but it happened simply because few people in a community had the time or inclination to learn the skills of every craft themselves. It was the beginnings of the division of labor.

The advantages of division of labor are manifold, though it is a principle that is also open to abuse. Adam Smith concluded, perhaps too strongly, that it was the market that was the driving force of economic development (Roll, 1942, p. 161). Exchange is certainly important, but it is important because it provides an environment wherein the division of labor can flourish and with it persons are able to refine specific skills toward excellence. It is the development of craft, *techné*, that actually produces economic development because it is *techné* that actually increases the efficiency of production and refines its quality and quantity. The market is just as capable of discouraging *techné*, as will be argued later.

It is in *techné* that we have the classical notion of professionalism and some of its complexities. Professionals have socially valuable abilities: they have an ethic of excellence and work their art as the result of specialized training and knowledge. Curiously, the classical notion strips income from professional practice, separating the performance of *techné* from the labor that attracts wages. While this is difficult for modern capitalist minds to grasp, it suggests which aspect of a professional's practice should be compromised when economic pressures exist. Hence, if a professional is aware that the time required to perform a task at the appropriate standard exceeds what the fees will cover, the concept of *techné* insists that the standard be maintained and income sacrificed.

This tension is common, especially as the professions move more and more into the market. Its resolution in favor of quality is the implicit expectation of society. Hence, medical general practicioners are expected to provide the same level of service regardless of whether they operate in a bulk billing clinic or a private practice situation. Price competition, the market, is implicitly premised on this expectation of comparable quality.

Market Theory

Modern market theory assumes that the market will set the correct price on a good (or service), but it also explicitly assumes full knowledge. The purchaser or consumer may inspect and compare competing goods and bid for them according to worth or quality. By definition, the consumer generally does not have the competence to judge professional services. This incompetence is a difficulty and one that many try to ignore. Some suggest that they know a good doctor when they see one or are able to select their solicitor on the basis of their ability, but does this assertion stand up to scrutiny? To some extent laypersons can identify gross outcomes, doctors whose patients don't recover, or a lawyer's tally of lost cases, but these are only gross indicators. Largely, it is only other members of the same discipline who can adequately identify professional quality.

Two examples, drawn from property development, will illustrate this. In structural and civil engineering, for example, a designer's fee is seldom more than 3 percent of the cost of the structure under consideration; however, poor design can add up to 50 percent to the cost. A cautious but market-driven engineer will always overdesign a structure; this takes less time, while ensuring against possible structural failure. A project manager who seeks to cut costs by competitive tendering for design may choose an engineer who may accept low fees for a given task. In Sydney's current market this could be down to half the profession's scale of fees.

The competitive tender has sliced perhaps 2 percent from the cost to construct through design cost savings, but it is likely to result in physical construction cost increases up to twenty times the saving. The project manager will never be aware of the inefficiency because the engineer's design and specification is the basis of the construction tender. The construction cost of an efficient design will never go to tender for comparison. At best, tradesmen on site may question apparent poor design, but their ability to do so is related in no small degree to their technical skill in virtually the same area as the structural engineer. Hence, only another person with engineering competence could detect poor design.

Similarly, land surveyors are registered by the state in NSW as a consequence of the Torren's title system, where under the state guarantees the existence of land contained within a particular land title. The state, and hence the community, have a stake in the surveyor's ability to competently measure out the land. However, it is the private client who retains the surveyor. From the client's perspective the best outcome is a low-cost plan. A low-cost plan is most easily achieved by using low-cost staff and methods that minimize the time spent on any one project.

Both these cost-saving techniques are employed by a large proportion of practicioners in Sydney, NSW, with the result that fees are commonly below that considered necessary for a professional result (Small, 1997, p. 193). The result does not impact on the client in this case but rather on the community, as poor-quality work greatly increases the probability of title errors that may not be apparent until decades into the future. Hence, tender pricing in land surveying subverts the integrity of the Torren's title tenure system.

Were the market able to competently evaluate the work of an occupation, it would not be a profession. This is illustrated in the courtroom, where expert witnesses are called when there is some question of professional competence. Hence in the case of the structural engineer, if the client wanted to claim damages as a result of costs of overdesign, another structural engineer would be called and not the tradesman who first called attention to the error. Similarly, nonprofessional staff cannot be held responsible for subprofessional work, even though they may actually be performing the particular activities. Hence, legal clerks may perform much of the work of conveyancing, but where a problem arises, they cannot be held liable in the same way as a professional staff attorney.

The professional therefore has a unique contribution to make to society, a duty carried out in trust, which is threatened by market pricing because the latter assumes full knowledge. To understand the pricing of professional services we again begin with Plato.

Just Price and the Guilds

The Greeks accepted that a craftsman acts simultaneously as an artist and as a laborer. However, there was no clear nexus between wages and skill. Plato's noted that insufficient wages would not attract skilled persons to practice their art and hence their wages must be higher than a nonskilled laborer. This still ignores the actual relativity.

The medievals resolved this problem in moral terms. A low fee would not attract persons to a craft, but a high fee was equated to theft. The medievals had a highly refined understanding of a person's moral obligations to society, and a person who charged in excess of a fair fee was considered to be stealing that portion of the fee that exceeded the fair price.

The term used for the fair price was *just price*, and there is a considerable literature on the concept and its contemporary applications (Blaug, 1991; Dempsey, 1935; Wilson, 1975; Worland, 1977).

The just-price doctrine protected society from overcharging and freed craftsmen to decide on the appropriate level of remuneration for their trade. It also freed them from the threat of fee undercutting because the set fees were recognized as just; lower fees were identified with lower quality. Craftsmen were consequently free to share their skills because such a technology exchange would not be used against them. The term *competition* relates to this form of relationship, from the Latin *com-petere*, "to seek together." This is opposed to the current connotation of *competition*, which in practice means "to seek against."

This mechanism gave rise to the guild system and its salient features of fee control, internal training, technology exchange, and quality control, which can all be seen to flow from the moral imperative of the just price. Additionally, the guilds extended the relationships between members beyond occupational issues to include para-welfare services for members and their families (Durkheim, 1957, pp. 15–25; Kurth, 1943/1978).

The rise of capitalism was based on the rejection of the just-price doctrine. Early mercantile capitalism used market opportunities to buy cheap and sell dear, using money as the focal object of the transaction. Marx drew attention to the process in *Das Kapital* using concepts borrowed from Aristotle and the scholastics. All recognized that licit exchange uses money as an intermediary in the essential exchange of equal goods (commodities); hence one producer exchanged products (commodities) for money and then the money for an equal value of another's product. Marx then revived the scholastic and Aristotelian criticism of the merchant who used money not as the means of exchange but as its termini. The merchant begins with money, which is exchanged for a commodity, which is then exchanged for a greater amount of money. This Marx abbreviated M-C-M', where the closing amount of money (M') exceeded the initial amount (M), necessarily resulting in an inequality (Marx, 18 vol. 3, pp. 339–343). The scholastics defined this type of nonproductive exchange as being "of the nature of evil but its exercise not necessarily evil" and permitted it within certain bounds; Marx was far less charitable.

Because the equality across the exchange is destroyed, the just-price constraint disappears. In addition, the implicit value of commodity quality disappears because capitalist exchange does not compare commodities (there is only one C term in the exchange). The capitalist can operate just as well on poor-quality goods as high-quality ones. The market is left to evaluate quality using the Roman law principle of *caveat emptor* ("let the buyer beware"). It is this latter aspect that is especially damaging for the professions.

Deprofessionalization

In many cases this transfer of quality control from the craftsmen and their guilds to the community (the market) was not problematic as the consumer could discern the quality of goods adequately. Many people could recognize the difference in quality—say, between two competing manufacturers of textiles—and price them accordingly. Skills that could be externally valued suit a market situation.

Other skills resist such general evaluation, and generally the latter have survived as the professions, retaining many of the characteristics of their guild origins. In this way the professions were identified as a vestige of older values that placed duty before profit (Duman, 1979) resulting in a location in the productive system distinct from those associated with land, labor, or capital. Durkheim recognized the need for this sector, its relationship to the guild system, and its necessity for the wider functioning of society (Durkheim, 1957, p. 29).

The erosion of professionalism (deprofessionalization) began at the beginning of the Renaissance when craftsmen were made accountable to the community and not their guilds. Its early victims have reemerged as trades. They confront the market using different tactics and relationships, such as labor withdrawal, which focuses on labor, not skill, and they make conscious decisions about the level of skill employed. Hence, a panel beater may be prosperous with a reputation for quick and cheap workmanship.

The survivors, the professions, rely on the obscurity and necessity of their arts. The community must trust them to perform services with an excellence that only they themselves can evaluate within their arcane associations. The issue of trust is central, and it produces a reciprocal responsibility analogous to an implicit social contract (Moore, 1987). Their income is set predominantly by confronting society with its need for the quality of their offering. The nineteenth century saw the establishment of the professional associations, often with state backing, which effectively replicated the guilds with some adjustments for the demands of the time (Brazier et al., 1993; Kronus 1976). In addition, new arts have emerged that do not suit the market and for which the guild morality is the most appropriate model.

The Location of Property Occupations

The real estate industry grew from the ashes of medieval feudalism. Under pure feudalism there could be no trading in land as it all belonged to the king, who used rent (in all the forms it was collected in medieval times) as the major source of public revenue. The baronial class in England arose as a group of land owners who essentially held the privilege of being able to privately appropriate land rent. This privilege was usually bestowed as a special gift or reward from the crown. As this class grew, revenue to the crown shrank, necessitating the introduction of other mechanisms for public funding. The result was the imposition of significant and regular taxation. The English popular response culminated with the signing of the Magna Carta, which although commonly cited as the start of citizens' rights in England, had as its principal beneficiaries the barons themselves.

With the barons came the structural possibility of private commerce in land and hence the foundation for the real estate industry.

Some real estate occupations existed before this time, however, as specialist officers of the medieval lords who dealt with the administration of land. The compiler of the *Domesday Book* was unquestionably a land economist. The English term for these skilled persons was *surveyor*, and the term lives on in the title of the English professional body, the Royal Institution of Chartered Surveyors (RICS). Surveying in this context originally meant all aspects of land evaluation, including boundary definition and rental determination (appraisal).

The early guild surveyors have come into this century as RICS members. There can be no debate regarding their status as professionals: they used specialist skills, had a relationship of trust with their community, and apparently were organized along guild lines.

The early surveyors did not encompas the entire set of occupations currently recognized as real estate occupations. In the absence of private profit in land, surveyors were not engaged in land brokerage, nor were they engaged in development in the same way that it exists today. The status of this portion of the real estate occupations is more closely related to general merchants than to real estate.

Merchants were organized into guilds, so the moral principles of the guilds would appear to have filtered down through tradesmen (originally those engaged in trading for their income—that is, merchants) to those specializing in the commerce of land transfer. Such a simple pedigree is problematic. Little has described the dynamics of the medieval belief that merchants were considered to be in a morally perilous situation. The exercise of their art was considered to constitute a serious and constant moral temptation, due to the ever present opportunity to succeed commercially by the use of immoral trading tactics (Little, 1978). Just price applies to both fees for service and goods themselves.

The just price of a good was considered to be the greater of either its cost to produce or its utility to the vendor—what was known as the *double rule of value* (Langholm, 1992). This basis of price explicitly excluded utility to the purchaser because *"the advantage accruing to the buyer is not due to the seller. . . . no man should sell what is not his, though he may charge for the loss he suffers"* (Acquinas, 1274/1920, Pt. 2-2, Q77/1, p. 1508). While the just price for land can be readily be seen to consist in its use value to the vendor, the temptation to set the price by the use value to the purchaser is an ethical tension shared with other merchants and brokers. It appears to have constituted the seed for the eventual undoing of the entire fabric of medieval economics, leading to the current market theory of price as the intersection of supply and demand (Fanfani, 1939/1955).

This tension finds expression in the contingent ethical difficulty underlying the doctrine of *caveat emptor*. This principle, although derived from Roman law, was not a part of medieval guild practice. If the product of the guilds could not be evaluated by the community, it would be unethical to leave the community with risk of poor quality in areas that the common person could evaluate. Its reintroduction into modern economics means that any merchant who relies on it is explicitly avoiding an area of trust, and the responsibility peculiar to professionals is betrayed. No tradesman who cannot be trusted by those purchasing from him, which is the case where *caveat emptor* is employed, is ethically professional. That person may still be retained and paid, but more in the way that one pays the cheap panel beater in the earlier example. The occupation cannot be a profession, though it does have a place in the society.

If real estate brokerage is to join the ranks of the professions, it would appear that it must be willing to separate itself from the principle of *caveat emptor* and be willing to undertake to represent the interests of the purchaser. In the classic salesmanship book *How I Raised Myself from Failure to Success in Selling*, Frank Bettger not only demonstrated how this transition into being a "buying adviser" rather than a salesman was a key to his success, but made a strong case for its adoption by others who wished to be respected and successful in the sales business (Bettger, 1949, p. 194). He was doing no more than pointing back to the ethics of the guilds and demonstrating how these were even desirable in terms of long-term self-interest. He was a professional salesman.

Professional Ethics

If the community trusts a profession, it empowers it to decide on issues that the community cannot evaluate. This necessitates ascribing status and income to professionals; status naturally flows from the responsibility handed over by the community, and income flows as an outcome of status and also as a sufficient incentive to attract professionals to the practice of their art. In return, professionals undertake to provide to the community with goods (including services) that are at the highest level of quality possible but that only the practitioners (or their professional body) understand.

This functionalist model explains the need for professional ethics and the absence of trade ethics. The existence of a code of ethics for an occupation does not mean that its practitioners necessarily follow them or for that matter that the profession has the answers to the problems that it is chartered by society to solve. The first is a problem with human nature that deserves close attention; the second is a problem with the incompleteness of human knowledge.

The inroads of the market and the commercial ethics of self-interest that Durkheim identified also had a negative aspect. Once behavior was controlled by the market and not by an individual's sense of duty, a wide range of abuses become possible. The nineteenth-century English professional was a gentleman and was afforded respect, authority, and income consistent with his station (Duman, 1979). These are attractive things in their own right and became identified with being a professional to the extent that many today would list them as core attributes of professionalism. The key distinction of the professional was a sense of duty, but this was becoming an anachronism, even last century. This is illustrated in education, where economic criteria are overtaking educational ones in a manner that seriously challenge professional outcomes (Helsby and Saunders, 1993).

More essentially, Warnock observed that moral philosophy has been effectively emptied over the last century (Warnock, 1967) with the process well under way in the nineteenth century. An ethic is no more than a set of morals: an empty moral set becomes a meaningless ethic. When duty is eliminated, what remains are professionals who retain the trust, respect, authority, status, and income but who feel no compulsion to practice what the community naively expects from them on trust—a powerful social position.

With moral erosion also comes an erosion of any understanding of *good*; a "*good* professional" is indeterminate. Good professionals may be good for the community, the client, the profession, or only their own self-interest, depending on the meaning of good. Where the predominant social ethic is based on self-interest, that becomes the ethic of the professional, for there is no reason for the professional to take on a moral discipline stricter that that of the surrounding society. Self-interest provides a definition of good that ignores all except self, unless attention to others has identifiable benefits for one's self. Psychology tells us that in evaluating such costs and benefits, humans tend to weigh very much in favor of the here and now, while discounting the future and effects on distant others.

The relationship between professionals and the community in this liberal system is no longer bound by duty to the former degree. When duty is not present, the relationship must be guided by other principles, such as political aspirations (Osiel, 1984) or economic security (Olson, 1983). Foucault (1976) identified power as a substitute principle driving professional and client relationships and extended a conflict theory that can be seen to have roots in Marx and Hegel. The client needs the expertise of the professional who in turn exercises power over the client. The relationship develops as a virtual contest for control of the relationship.

When the behavior of a profession takes on this appearance, it has clearly passed out of the trust and duty dynamic that is the fundamental of professionalism. Although Foucault's analysis could be accepted only by a fellow Hegelian, he does identify the real phenomenon of power abuse. Broadly this is the distraction of the professional activity from what Aristotle would term the *common good*. It means that professionals no longer seek the best exercise of a skill, whether medicine or engineering, for its own sake, but rather only to the extent that such exercise maximizes the benefits to the professionals or their social group.

The behavior of medical practicioners in the care of the aged in Sweden illustrates this abuse of power. The younger working community (of which doctors are a part) are benefited in many way by the practice of euthanasia. Pollard observed that studies of supposedly *voluntary* euthanasia reveal that it is for the convenience of family and medical staff that most acts of euthanasia are committed (Pollard, 1989). It is seldom the patient who makes the deadly request but their families. The practice is supported by a utilitarian ethic[1] and those who value reduced health expenditure. The legal difficulty of the practice's criminal nature is set aside by the younger community's doctors as unjust law.

When the aged are forced to rely on doctors for their health, there is an unfair power balance. Where doctors feel no duty to their clients with respect to the object of medicine, health, Foucault's criticisms are apt. The result is a power struggle that is commonly lost by those whose signature is posthumously attached to consent forms. Power may be used for many ends, but the fact that it is now used by professionals for their own ends marks a serious rupture in the relationship between the community and the professions resulting from the conflict of sets of ethics in a pluralistic culture. It signals that the term *good* no longer can be assumed to mean the same thing to different people, a dangerous development.

Ethical Responsibility and Brokerage

In real estate the balance of objectives and power is critical in the transition to true professionalism. The objectives of a professional are framed by the necessity for trust, and the party who must extend this trust is an important consideration. In agency (brokerage) practice, for example, the object may be the most advantageous material outcome. Both vendors and purchasers trust practitioners to inform them how to realize this goal. It is this specialist knowledge that distinguishes the agent. Agents must consider in which ways and by whom they will be trusted by others.

Four parties may be identified—the practitioner, the vendor, the purchaser, and the community. Only the last is the genuine object of professional accountability. Commonly, the interests of the vendor are promoted unduly, which compromises honesty to other players and hence trust. Similarly, competition for listings is tending to overtake competition for sales, which reflects a distortion of professional objectives as practitioners focus on their own interests rather than any other parties.

In Australia, it appears accepted that several practices exist in common agency practice ordered to obtaining a sale at the expense of others. These include (1) initial overestimation of value to gain a listing, (2) misrepresentation of the property, mainly through omission, to purchasers, and (3) talking down vendor expectations during the sale period to facilitate acceptance of a lower offer. These reveal an order of responsibility that has self first, the vendor second, and the purchaser exposed to the uncertainty of *caveat emptor*.

The inappropriateness of *caveat emptor* in professional practice is illustrated in medicine. Few would take pills from a doctor if the label read "Let the buyer beware." In any sale the community is represented by the purchaser. For a person to warrant the title professional, they must uphold the trust invested in them by the community and not merely a small interest group with whom they collude. This was the key to Bettger's professionalism, and its exposition within what was essentially a manual on self-interest is a curious anomaly.

A further anomaly in regard to self-interest is fee control. Standardized fees appear monopolistic, serving the professionals alone. However, this analysis is too simplistic and ignores the fact that it is quality that is paramount in professional activity, even though such quality may not be fully understood by the layperson.

The market has made direct inroads into the professions, both by entrepreneurial practitioners within and by trade practice (antitrust) legislation outlawing standard fees from without. Most professions are now prevented from standardizing their fees, with the result that it is only professional ethics that ensure quality. In a tight market, ethics become a weak control, as practicioners battle to survive, and we seem to be awash with tales of professionals who opt for a reasonable balance between quality, ethics, and fees.

This balancing follows from the ethical mechanism of proportionalism. Proportionalism is a contentious strategy that holds that moral decisions may be made by balancing the desirable versus undesirable outcomes of an action. Proportionalism is fundamental to utilitarianism but opposed categorical ethical systems such as those of Aristotle, the scholastics, or Kant. The quality and fee balance is a proportionalist approach that balances the risk of negligence against the enhanced returns from cutting corners. Many sense that it is not professional.

Professional Indemnity Insurance

The fee and quality balance is further complicated by the recent development of the insurance of professionals against their own negligence. Negligence is distinct from error because the former is that error arising from faulty practice below the commonly accepted standards.[2] This type of insurance, often known as professional indemnity (PI) insurance, is actually an insurance against the practicioner chosing to dispense with *techné*. If the error was one that no reasonable practitioner would be able to avoid, or an error that occurred even though the practicioner took reasonable measures to avoid it, the client would have no claim, and there would be no need for PI insurance. It is actually a commercial tactic to avoid the economic sanction associated with a failure of professional duty. Twenty years ago PI was widely abhorred by most professions as an indication of a professional's abdication of duty, but today it is widely embraced as a professional necessity.

The economic implications of PI are complex, but at the simplest level it allows a high degree of price competition because many professions now economize on the resources devoted to clients and pass on the cost savings. As earlier noted, clients expect excellent professional conduct, *techné,* regardless of discounting, and now the professions can discount, knowing that where poor quality is detected, the penalties can be passed on to the insurer. In this way the special duty of many professionals has been commercially diverted to insurers, and professional services have become commodities to be traded in the market under Marx's M-C-M' model. This process has made inroads into medicine but is most widespread in professions such as engineering and accounting (Bernard and Hamel, 1982; Richardson, 1987).

PI insurance is widely relied on in the real estate industry. While its adoption may be for the most noble grounds, such as client protection, its use cannot but tempt some practicioners to overrely on it. This overreliance will facilitate lower cost structures, enabling lower fees, which in turn increases market success. Unfortunately, this commercial success is effectively at the expense of quality practitioners who may be squeezed out of the industry because they are not fee competitive. There appears to be reasonable evidence of this process in some real estate–related professions, at least in some markets. It is very difficult to monitor but deserves closer study.

Current and Future Directions

The nature of professional bodies is also changing with a tendency for more professional associations to approach the market using trade union tactics and more professionals to seek union-like association. Hence, the last two decades have seen doctors effectively strike, teachers (a *nouveau* profession) adopt widespread industrial tactics, and employed professionals, such as public service professional staff and university academics, enlist in industrial associations (Oppenheimer, 1973).

While recognized professions appear to be compromising their professionalism, new occupational groups are attempting to appropriate the professional title. These cover a wide spectrum, from pure abuse of the term *professional* to genuine new occupations that do not suit the trade model. This status ascendency is often associated with upgrading of qualifications to degree level. There is almost a *cargo-cult* mentality that seems to believe that holding a degree will cause professional recognition to materialize, with all the wealth, status, authority, and respect that come with that title.

Medicine has spawned a large number of occupations that now describe themselves as semiprofessional, such as nursing, physiotherapy, and occupational therapy. The real estate industry includes several occupations now termed professions. Finance and business, as professions, are curious because they are founded on the very factor that most corrodes classical professionalism but currently lead as ascending professions. Perhaps it is indicating a continued moral association but one redirected to a new morality.

Alternatively, if the contemporary professional is a degreed practicioner who exists within the market, uses PI insurance, and is distinguished principally by status and income, the notion of professional may be evolving as a social construct, into what could be called *postmodern professionalism.*

While its meaning may once have connoted *techné* and inspired trust in a gentlemanly sense of duty, tied to the positive attributes of status, that meaning of professionalism may have belonged to a moralistic world, perpetuated for a time by a romantic one. The twentieth century, with the ascendency of the market as the dominant ethical symbol may be remaking professionalism in a form consistent with self-interest, as observed by Smith, Durkheim, and Foucualt. In such a world, a professional is merely someone whose activities have to be more carefully checked by the client and who may be sued for greater amounts when found wanting.

In medicine, more patients are critical of the performance of their practitioners. In the construction industry, contract law and litigation are rapidly rising to dominate the relations between consultants and their clients. In other areas, new semi-, pseudo- and self-proclaimed professions abound, ascending the status ladder as traditional professions pass on the way down to a common new understanding of what it is to be professional. There is certainly no question that professions are disappearing, as some have suggested; rather, the new-look professional is someone who uses some skill, has some association, and is just as entrepreneurially hungry as the merchant-turned-business-graduate who is our culture's prototype for personal success.

The only losers are those who naively expect the term to mean what it did in some lost past—the geriatrics who trust their doctor to give health not death, the patients who think they are being attended by doctors who uphold the Hippocratic oath, or the builders who think the cut-price designer will save them money. The new definition of professional is just as serviceable as the old, though it connotes a very new idea.

Perhaps, in the future, a new word will be needed to denote those who are dedicated to *techné* and the ethics of the guilds, just as the term *professional* emerged out of the decay of the concept of *master craftsman,* following the violence of the encyclopaedists and capitalism. Such a new word will no doubt become necessary as some in the community consider the risk of trusting professionals too great. That time is far off in the future, for although the demise of professional trust has begun, it is only a small part of all professional relationships at present. The use of such a new word will indicate a renewed interest in, and commitment to, the values of trust and duty, which the ancients saw as the hallmarks of civilization.

It is within these parameters that the real estate industry finds itself.

While we are all keen to assert the term *real estate professional*, what is actually being meant? It appears that in real estate the stigma of being associated with occupational practices that are neither honest nor honorable is something most want to leave behind. The mere upgrading of qualifications is hardly the solution, unless this is somehow associated with an enhanced sense of social responsibility, though there is no clear nexus here. To seek postmodern professionalism is an illusion, though an attractive one. It succumbs to the age-old human desire to have the benefits of a just world while living above the personal limitations that such a world requires. It is incumbent on educators to communicate to students the two directions for professionalism and inspire them to lift the real estate occupations into genuine professionalism, rather than allow our industry to be but one further example of the social blight that is postmodern professionalism.

Notes

1. Utilitarianism, under J.S. Mill's parameters, asserts that harm (evil) is pain, so painless death harms no one, but as a *contra-evil* is actually good. Eliminating the possibility of pain is actually a good (Mill, 1962). Euthanasia is thoroughly consistent with Mill's ethics but leads to macabre possibilities. A utilitarian community would increase its sum of good per citizen if the most miserable members were painlessly killed, regardless of the source of their misery. Miserable aged are the current focus of euthanasia, but this could be extended to psychologically miserable, economically miserable, and so on. If a community passed a law to improve the lot of its members by the elimination of the most miserable 1 percent of the population, the average happiness of the community would improve. Unfortunately, depending on the frequency of the culling, the community would eventually kill itself off. Those with the power to drive the law would have the power to set the limit. It was precisely this ethic that validated the extensive but little publicized Nazi cull of Germany's own intellectually handicapped and war disabled before turning on their resident Jews.

2. These standards are usually expressed in terms of those levels of competence that are expected from typical reputable practitioners. They are not framed by the leaders in the field but more by public expectations of the profession. For example, for a particular surgical operation typical surgeons may have a generally recognized success rate of 90 percent. This would become the commonly accepted standard even if the best surgeon in the field may have a 100 percent success rate. A surgeon could not be sued for negligence for a failed outcome because it may have been part of the 10 percent of expected failures, unless it could be shown that the surgeon was behaving in a way objectively deficient compared to normal practice.

References

Acquinas, Thomas. (1274/1920). *Summa Theologica*. Westminster, MD: Christian Classics.

Bernard, Francine, and Pierre J. Hamel. (1982). "Toward a Deprofessionalization of the Profession of Accountant? The Situation in Quebec." *Sociologie du Travail* 24(2): 117–134.

Blaug, Mark, ed. (1991). *St. Thomas Aquinas* (vol. 3). Elgar.

Brazier, Margaret, Jill Lovecy, Michael Moran, and Margaret Potton. (1993). "Falling from the Tightrope: Doctors and Lawyers Between the Market and the State." *Political Studies* 41(2): 197–213.

Dempsey, B.W. (1935). "Just Price in an Unjust World." *American Economic Review* 25 (September): 471–486.

Duman, Daniel. (1979). "The Creation and Diffusion of a Professional Ideology in Nineteenth Century England." *Sociological Review* 27(1): 113–138.

Durkheim, Emile. (1957). *Professional Ethics and Civil Morals*. Ed: led by W.J.H. Sprott. London: Routledge and Kegan Paul.

Fanfani, A. (1939/1955). *Catholicism, Protestantism, and Capitalism*. London: Sheed & Ward.

Foucault, Michel. (1976). "Disciplinary Power and Subjection." In Colin Gordon (ed.), *Selected Interviews and Other Writings 1972–1977*. Pantheon.

Helsby, Gill, and Murray Saunders. (1993). "Taylorism, Tylerism and Performance Indicators: Defending the Indefensible?" *Educational Studies* 19(1): 55–77.

Hurley, Neil. (1996). "Ethics and Ethical Behaviour in the Property Valuation Profession." *Appraisal Journal* 64(2): 125.

Kronus, Carol L. (1976). "The Evolution of Occupational Power: An Historical Study of Task Boundaries Between Physicians and Pharmacists." *Sociology of Work and Occupations* 3(1): 3–37.

Kurth, Godfriod. (1943/1978). *The Workingmen's Guilds of the Middle Ages*. Translated by Denis Fahey and Stephen Rigby. Hawthorne, CA: Omni.

Langholm, Odd. (1992). *Economics in the Medieval Schools: Wealth, Exchange, Value*. New York: Brill.

Little, Lester K. (1978). *Religious Poverty and the Profit Economy in Medieval Europe*. New York: Cornell University Press.

Marx, Karl. (1867/1909). *Chicago: Kerr Capital*.

Mill, J.S. (1859/1978). *On Liberty*. London: Fount.

Moore, Nancy J. (1987). "Professionalism Reconsidered." *American Bar Foundation Research Journal* 4: 773–789.

Olson, Paul A. (1983). "Credentialism as Monopoly, Class War, and Socialization Scheme: Some Historical Reflections on Modern Ways of Determining Who Can Do a Job." *Law and Human Behaviour* 7: 2–3.

Oppenheimer, Martin. (1973). "The Proletarianization of the Professional." *Sociological Review Monograph* 20: 213–227.

Osiel, Mark J. (1984). "The Politics of Professional Ethics." *Social Policy* 15(1): 43–48.

Pollard, Brian. (1989). *Euthanasia*. Sydney: Regeant House.

Roll, Eric. (1942). *A History of Economic Thought*. New York: Prentice-Hall.

Richardson, Alan J. (1987). "Professionalization and Intraprofessional Competition in the Canadian Accounting Profession." *Work and Occupations* 14(4): 591–615.

Small, G.R. (1997). "The Ethical Context for Land Economics Professions." In
   Pacific Rim Real Estate Society Conference in Massey University, New Zealand.
Warnock, G.J. (1967). *Contemporary Moral Philosophy.* London: McMillan.
Wilson, G.W. (1975). "The Economic of the Just Price." *HOPE* 7(1) (Spring): 56–74.
Worland, S.T. (1977). "Justum Pretium: One More Round in the Endless Series."
   HOPE 9(4) (Winter): 504–521.

4 TOWARD A COMMON PERCEPTION OF ETHICAL BEHAVIOR IN REAL ESTATE

Marvin L. Wolverton

Department of Finance, Insurance and Real Estate
College of Business and Economics
Washington State University at Pullman

Mimi Wolverton

Department of Educational Leadership and
Counseling Psychology
College of Education
Washington State University at Pullman

Abstract

Even though an underlying commitment to morality is clearly stated in most professional real estate organization codes of ethics and most standards of practice provide detailed guidelines and rationale for proper professional conduct, these provisions are often ignored, and the common perception of unethical behavior in real estate persists. This essay examines ethics and ethical conduct in the real estate profession, going beyond rule ethics and end-point ethics into the uncharted waters of habitual behavior and integrity. The goal is to stimulate dialogue among real estate professionals about the value of striving for creation of professional real estate organizations that are self-selected by discriminating members. These sort of organizations are seen as a means to establish a common perception of ethical behavior in real estate.

People speak of ethical behavior and hear of ethical misconduct. Trade societies espouse professional codes of ethics. But what is *ethics*, and what bearing does it have on the enterprise called real estate? This chapter examines the basics of ethical reasoning in an attempt to shed light on ethics and ethical conduct as they pertain to real estate professionals and the way in which they carry out their business. The objective is to enhance understanding of codes of ethics and their shortcomings. In addition, the need for integrity in organizational decisions is stressed with a goal of stimulating a dialogue among real estate professionals about these issues.

"Ethics deals with the most fundamental principles by which individuals and organizations act" (Pastin, 1988, p. 16). Practice-based ethics finds its philosophical beginnings in the work of Socrates. Socrates grounded his code of behavior in what he termed *virtue*, a sense of reason, which enables an individual to do the right thing. His reasoning went something like this. If a person thinks that he or she possesses a certain kind of knowledge but really does not, then the person forms a false belief. He or she supports this false belief's legitimacy by building a complimentary series of confirming misbeliefs. The person can now act, based on this set of beliefs, without admitting to being misdirected and, thus, is prevented from "doing the right thing" (Pastin, 1988).

Early Greek philosophers, like Plato and Aristotle, extended Socratic thinking by delineating specific virtues that, when followed, lead individuals and organizations to the realization of the common good. The moral and ethical person sought to "do the right thing" by balancing four virtues: *fortitude*—the patience and strength of endurance against adversity; *temperance*—self-restraint and moderation; *justice*—honesty, fairness, the quality of being right; and *prudence*—wisdom applied to practice, the ability to make sound judgments and right choices using discretion and caution (Durrant, 1961; MacIntyre, 1984; Wilson, 1993; Woodward, 1994). As these early philosophers refined their views of moral behavior and virtue, the debate became academic, which, in turn, distanced discourse about ethics from the applied arena. The ensuing gap that emerged between ethics and practice is one we have been trying to close ever since (Pastin, 1988; Durrant, 1961).

Between 1600 and 1900, ethicists began to address this rift, and much of what we recognize today as the body of ethical theory stems from their efforts. Ethics during this period took two primary forms—rule and end-point—which provide the framework for the following discussion (see Figure 4.1).

A First Look at Professional Ethics: Rule Ethics

The idea of codes of ethics derives directly from rule ethics. Rule ethics proponents state that basic rules can be employed to determine the rightness

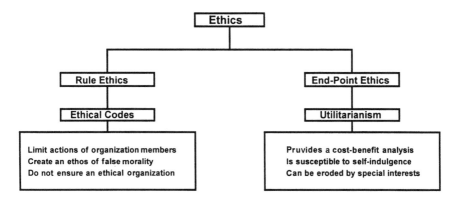

Figure 4.1.   Two primary ethical forms

or wrongness of our actions. As such, their concerns are procedural, and end results are viewed as being fair as long as the process used to arrive at the outcome is fair. John Locke's (1632–1704) *social contract ethics* provides the most forceful example of rule ethics. Locke challenged the political structure of his day by attacking the concept of divine right, which the English monarchy used to justify its claims to power. Social contract ethics stipulates that the rules that ought to govern the lives of people are the rules to which people would agree given the opportunity to make a choice based on reason and knowledge (Locke, 1690/1980; Durrant, 1961; Pastin, 1988). In other words, an ethical code's legitimacy arises out of its ability to reflect the reasoned choice of free people and on the assumption that the decision to abide by its rules must be voluntary.

Ethical Codes and the Professional Organization

Ultimately, a central function of rule ethics is to gain control over and to limit others (Pastin, 1988). A need to limit the actions of individual members of professional organizations stems from the idea of the organization as a *commons* (Hartman, 1994) and its vulnerability to the "tragedy of the commons" (Hardin, 1968). A commons exists any time a resource is jointly consumed and no corresponding sense of responsibility for the resource exists. Hardin's description of the commons paints a word picture. A community has a pasture that is open to everyone. Each herdsman in the community expects to freely choose how many cattle to graze on the common pasture. Since immediate benefits accrue to the individual (for instance, more cattle producing more milk, which leads to a better living for the herdsman) with no readily apparent costs, each herdsman makes the rational choice to maximize his or her personal gain by grazing more and more cattle on the commons (a practice often referred to in a more general sense as *free-riding*). This continues until overpopulation leads to the depletion of the pasture.

The tragedy (intended here to mean "the remorseless working of things") stems from every community member reaching the same rational conclusion—maximized use of the commons (Whitehead, 1948). On one hand, the individual herdsman benefits, in the short run, from the production of one additional cow unit. On the other hand, the herdsmen, as a whole in time, suffer from the harmful effects of overgrazing (Ault, 1994). Ultimately, free use of the commons by all, coupled with rational choice logic, exhausts the limited resources of the commons, thereby destroying the livelihood of all.

An organizational commons can be interpreted as the rights and benefits derived from membership in a professional organization. These include enhanced credibility, reputation sharing, national exposure through organization-level advertising and promotion, quality education, information sharing, lobbying efforts, and sharing of knowledge. To the extend that there is a moral obligation to preserve the "organizational commons" serving a group of professionals, a system is required to control the ravages of self-interest and preserve the commons. In order to prevent members from overgrazing the "organizational pasture," professional groups establish codes of ethics that spell out each member's share of responsibility for the group's organizational commons. Each code encourages members to give back to the group and discourages behaviors by individuals that soil the reputation of the organization and thereby devalue the benefit of membership for all.

The National Association of Realtors (NAR) and the Appraisal Institute (AI) are examples of commons that serve the real estate community. These organizations actively promote their members' interests through lobbying, educational programs, publications, and granting of designations indicative of professional expertise and achievement. Both organizations employ codes of ethics[1] in an attempt to inhibit objectionable behaviors on the part of their members. These codes—NAR's Code of Ethics and Standards of Practice (National Association of Realtors, 1995) and the AI's Code of Professional Ethics (Appraisal Institute, 1996a) and the Uniform Standards of Professional Appraisal Practice (Appraisal Institute, 1996b) adopted by the AI—are steeped in rule ethics.

Much of the content of these codes of professional ethics and standards of professional practice deals with myriad rules governing what to do and what not to do as a practicing professional.[2] For example, Article 1 of the NAR Code of Ethics and Standards of Practice states, "When representing a . . . client as an agent, REALTORS® pledge themselves to protect and promote the interests of their client" (Pivar and Harlan, 1995, p. 183). Canon 3 of the Code of Professional Ethics of the Appraisal Institute (Appraisal Institute, 1996a) says, "In the performance of an assignment, a member must develop and communicate each analysis and opinion without . . . bias . . . and without the accommodation of his or her own interests" (p. 5).

Deinhart (1995) suggests that this tendency for rule ethics to be reduced to a "codified system of concrete rules that imposes values on others" (p. 426) represents the first of three criticisms of ethical codes—conceptual and ethical incoherence. Ethical codes are accused of incoherence because they attempt to apply technical (rules-based) solutions to problems of human values and morality (Hardin, 1968; Deinhart, 1995). For instance, consider a broker who has a highly marketable listing and a buyer who is ready to make an offer. Imagine that the broker receives an offer procured through the efforts of a subagent prior to obtaining an offer from his or her own buyer. If the broker is a REALTOR®, then the broker is bound to uphold Standard of Practice 1-6, a corollary to Article 1, which states that offers shall be submitted "as quickly as possible" (Pivar and Harlan, 1995, p. 183). Too quick of a submission may, however, result in an outcome that may be against the interests of the seller—a violation of Article 1—and could be against the interests of the listing broker. The seller may be harmed if the listing broker's buyer would have offered a higher price but delays too long or decides not to make an offer in competition with someone else. The listing broker will be harmed by having to share the commission if the sub-agent's buyer ultimately purchases the house. This provides an incentive, potentially in conflict with the seller's interests and certainly in violation of Standard of Practice 1-6, to not present the subagent's offer as quickly as possible in order to obtain the additional offer from the listing broker's potential buyer.

Rutledge (1994) suggests a similar scenario that relates the appraisal field to real estate investment management and points to the potential for conflicts of interest. Investment managers typically adopt compensation schemes requiring their clients to pay fees based on the value of the real estate they manage. He notes two resulting financial incentives for invest-ment managers to "play a principal role in measuring investment perfor-mance" (p. 17). First, appraisals with an upward bias have a favorable impact on the investment performance (return) reported to the client and hence are "critical to the success of a manager's survival and growth" (p. 17). Second, investment management fees are positively correlated with asset values. He further comments that, although the appraiser may be committed to maintaining his or her objectivity, "it cannot be far from his (her) mind, however, that his (her) client . . . will be both evaluated and compensated . . . based partly on the results of the appraisal."

This dilemma is more fully illustrated by the following, real-world example. Appraisers are often commissioned to prepare a "draft" appraisal report, which is sent to the client for "review" prior to completing and signing the final report. If the draft report does not fulfill the investment manager's needs, then the appraiser is given the option of (1) terminating the contract for services and negotiating a partial fee for the "preliminary draft report" or (2) adjusting the appraised value and completing the assignment at the agreed on full appraisal fee. Terminating the contract may also result in removal of the appraiser's firm from the investment manager's approved roster of appraisers, effectively costing the firm a client. So the appraiser is forced to choose either to knowingly violate an ethical rule in order to satisfy a client of the firm[3] or to honor the ethical code and risk losing a client.

Deinhart (1995) presents two more criticisms of ethical codes beyond those based on conceptual and ethical incoherence. First, he argues that codes cannot and do not alter behavior. This is because, as Ladd (1985) notes, "Those to whom it [a code] is addressed and who need it most will not adhere to it anyway, and the rest of the good people in the profession will not need it because they already know what they ought to do" (p. 11). In effect, as code makers draft a comprehensive system of concrete, technical rules designed to protect the professional organization members' common good, they attempt to impose what they perceive to be good-member values on the members who are least likely to adhere to the rules. Hence, they violate the fundamental Lockean ideal, which says rules that ought to govern the lives of people are the rules people would voluntarily agree to given the opportunity to make a reasoned choice.

Second, Deinhart notes that codes "promote unethical behavior, because the true aim of such codes is to serve the interests of those who write them" (p. 427) rather than to promote the common good. In other words, simply reading rules and being lectured to about codes at continuing education sessions do not guarantee that an organization's members will put them into practice. If codes did alter behavior, then investment managers, for example, would be unsuccessful in finding appraisers who are willing to adjust their opinions of value to meet the manager's needs, and the threat of removal from an investment manager's approved list would eventually become ineffective.[4] In the end, the primary objection to codes revolves around the ethical inadequacy of codes—that is, the inability of codes to inspire ethical conduct (Deinhart, 1995).

The Moral Component

Further criticism of rule ethics stems from early disapproval of Locke's social contract ethics. Commentators noted that Locke's "free people making reasoned choices based on false beliefs or influenced by ingrained prejudices fail to recognize social injustice" and, instead, create an ethos of false morality (Pastin, 1988, p. 20). In addressing this shortcoming, Immanuel Kant (1724–1804) added a moral dimension to ethics. According to Kant, what guides our willingness to adhere to rules is an innate, absolute moral sense—an inescapable feeling that something is either right or wrong (Durrant, 1961). This view stresses morality above happiness. In fact, Durrant quotes Kant: "Seek happiness in others, but perfection in ourselves, even if it brings us pain" (p. 277).[5]

Kantians confront the issue of false morality by suggesting that only rules that apply equally to everyone and are purely moral in motive are ethical. So devised, codes strive to instill a desire for voluntary compliance on behalf of an organization's members and to inspire ethical conduct. Identifying motive is the key to uncovering false morality. If a code's underlying motive is to enhance the image of the organization as a means of promoting the marketability of its members' services, then the code is immoral in a Kantian sense (L'Etang, 1992). As Paton (1986, pp. 55–56) says, "For, if any action is to be morally good, it is not enough that it should conform to the moral law—it must also be done for the sake of moral law." Therefore, in Kantian terms, if organization members are to be inspired to make a reasoned choice to adhere to an ethical code, then the code must be a moral code.

Moral codes imply moral communities. A professional organization is a community that expects its members to conduct themselves in a certain way and finds certain other ways unacceptable. An organization uses codes to maintain the basic constructs of its "right kind of community." Herein lies the problem: we cannot legislate the moral fiber of the person solely, or even chiefly, by imposing rules of conduct. At best, rules draw lines in the sand over which organizational members fear to tread (Garcia, 1994, p. 44). At worst, they "immunize institutionalized practice against criticism"

(Putnam, 1995, p. 268). In effect, rigorously enforced rules in some instances afford an organization's members the opportunity to abdicate their ultimate moral responsibility—personal integrity.

Long (1998) provides an illustrative example of a conflict between rules and personal integrity. She presents a murder-suicide case where a house is being sold by the estate of a person who murdered his family in the home and subsequently committed suicide there. Long poses the question, "should the agent disclose this information?" (p. 40) when buyers ask why the house is being offered for sale, if disclosure is apt to reduce the price buyers are willing to pay. As the case is written, there is no state law or legal precedent to guide the agent. Furthermore, the office policy and procedures manual and the professional code of ethics call for the agent to elevate the seller's interests above all others, but the code of ethics also cautions agents to be honest with buyers. While nondisclosure can be rationalized within the bounds of the relevant rules, Long points out that the agent's conscience says that "buyers have a right to know . . . anything within reason that might adversely affect the future value of the home" (p. 43).

Exit, Voice, and Loyalty.   A professional organization that is the "right kind of community" must, at a minimum, provide for *exit*, *voice*, and *loyalty* (Hirschman, 1970; Hartman, 1994). By right kind of community it is meant one where the commons is preserved and members of the organization freely share experiences about morality "from which moral progress may emerge" (Hartman, 1994, p. 260).[6] *Exit* is the right of a dissatisfied member to leave the organization. The ability to freely leave the organization provides two benefits. First, those who leave and then return may be viewed by other, less adventurous members as worldly and sophisticated judges of various alternative organizations, rather than an "uncritical prisoner of any local values" (Hartman, 1994, p. 261). In other words, a returning member who has searched for a better organization and failed to find one, strengthens the organization to which he or she has returned. Second, the right of exit pressures an organization to continually strive to provide a good community for fear of losing all of its members and ceasing to exist.

Voice refers to the rights of organization members to provide input and to experience due process. This kind of political power must be vested in grassroots members, and individual members must feel that the organization's leaders are responsive to members' needs and concerns. Hartman (1994, p. 261) stresses also that "the organization be hospitable to those whose ways of seeing and interpreting life are different." For professional communities, this means defining and pursuing a common purpose that has been shaped by multiple views. The engagement of such diversity strengthens and nurtures the community through open communication and a growing sense of mutual understanding.

The third, and most essential, ingredient of right kinds of communities is *loyalty*. Members must be bound to each other by more than self-interest. There must be a sense of communal accomplishment that all members realize could not be achieved by a noncohesive collection of individuals, all of whom are striving solely to achieve self-elevating goals. Loyal members are motivated by the interests of the organization, and they make personal sacrifices for the benefit of the organization, thereby preserving the commons. However, as Hartman (1994) points out, the right degree of loyalty is a delicate balance that is difficult to achieve and sustain. There must be enough loyalty to preserve the commons but not so much loyalty that voices are stilled and exiters are ostracized.

Rationale and Sanctions. If a code is moral, can an organization automatically expect voluntary compliance with the code by its members? The answer to this question is, of course, "No, it isn't that simple." Consider, for example, the Socratic idea of virtue—knowing what we do not know—that motivates the Competency Provision of the Uniform Standards of Professional Appraisal Practice (USPAP). The Competency Provision requires an appraiser to consider the expertise that will be required to complete an appraisal and to either have the requisite knowledge and experience or arrange to collaborate with another appraiser who does have the requisite expertise (Appraisal Institute, 1996b). Although this is a highly virtuous organizational ideal, it is often ignored by appraisers. Indeed, when the authors posed a related question, "What does the appraisal community see as the important ethical issues impacting the appraisal business today?" to a group of appraisal professionals, the violation of the competency provision was the issue that arose most often.[7] One respondent commented that "almost every appraiser I have run into has been willing to take on almost any assignment." Another appraiser indicated that in his area of the country certified residential appraisers are doing commercial appraisal work and then finding certified general appraisers to "co-sign (the report) after the fact." A third appraiser answered that he has "found very few appraisers who will turn down any job . . . even if they never performed an assignment of that type before."

Weaver (1995) suggests two ways to achieve code compliance: include both rationales and sanctions against transgressions within the body of a written code. He conducted a study designed to measure the relationship between code design, content recall, and perceptions of justice, emphasizing that "perceptions of organizational justice . . . have been theoretically and empirically linked to . . . important actions and attitudes on the part of organization members" (p. 369). Weaver's pioneering empirical study provides mixed messages regarding the connectivity between code design and effectiveness. It finds a significant relationship between inclusion of a rationale within a code and perceptions of justice, but it also discovers that the perception-of-justice influence of sanctions alone or sanctions combined with rationales is insignificant. Furthermore, the study finds no significant relationship between rationales or sanctions and code content recall. Thus, a moral code that includes sanctions and an explicitly stated rationale may bring about some degree of compliance, but it will not necessarily lead to the creation of Hartman's (1994) "right kind of community."

For example, an underlying commitment to morality is clearly stated in NAR's Code of Ethics and Standards of Professional Practice, which says dedication to "social responsibility and . . . moral conduct in business relations . . . can take no safer guide than that which has been handed down through the centuries, embodied in the Golden Rule" (Pivar and Harlan, 1995, p. 182). The NAR code also provides plenty of rationale. Its preamble emphasizes the connection between the interests of the nation and a wide distribution of land ownership, and it emphasizes the obligation of REALTORS® to help ensure that citizens have adequate housing, functional cities, productive industries, and a healthy environment. As for the appraisal profession, the Competency Provision of USPAP includes clearly stated explanatory comments saying, "If an appraiser is offered the opportunity to perform an appraisal service but . . . (cannot) complete it competently, the appraiser must disclose his or her lack of knowledge to the client . . . and then take necessary and appropriate steps to complete the appraisal service competently" (Appraisal Institute, 1996b, p. 5). Nevertheless, the foregoing provisions are often ignored, and the common perception of unethical behavior in real estate appraisal and real estate brokerage persists.[8]

Codes and the Ethical Organization

Clearly, the adoption of ethical codes does not ensure the existence of an ethical organization. An ethical organization can exist with or without ethical codes. Codes serve as a means of formalizing the moral tenets of the organization, and they form the basis for an enforceable agreement among members through a system of sanctions. However, a commons cannot be preserved by imposition of a set of values on an organization's members. Rather, the codified set of values must be freely embraced by the members. As a necessary, but insufficient, condition of commons preservation and free-rider minimization, codes must be adopted for the sake of moral law, rationale must be self-evident, and codes must uphold the rights of exit and voice in order to instill loyalty. The ethical organization's codes should, therefore, both reflect and nurture the morality of its members. But how does one determine which choices constitute moral behavior?

A Second Look at Professional Ethics: End-Point Ethics

End-point ethics emerged in response to societal shifts brought on by the advent of the industrial revolution when extended families collapsed into smaller nuclear ones, government agencies became more involved in commerce, and industrialists replaced merchants. People began to realize that some choices freely made are "better than others, some are highly objectionable and others are simply intolerable" (Garcia, 1994, p. 23). End-point ethics takes this conclusion into account. Its basic premise rests on the notion that society should do what promotes the greatest balance of good over harm. In 1861, John Stuart Mill (1806–1873) integrated this ideal into the theory of *utilitarianism*, which suggests that we look at an action's likely consequences to determine its appropriateness. Of each rule or institution, Mill asked, "Does it promote a greater balance of benefit over harm than do other rules (or institutions) by which we live?" (Pastin, 1988, p. 21).[9] Twentieth-century variants of utilitarianism include cost-benefit analysis and risk-benefit analysis.

Although overall societal good is the end goal of utilitarianism, a drawback to end-point ethics is that a short-sighted, self-indulgent generation may pursue immediate gratification at the expense of future generations. Self-indulgence aptly describes the role played by special-interest groups in the political process. For example, the United States League of Savings Institutions lobby was instrumental in soliciting former Speaker of the U.S. House of Representatives Jim Wright's leadership in a fight against a 1986 bill, endorsed by the Federal Home Loan Bank Board and the Treasury Department, which was designed to recapitalize the Federal Savings and Loan Insurance Corporation. Their self-motivated effort succeeded in delaying the fight to clean up what is now referred to as the S&L scandal for fifteen additional and crucial months (Adams, 1990).

For the appraisal industry, the upshot of the S&L scandal was the advent of licensing, certification, USPAP, and the Appraisal Foundation. According to a 1986 Report of the House Government Operations Committee's Subcommittee on Commerce, Consumer and Monetary Affairs, "inaccurate appraisals had contributed to the insolvency of financial institutions and caused substantial losses" (Dennis, 1992, p. 333). In 1987, in an attempt to forestall government intervention into the industry, appraisers took measures designed to upgrade the practice of appraisal. By 1988, the nation's leading appraisal organizations had formed the Appraisal Foundation (Bailey-Seas, 1994). Meanwhile, Congressman Barnard, who had been promoting appraisal regulation, succeeded in sponsoring an amendment eventually adopted as Title XI of the Federal Institutions Reform, Recovery and Enforcement Act of 1989 (FIRREA).[10] The appraisal industry has struggled since that time with passage of licensing and certification laws in all fifty states, analyzing the impact of licensing and certification and the quality of appraisers' work product and sanctioning appraisers who violate the rules set forth in USPAP (Colwell and Trefzger, 1992; Evans, 1994; Rudolph, 1994; Dotterweich and Myers, 1995).

People often speak of the common good when making decisions restricting property rights or the activities of members of society—an end-point ethics consideration. However, as the multibillion dollar S&L scandal and the current disarray of the appraisal industry reveal, utilitarian political solutions to ethical problems suffer from vulnerability to self-indulgent, self-interested, special interests. Resulting legislation and regulations may not have the desired effect or, as some argue in the case of appraisal, may have an effect that runs counter to the stated purpose by expanding the pool of less qualified appraisers and thereby constraining "appraisal quality at the high end" (Colwell and Trefzger, 1992, p. 429). The consequences of the savings and loan scandal and the subsequent regulatory legislation clearly demonstrate that the fruits of end-point ethics are no more (or perhaps less) satisfying than those of rule ethics.

A Third Look at Professional Ethics: Uncharted Waters for Real Estate

So far this discussion appears to lead to an impasse. Real estate practitioners have professional codes to regulate ethical conduct, and decision makers assess situations to determine monetary and political costs and benefits in order to determine courses of action. In spite of this, the outcomes of rule ethics and end-point ethics seem to be less than satisfactory. Ethical codes are not totally effective at preventing potential conflicts of interest, and the utilitarian political process is mired in the status quo by self-interested, special-interest tactics.

Overcoming Self-Interested Habitual Behavior

Émile Durkheim says that "habits are the real forces which govern us . . . and as they acquire force they are transformed into rules of conduct" (Camic, 1992, pp. 197, 198). Durkheim implies that habits of self-interest and rugged individualism permeate today's society. John Dewey (1859–1952) follows a similar train of thought in *Nature and Experience* (1958). He warns that when we take into account only special or partial interests, we run the risk of being "insincere in the name of peace [and in doing so] of fostering divisions that lead to strife or [of being] deceitful in the name of loyalty [and in doing so] of promoting unholy alliances and secret understandings" (p. 410). He further suggests that sole reliance on common sense—a cornerstone of rugged individualism—"is sound as to the need and possibility of objective criticism of value . . . but weak as to the method of accomplishing it" (p. 426). This is because, in his estimation, common sense relies on "half-judgement, uncriticized products of custom, chance circumstances and vested interest" (p. 426).

Consider, for example, the practice—now required by law under FIRREA—of routinely disclosing the sale price of a property being appraised as part of the process of underwriting a new mortgage. There is a school of thought that maintains that reliance on the normative, appraisal process model will facilitate separation of an appraiser's "personal beliefs, perceptions, biases, attitudes, or emotions" (Mundy, 1992, p. 494) from the analytical process. But are self-reliant appraisers capable of ignoring the potentially biasing influence of sale price knowledge when solving valuation problems? One empirical study, critical of the practice of routinely disclosing sale price, suggests that they cannot (Gallimore and Wolverton, 1997). Gallimore and Wolverton utilize controlled, completely randomized experiments to test the effect of sale price knowledge on comparable sale selection. They find significant comparable sale selection bias when comparing appraisal-problem processes and solutions of a sale-price-knowledge treatment group with those of a no-price-knowledge control group. Reliance on routinely provided sale price information, as required by law, appears to result in biased value judgments directly counter to the intentions of Canon 3 of the Code of Professional Ethics of the Appraisal Institute, which requires that valuations be developed without bias.

Durkheim suggests that societal institutions, such as business and education, can lessen the impact of habits born of self-interest and individualism by encouraging "self-forgetfulness" and a devotion to "collective ideals" and by supporting continual reflection on ethical principles (Camic, 1992). Dewey (1958) seems to concur when he asserts, "To define value is to begin a process of discrimination" (p. 398). Discrimination, in this case, implies a need for reflective criticism and, to a great extent, moral reasoning. Whether determining a strategy regarding presentation of offers to purchase, confronting an investment manager promoting a self-interested objective, or dealing with the biasing effects of price knowledge, an innate sense of what is moral seems a more reliable means of discriminating between right and wrong choices than reliance on today's codified rules of behavior.

The Missing Ingredient: Integrity

Professional organizations initiate codes in attempts to regulate role morality—how we should act in a certain capacity. They do so by trying to bind professional competence to professional integrity, thereby relaxing the requirement that individual members exercise the higher degree of intelligence, which is typically an integral part of moral reasoning. In effect, codes allow us to meet the letter of the law while avoiding its spirit. Even if this were not the case, many current ethical theorists contend that ethical behavior will not result from moral reasoning alone (Gilligan, 1977, 1982; Noddings, 1984; Belenky, Clinchy, Goldberger, and Tarule, 1986; Pastin, 1988). People must, in their estimation, start with a moral attitude—a longing for goodness. Such moral excellence intertwines the logic of moral reasoning with a sense of caring, which results in individual integrity. It is this moral attitude on which professional organizations can build. The ethical underpinnings become a desire for success, a desire to serve others, and a desire for personal integrity (Emmet, 1989) and the overall organizational goal—collective integrity. Professional education, university business programs, and real estate training opportunities must strive to instill in students and members the ability to define values (individually and collectively) and learn habits that foster integrity and moral behavior.

Closing Remarks

Both of the primary branches of ethics, rule and end-point, seem to offer less than satisfying resolution to the common perception of unethical behavior in real estate. Codes of ethics, alone, do not alter behavior, and utilitarianism is susceptible to self-indulgence and special interests. Truly moral, and hence revered, professional organizations are not the ones that flaunt rigid rules and openly sanction their members. Rather, they are organizations consisting of members who possess integrity, both in reasoning and in attitude—members who agree on clearly stated fundamental rules of behavior that have been devised for the sake of morality and the common good and not for individual or organizational image enhancement. If practicing professionals in real estate can strive to create organizations that are self-selected by discriminating members on the basis of values grounded in morality, then the industry will be well on its way toward a common perception of ethical behavior in real estate.

Notes

1. Many other real estate organizations have codes as well—the Counselors of Real Estate (CRE), Building Owners and Managers Institute (BOMI), and the Appraisal Foundation's Uniform Standards of Professional Appraisal Practice (USPAP). The National Association of Realtors and the Appraisal Institute were selected as examples for this study because they are more visible, hence more often criticized, organizations.

2. NAR's Code of Ethics and Standards of Practice encompass seventeen Articles and sixty-three corollary Standards of Practice. AI's Code of Professional Ethics and Standards of Professional Appraisal Practice includes six Canons with thirty corollary Ethical Rules, plus adoption of USPAP with ten Appraisal Standards with eight Explanatory Statements, and fifteen Advisory Opinions. In addition, USPAP includes an Ethics Provision, Competency Provision, Departure Provision, Jurisdictional Exception, Supplemental Standards, and Definitions.

3. If the assignment is completed and a biased appraisal or conflict of interest occurs as a result, then the appraiser has violated Canon 3 of the AI Code of Professional Ethics.

4. For a recent, highly publicized example of appraisers who were influenced by client pressure, appraisers who failed to adhere to rule ethics, and the personal price borne by a whistleblower at Prudential Real Estate Investors' PRISA and PRISA II commingled funds, see Connolly (1994), Vinocur (1994), and Williams (1994). Also see Smolen and Hambleton (1997) for survey data on the extent of client pressure and coercion in the practice of real estate appraisal, and the Appraisal Institute (1997) for a summary of the General Accounting Office's finding that client (lender) pressure has increased substantially since 1995.

5. See Kant (1785/1981) for further discussion of utilitarian rule ethics.

6. Bowen H. "Buzz" McCoy (1994), in an ethics orientation class taught to incoming MBA students, urges "students to develop their own awareness of ethics . . . to develop a community in which they can comfortably discuss and share ethical concerns . . . without having to 'go public' every time they are uncomfortable" (pp. 1, 2).

7. The question was posted in May of 1996 on the aiforum electronic bulletin board (aiforum@realworks.com).

8. See essays by Fiedler (1996), Long (1995), White (1994).

9. See Mill (1861/1948) and Ryan (1970) for further discussion.

10. On March 16, 1992, the Office of Management and Budget (OMB) issued OMB Bulletin 92-06, Guidance on Real Estate Appraisal Standards and Practices, which extended Title XI appraisal standards to the eighteen federal agencies formerly covered by Uniform Standards for Federal Land Acquisition, the Uniform Act of 1970 (Bailey-Seas, 1994). Consequently, all federally related transactions and federal agencies were subjected to the "minimum standards for appraisals in conformity with . . . USPAP" (Bailey-Seas, 1994, p. 36) and were required to use state-certified or licensed real estate appraisers.

References

Adams, J.R. (1990). *The Big Fix: Inside the S&L Scandal.* New York: J Wiley.

Appraisal Institute. (1996a). *Code of Professional Ethics of the Appraisal Institute.* Chicago: Appraisal Institute.

Appraisal Institute. (1996b). *Standards of Professional Appraisal Practice of the Appraisal Institute.* Chicago: Appraisal Institute.

Appraisal Institute. (1997) "GAO Report Signals FHA Fraud, Mismanagement, and Abuse; Calls for Stricter Review." *Appraiser News in Brief* 4(6): 1.

Ault, C.R., Jr. (1994). "Citizens and the Conduct of Ecological Science." In C. Brody and J. Wallace (eds.), *Ethical and Social Issues in Professional Education* (pp. 147–167). Albany: State University of New York Press.

Bailey-Seas, A.K. (1994). "Evolution of Appraisal Reform and Regulation in the United States." *Appraisal Journal* 62(1): 26–46.

Belenky, M., B. Clinchy, N. Goldberger, and J. Tarule. (1986). *Women's Ways of Knowing: The Development of Self, Voice and Mind.* New York: Basic Books.

Camic, C. (1992). "The Matter of Habit." In M. Zey (ed.), *Decision Making: Alternatives to Rational Choice Models* (pp. 185–232). Newbury, CA.: Sage.

Colwell, P.F., and J.W. Trefzger. (1992). "Impact of Regulation on Appraisal Quality." *Appraisal Journal* 60(3): 428–429.

Connolly, J. (1994). "Restitution on Overvaluations May Cost Pru $50M." *National Underwriter* (May 9): 4.

Deinhart, J. (1995). "Rationality, Ethical Codes, and an Egalitarian Justification of Ethical Expertise." *Business Ethics Quarterly* 5(3): 419–450.

Dennis, K.A. (1992). "Regulatory Requirements for Appraisals." *Appraisal Journal* 60(3): 331–346.

Dewey, J. (1958). *Experience and Nature.* New York: Dover.

Dotterweich, D., and G. Myers. (1995). "Appraiser Attitudes Toward Industry Changes." *Appraisal Journal* 63(3): 291–297.

Durrant, W. (1961). *The Story of Philosophy.* New York: Washington Square Press.

Emmet, D. (1989). "Roles, Professions and Moral Responsibility." In M. Bayles and K. Henley (eds.), *Right Conduct: Theories and Applications* (2nd ed.) (pp. 322–329). New York: Random House.

Evans, R.C. (1994). "Impact of State Certification on the Commercial Appraisal Market." *Appraisal Journal* 62(2): 217–221.

Fiedler, L.E. (1996). "The Problem with Commercial Property Appraisals Today." *Real Estate Review* 25(4): 33–36.

Gallimore, P., and M.L. Wolverton. (1997). "Price Knowledge Induced Bias: A Cross-Cultural Comparison." *Journal of Property Valuation and Investment* 15(3): 261–273.

Garcia, J. (1994). "The Aims of the University and the Challenge of Diversity: Bridging the Traditionalist/Multiculturalist Divide." In M. Sellers (ed.), *An Ethical Education* (pp. 21–48). Providence, RI: Berg.

Gilligan, C. (1977). "In a Different Voice: Women's Conception of the Self and Morality." *Harvard Educational Review* 47: 481–517.

Gilligan, C. (1982). *In a Different Voice.* Cambridge, MA: Harvard University Press.

Hardin, G. (1968). "The Tragedy of the Commons." *Science* 162 (December 13): 1243–1248.

Hartman, E.M. (1994). "The Commons and the Moral Organization." *Business Ethics Quarterly* 4(3): 253–269.

Hirschman, A.O. (1970). *Exit, Voice, and Loyalty: Responses to Decline in Firms, Organizations, and States.* Cambridge, MA: Harvard University Press.

Kant, I. (1785/1981). *Grounding for the Metaphysics of Morals.* Translated by (J. Ellington.) Indianapolis: Hackett.

Ladd, J. (1985). "The Quest for a Code of Professional Ethics." In Deborah G. Johnson and John W. Snapper (eds.), *Ethical Issues in the Use of Computers.* Belmont, CA: Wadsworth.

L'Etang, J. (1992). "A Kantian Approach to Codes of Ethics." *Journal of Business Ethics* 11(10): 737–744.

Locke, J. (1690/1980). *Second Treatise of Government.* Indianapolis: Hackett.

Long, D. (1995). "The Real Estate Educator as Moral Leader." *Real Estate Educators Association Journal* (Spring): 31–36.

Long, D. (1998). *Doing the Right Thing: A Real Estate Practitioner's Guide to Ethical Decision Making.* Upper Saddle River, NJ: Gorsuch/Prentice-Hall.

MacIntyre, A. (1984). *After Virtue* (2nd ed.). Notre Dame, IN: University of Notre Dame Press.

McCoy, B.H. (1994). "On Business Ethics." *Real Estate Issues* 19(3): 1–7.

Mill, J.S. (1861/1948). *Utilitarianism.* Edited by O. Piest. New York: Liberal Arts Press.

Mundy, B. (1992). "The Scientific Method and the Appraisal Process." *Appraisal Journal* 60(4): 493–499.

National Association of Realtors. (1995). *Code of Ethics and Standards of Practice.* Chicago: National Association of Realtors.

Noddings, N. (1984). *Caring: A Feminine Approach to Ethics and Moral Education.* Berkeley: University of California Press.

Pastin, M. (1988). *The Hard Problems of Management: Gaining the Ethics Edge.* San Francisco: Jossey-Bass.

Paton, H.J. (1986). *The Moral Law: Kant's Groundwork of the Metaphysics of Morals.* London: Hutchinson.

Pivar, W.H., and D.L. Harlan. (1995). *Real Estate Ethics: Good Ethics = Good Business* (3nd ed.). Chicago: Dearborn.

Plato. (387–367 B.C./1981). *Five Dialogues.* Translated by G. Grube. Indianapolis: Hackett.

Putnam, H. (1995). "Pragmatism, Relativism and the Justification of Democracy." In J. Arthur and A. Shapiro (eds.), *Campus Wars: Multiculturalism and the Politics of Difference* (pp. 264–273). Boulder, CO: Westview Press.

Ryan, A. (1970). *John Stuart Mill.* New York: Pantheon Books.

Rudolph, P.M. (1994). "Will Bad Appraisals Drive Out Good?" *Appraisal Journal* 62(3): 363–366.

Rutledge, J.K. (1994). "Conflicts of Interest or 'Thou Shalt Not Steal' Revisited." *Real Estate Issues* 19(3): 15–19.

Smolen, G.E., and D.C. Hambleton. (1997). "Is the Real Estate Appraiser's Role Too Much to Expect?" *Appraisal Journal* 65(1): 9–17.

Vinocur, B. (1994). "Pru's Appraisal Mess." *Barron's* (May 16): 50–51.

Weaver, G.R. (1995). "Does Ethics Code Design Matter? Effects of Ethics Code Rationales and Sanctions on Recipients' Justice Perceptions and Content Recall." *Journal of Business Ethics* 14(5): 367–385.

White, J.R. (1994). "Lofty Expressions of Ethical Conduct Do Not Insure Adherence." *Real Estate Issues* 19(3): 26–33.

Whitehead, A.N. (1948). *Science and the Modern World.* New York: Mentor.

Williams, T. (1994). "Prudential Dismisses Jorgensen." *Pensions and Investments* (February 21): 4, 39.

Wilson, J. (1993). *The Moral Sense.* New York: Free Press.

Woodward, K. (1994). "What Is Virtue?" *Newsweek* (June 13): 38–39.

II INDUSTRY PRACTICE

5 "AND THEIR RIGHT HAND IS FULL OF BRIBES"
Corruption and Real Estate

Jeroen Broeders

Trouringhstraat 8-hs 1055 HA Amsterdam

Jacco Hakfoort

Department of Geography and Planning
Faculty of Geographical Sciences
Utrecht University

Gather not my soul with sinners,
Nor my life with bloody men:
In whose hand is mischief,
And their right hand is full of bribes.

Psalms 26: 9–10

Abstract
Where private and public sectors interface, there is always the risk of personal enrichment at the public's expense. Many real estate transactions and construction projects are characterized by such interactions, which usually involve considerable sums of money. It is therefore not surprising that the real estate business is relatively vulnerable to corrupt activities. In economic models of corruption, the decision to engage in corrupt activities is seen as a tradeoff between the expected gains and costs of such behavior. Using this framework, we address some of the following questions: What factors determine the level of corruption? Why do some sectors of the economy seem more prone to corruption than others? And what should we do about it?

Introduction

It is not hard to think of instances where there is an incentive for real estate firms (or their employees) to bribe public officials to obtain building permits or public contracts. The real estate business seems, perhaps more than most other lines of business, vulnerable to corrupt practices. Considerable sums of money are involved in development and trading, while business transactions in this industry have a rather intricate character.

Corruption can be defined as a transaction in which a public official, while interacting with a third party, acquires private benefits and at the same time breaches the loyalty to his employer.[1] Corruption occurs whenever a public servant *intentionally* acts in contradiction with the objectives and rules of his organization by putting his private interests, financial or otherwise, before the well-being of the organization. A public official can act against the interests of his organization by delivering inefficient or bad work, but he can be called corrupt only when he deliberately acts in this way to further his own interests.[2]

The benefits of corruption for a public servant can take different shapes. For example, an envelope of money can change hands, or goods and services can be delivered at a discount or even free of charge. In exchange, the official delivers a certain favor, such as a permit, a contract, or a discharge. Corrupt behavior can lead to large personal benefits for public officials. One of our favorite examples from the corruption literature (see Table 5.1) is taken from Gould (1983).

Corruption has always been with us. It is an ineradicable fact of social life. Within every nonanarchistic society, a partial transfer of sovereignty will take place from the community as a whole toward certain selected individuals, the public officials. History has taught us that it is *de facto* impossible to ensure that those individuals will *always* let the public interest prevail over their specific (often financial) private interests. Historical evidence from the real estate and construction industries shows that this is a constant phenomenon in these sectors as well. Present-day evidence suggests it to be a big problem for foreign investors in Eastern Europe and China.

This article explicates the characteristics of corruption for both perpetrators and fighters of corruption. We start with some anecdotal evidence from corruption cases in the real estate and construction industries. In the next section, an economic model is presented in which we use the so-called principal-agent model to analyze the phenomenon of corruption (see also Besley and McLaren, 1993; Shleifer and Vishney, 1993; Broeders and Hakfoort, 1994). According to this model, corruption is possible because the

Table 5.1.   Regional finance officials' salaries and automobile ownership, Lubumbashi, Zaire, May 1977

Position	Monthly Wages (in zaires)	Automobiles owned	1977 Value (in zaires) New	Used
Sixth bureau: Customs verification				
Head of office	115	Renault 17	8,000	6,000
		Mustang	10,000	7,000
		Volkswagen	7,000	4,000
		Pick-up truck	10,000	7,000
		Kombi	12,000	8,000
Office worker	90	Mercedes	30,000	15,000
Office worker	90	Renault 4	7,000	4,000
Temporary worker	39–66	Fiat (station wagon)	10,000	4,000
Third bureau: Tax collection				
Head of office	115	Toyota	10,000	7,000
Collection agent	90	Volkswagen	7,000	4,000
Accountant	72–90	Peugeot 404	12,000	8,000
Teller	39–66	Peugeot	12,000	8,000
Clerk	22–26	Ford Capri	9,000	6,000
Clerk	22–26	Fiat	8,000	6,000

Source: Gould (1983, p. 11).

management of any governmental organization (the *principal*) finds it impossible or undesirable to continuously monitor every employee (the *agent*). In this model both the agent and the principal are considered to be rational maximizing actors. Monitoring involves costs, and therefore it might be optimal to accept a certain level of corruption. The tradeoff that individual public servants make between the perceived costs and benefits of corruption determines the actual level of corruption in an organization. Differences in levels of corruption between organizations and societies are therefore the logical outcome of this tradeoff.

In the next part of this article we address the question of whether corruption is a good or a bad thing for society at large. This is a rather controversial matter. In the economic literature two different strands of thought can be discerned. Several authors have in the past laid down the view that corruption can have a positive effect on economic growth and development. However, we show that the economic costs of corruption usually exceed the benefits, especially when one also considers the indirect costs, an element that is normally not considered by economists. In the final part of this chapter we give an overview of the policy options open to government whenever it wants to fight corruption.

Some Anecdotal Evidence

The real estate and construction industry is prone to corruption. The stakes are high, the procedures and transactions relatively opaque for outsiders, while individual public officials typically have large discretionary powers. Therefore, in the last couple of decades many cases of corruption and fraud have become known, both in the Western world and in industrializing countries.

The last few years major cases of corruption have been reported from many countries, and especially from countries like China, Russia, and Indonesia. However, corruption is not restricted to the third world or to former communist countries. The large number of investigations into and court cases about the existence of corruption and fraud in the North American real estate and construction industries does suggest widespread corrupt activities. And because there is always more corruption than meets the eye, those cases might only be the proverbial tip of the iceberg.

Some examples: already in the 1920s the Lockwood Commission was set up to investigate illegal activities in the New York construction industry (see, for instance, Ichniowski and Preston, 1989). In the 1950s the New York City Waterfront Commission was set up to combat systematic corruption and racketeering in the same industry in the same city (see, for instance, Levy, 1989). This Commission revealed among other things that the New York longshore industry suffered from six categories of fraud and corruption: collusion, shape-up, public loaders, theft, misrepresentation of workers, and misuse of office for private ends.

A number of hearings in the late 1950s by the U.S. Congress, commonly known as the McClellan Committee hearings, investigated corrupt activities in the whole of the United States. In the 1970s in Quebec, Canada, the Cliche Commission was set up to investigate in particular union corruption in the real estate industry (see, for instance, Sexton, 1989). And more recently, the New York State Organized Crime Task Force, set up in the 1980s, was to deal again with what might be an inevitable characteristic of the New York construction industry: corruption.

Although there is no reason to assume that these cases are representative of the corruption in real estate and related sectors in North America, they do suggest that corruption matters and that its importance is probably more easily understated than overstated.

The Principal-Agent Model

The essence of corruption is that information is costly. It can occur only because the people who formulate the policy goals or have to uphold the law (the voters, the legislature, or high-ranking public officials) can never be completely sure that the bureaucracy will carry out its task in good faith. It is either too expensive, simply impossible, or maybe not even desirable to keep all public officials under full surveillance. Therefore, officials always have a certain leeway to use the government goods or services that are put under their care for their own private interests.

Each principal-agent model involves three actors: the principal, the agent, and a third party. In the case of corruption, the agent is a bureaucrat who is trying to further his personal interest by deciding whether to become corrupt. The principal is his supervisor whose prime interest is to minimize the occurrence of corruption, given the costs of fighting it. The third party is the person who is willing to offer a bribe to lay his hands on a public good or service over which the agent has discretionary powers. Figure 5.1 presents the relations between the actors.

This model of corruption potentially deals with all kinds of corruption, including bureaucratic and political corruption. When one uses this model, there is no need to differentiate between bureaucratic and political corruption, as some authors do (see, for instance, Rose-Ackerman, 1978). When the agent is no longer a low-level official but a top-level civil servant, the legislature is the principal. When the agent is a politician, the electorate is the principal. However, the problem of information will increase with the level of the agent. For instance, it is much more difficult for an individual voter to control a politician than it is for a high-ranking public official to control one of his employees.

Let us assume a homogeneous good—for instance, a permit—which can be issued by an individual official. This official has to decide to which party this permit will be granted. Furthermore, the demand curve for this permit is a negative function of the price of the good. Finally, we assume that the agent wants to maximize his personal well-being, which is a function of discounted income.

Given the problem of information mentioned above, the official can potentially grant permits for unjust causes without being discovered by his superiors because the probability of detection is less than one. He selects

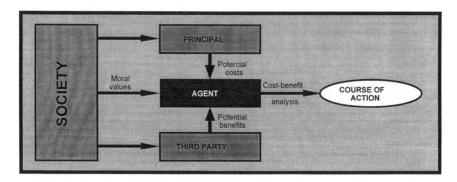

Figure 5.1.   The basic model

his course of action based on an analysis of his potential costs and benefits. Given the demand curve for the permit, the official acts as a monopolist in issuing this permit. His goal is to maximize the bribes he receives, given the detection probability and the costs involved in detection. However, in almost all cultures and religions corruption has a negative connotation, and a corrupt official has to live with a bad conscience. Therefore, the official will also take his moral costs into account when he decides whether to become corrupt.

The principal-agent model is essentially a static one. However, in the real world corruption is not a static affair. Corruption is linked in time. Often corruption is not a once-in-a-lifetime experience. Why do corrupt officials tend to repeat their corrupt acts? The answer to this question is simple: nothing corrupts more than corruption itself. Or, to put it in an economic framework: the profitability of corruption tends to increase with its established frequency. A model like this was developed by Andvig and Moene (1990). According to their model, the number of corrupt bureaucrats is higher

- The higher the perceived fraction of corrupt bureaucrats,
- The higher the bribes,
- The lower the salary of the bureaucrats,
- The lower the detection probability,
- The higher the discount rate.

The dynamic element in the model is that the detection probability decreases with a higher (perceived) number of corrupt bureaucrats. This number of bureaucrats can increase due to some exogenous shock—for example, a change in wages.

Different Levels of Corruption: Goods, Organizaitons, Societies

Characteristics of goods and services matter when it comes to explaining the differences in levels of corruption between organizations and between societies. Corruption involving nonbulk goods and services like building projects or advanced weaponry is much harder to detect than corruption that occurs when a government organization orders bulk goods like paper and pencils. Corruption in the first group of transactions is difficult to detect due to the detailed technical and financial knowledge needed. Paper and pencils can be bought at every ordinary shop, and every one will recognize an inflated price if an organization pays too much for them.

But not only the characteristics of the goods and services are important. Differences in organizational design may also explain different levels of corruption. Because of the nature of their activities, some government organizations are more vulnerable to corruption than others.[3] Organizations that grant subsidies or permits or review tax returns are more prone to corruption than government agencies that have no executive tasks and therefore no direct interaction with the public.

The characteristics of the economic system at large also make a difference. When a government strongly regulates an economy, there are many possibilities for public officials to develop corrupt activities. Therefore, in a planned economy the level of corruption is often high. Apart from that, corruption also tends to flourish in periods of economic transition—for instance, from a planned economy to a market economy, or from a traditional system to a modern economic system (see, e.g., Riggs, 1964).

It is rather difficult to compare levels of corruption in between countries. However, an interesting attempt to do just that has been developed by *Transparency International*, a worldwide organization whose mission it is to fight corruption (see Table 5.2).

Costs and Benefits of Corruption for Society at Large

We have discussed the cost-benefit analysis of the individual official. In this part of the article we discuss the costs and benefits of corruption for society as a whole (see Table 5.3).

Table 5.2.   Corruption in fifty-two countries: A ranking from "good" to "bad," 1997

Country	Score[a]	Number of Surveys[b]	Variance[c]	Country	Score[a]	Number of Surveys[b]	Variance[c]
1. Denmark	9.94	6	0.54	26. Belgium	5.25	6	3.28
2. Finland	9.48	6	0.30	27. Czech Republic	5.20	5	0.22
3. Sweden	9.35	6	0.27	28. Hungary	5.18	6	1.66
4. New Zealand	9.23	6	0.58	29. Poland	5.08	5	2.13
5. Canada	9.10	5	0.27	30. Italy	5.03	6	2.07
6. Netherlands	9.03	6	0.23	31. Taiwan	5.02	7	0.76
7. Norway	8.92	6	0.23	32. Malaysia	5.01	6	0.50
8. Australia	8.86	5	0.44	33. South Africa	4.95	6	3.08
9. Singapore	8.66	6	2.32	34. South Korea	4.29	7	2.76
10. Luxemburg	8.61	4	1.13	35. Uruguay	4.14	4	0.63
11. Switzerland	8.61	6	0.26	36. Brazil	3.56	6	0.49
12. Ireland	8.28	6	1.53	37. Romania	3.44	4	0.07
13. Germany	8.23	6	0.40	38. Turkey	3.21	6	1.21
14. United Kingdom	8.22	6	1.43	39. Thailand	3.06	6	0.14
15. Israel	7.97	5	0.12	40. Philippines	3.05	6	0.51
16. USA	7.61	5	1.15	41. China	2.88	6	0.82
17. Austria	7.61	5	0.59	42. Argentina	2.81	6	1.24
18. Hong Kong	7.28	7	2.63	43. Vietnam	2.79	4	0.26
19. Portugal	6.97	5	1.02	44. Venezuela	2.77	5	0.51
20. France	6.66	5	0.60	45. India	2.75	7	0.23
21. Japan	6.57	7	1.09	46. Indonesia	2.72	6	0.18
22. Costa Rica	6.54	4	1.73	47. Mexico	2.66	5	1.18
23. Chile	6.05	6	0.51	48. Pakistan	2.53	4	0.47
24. Spain	5.90	6	1.82	49. Russia	2.27	6	0.87
25. Greece	5.35	6	2.42	50. Colombia	2.23	6	0.61
				51. Bolivia	2.05	4	0.86
				52. Nigeria	1.76	4	0.16

Source: Transparency International (1997). This index can also be found on the Internet at http://www.transparency.de.
Note: Scores are based on seven surveys and are average scores.
a. A 10 score indicates a perfectly clean country, whereas a 0 score refers to a country where business transactions are entirely penetrated by corruption involving immense sums of kickbacks, extortion, fraud, and so on.
b. The amount of surveys in which the particular country has been included (four to seven).
c. The variance of the rankings. A high number indicates a high degree of deviating opinions.

Benefits of Corruption

In most cultures the notion of corruption has a negative connotation. Nevertheless, in the economic literature several authors stress the (alleged) positive side-effects of corruption (see, for instance, Leff, 1964; Huntington, 1968). Their argument develops along both economic and noneconomic lines.

Table 5.3. Costs and benefits of corruption

	Benefits	*Costs*
Economic	Increase in economic efficiency Reduction of uncertainty	Direct: Higher prices Loss in time and energy Flight of capital Bad projects, wrong projects Indirect: Higher control costs

Political	Influence on decision making
	Nonviolent entry into the political
	    system
		Loss of legitimacy
		Leaders get caught in a
		    corruption trap

The main argument is that corruption is justifiable because it leads to an optimal allocation of government services and in general to a more efficient economy. The most efficient and entrepreneurial company can and will pay the highest bribes. Because of this, corruption can work as a corrective mechanism for a less efficient governmental decision-making process. But it would also have other positive economic side-effects. For instance, it could also reduce the uncertainty attached to investments because it reduces the burden of bureaucratic obstacles.

According to this line of thought corruption could also have some other positive effects of a more political nature. Especially in a transitional period it would increase the faith people have in the political system because it gives them the possibility of influencing the decision-making process. Furthermore, in a stable period bribery could establish a nonviolent entry into the political system, whenever traditional political channels are clogged.

Direct Economic Costs of Corruption

This argumentation ignores some important negative side-effects of corruption. To start with, corruption can be inefficient because, while rendering a corruptive service, costs are made by both the public servant and his client that would not have been made had the transaction been performed legally.[4] Often goods are purchased at a higher price than strictly necessary, and the process consumes time and energy that could have been used for other, socially more productive activities. And when products are purchased at a below market price, society at large will pay the difference.

Furthermore, the bribes collected in the corrupt activities are often siphoned off and exported to foreign bank accounts. This money is no longer used productively in the country of origin. Substantial amounts of money are involved in this process. For instance, according to some reports, in Switzerland alone some $20 billion (U.S.) are stacked away in the bank accounts of present and former African leaders. Another good example concerns the Indonesian state-owned enterprise Pertamina, which was responsible for constructing a steel works at Cilegon, West Java, in the 1970s. At no stage did the salary paid to the assistant who authorized payments under the various contracts exceed $9,000. When he died in 1976, it was discovered that he held nineteen bank accounts in Singapore, with credits totaling nearly $36 million (Genthe, 1994).

There are also less obvious but even more important direct economic costs involved with corruption. They can be summed up under the heading of "bad projects or wrong projects." First of all, there are bad projects—projects in which, for instance, inferior materials are used. The collapse of a number of blocks of flats in South Korea in recent years has been linked to this kind of corruption. And then there are wrong projects—projects like a big hydroelectric dam in an underdeveloped region, which never would have been built if the decision making in the public sector had not been distorted by bribes.

Indirect Economic Costs

Besides direct negative economic effects there are also indirect negative effects. When cases of corruption become known to the public, citizens lose their trust in government, and control problems arise. If a government's legitimacy is questioned, the rightfulness of government actions is no longer a priori accepted, and the authority of the administration decreases. Legitimacy can be defined as the belief that the members of a political system have in the rightness of the political institutions. When this belief is existent, citizens accept (most of) the rules laid down as binding. They believe that the institutions that issue the laws are justified in doing so, although not everyone may agree with every specific element (Daalder and Daudt, 1993, p. 153).

Legitimacy is just one of the mechanisms used by an administration to influence the population. Other mechanisms include legislation, education, subsidization, inspection, and taxation. But legitimacy is probably the most efficient control mechanism around. In any case, it is the cheapest one. As the eminent American political scientist Robert Dahl (1976, p. 60) observes: "It is easy to see why leaders strive for legitimacy. Authority is a highly efficient form of influence. It is not only more reliable and durable than naked coercion, but it also enables a ruler to govern with a minimum of political resources."

Consequently, when the authority of an administration decreases, the costs of governing increase. An increase in the size of the bureaucratic apparatus might be necessary. For instance, when more people send in false tax returns, a government has to hire more tax officials to get the same revenue. Something similar applies to the police force: the police lose legitimacy when a case of a corrupt police officer becomes public. Then it becomes more difficult to uphold the law and maintain order. More police officers have to be put on the streets.

When corruption becomes public, the integrity of an administration is at stake. As the late Ms. Ien Dales, a former Dutch Secretary of the Interior, once stated eloquently: "The government has integrity or not. Having a little bit of integrity is impossible. And without integrity, government fails. The undermining of integrity means the loss of our people's trust. And without trust democracy cannot exist" (Noppen, 1994, p. 6).

Political Costs

Besides economic costs there are also some political costs associated with corruption. To a large extent these are in a direct line with indirect economic costs because they are a result of the loss of legitimacy of the bureaucracy. Furthermore, corrupt bureaucrats may be caught in a corruption trap. They invest much of their time, energy, and other scarce resources to stay in power because they know they will be prosecuted when they lose their position. And because staying in power tends to be costly for them, they often have to increase their corrupt activities to finance this power struggle, thereby making it even more important for them to stay in power.

Fighting Corruption

Someone once observed that "the Judea-Christian tradition begins with the temptation of an innocent by a serpent, with disastrous and enduring consequences for all of humankind" (Genthe, 1994, p. 1). Corruption might to a certain extent be endemic to the human condition, but it most certainly is endemic to any nonanarchistic model of social organization. Whenever private and public sectors interact, there will always exist possibilities for personal enrichment at the public's expense.

According to some views, corruption undermines the basis of the modern constitutional state and must therefore be fought at *any* price. However, from an economic point of view the argument is a different one. One should decide what resources to spend on fighting corruption based on a cost-benefit analysis. However, making such an analysis is extremely difficult, since particularly the political costs and benefits of corruption are hardly quantifiable. To a large extent this also applies to the economic costs and benefits.

A Cost-Benefit Analysis

Klitgaard (1988, pp. 26–27) proposes such a cost-benefit analysis. He assumes that the marginal social costs of corruption increase as corruption occurs more frequently and that the marginal costs of discovering and fighting corruption become higher as it occurs less. Based on those assumptions, an optimal level of corruption can be distinguished (see Figure 5.2).

When corruption is considered undesirable from a social point of view, it must at least be fought until the point is reached where the marginal costs of fighting it are outweighed by the marginal benefits of forcing back corruption. The exact optimal level of corruption depends on the steepness and forms of the curves, of which we have no detailed knowledge. However, if one believes, as we do, that the loss of legitimacy is too high a price, the optimal level of corruption is probably a very low one.

Which instruments are available for governments to fight corruption? Any government has several options to decrease the level of corruption or at least the probability of corruption. Most of them refer to incentives to change the behavior of the agent (the public official) (see Klitgaard, 1988, p. 24), and some of them also target the third party.

Five different kinds of options can be discerned. All five of them try to influence the decision-making process of the public official by reducing the perceived benefits or increasing the expected costs:

- Changes in the payment and punishment systems to reduce the incentives to engage in corrupt activities,
- Intensified supervision to increase the probability of detection,
- Changes in the organizational structures to reduce the leeway of individual bureaucrats,
- Changes in the societal values to make corruption more reprehensible from a moral point of view, and

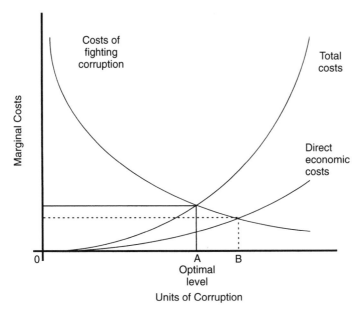

Figure 5.2. The "optimal" level of corruption in a society
Notes: In this figure we assume that the marginal costs of corruption are always positive, although it would not make any difference for the analysis if this is not the case. In this figure the optimal level is at point A. However, when only the direct economic costs are taken into account and no attention is paid to the loss of legitimacy, one would arrive at point B as the optimum.

- Changes in the selection procedures to prevent potentially corrupt citizens from becoming public officials.

Payment and Punishment

One way of fighting corruption is by increasing the wages of public officials. By paying wages above the comparable wages in trade and industry—as already suggested by Becker and Stigler (1974)—the stimulus to develop corrupt activities will decrease. Corrupt public servants will have more to lose when they are paid higher wages. Such a change in the wage structure is effective because it increases indirectly the costs of sanctions, while at the same time it decreases the relative importance of the benefits (especially regarding the nonmonetary moral costs). Table 5.4, taken from Hoetjes (1982), indicates that differences between what society and the public official consider the right wage and the actual wage may cause corruption through a number of mechanisms.

A second option a government has to fight corruption is sharpening the sanctions on detection of corruption. When enforcement of these rules then also becomes more strict, the expected costs of rendering a corruptive service will increase, and that will lead to a decrease in corruption.

Table 5.4. Wage structure and corruption

Opinion About Appropriate Salary for Public Officials

In Society	Within the Group of Public Officials	"Real" Salary	Effects on Corruption
High	High	High	Agreement—keeps corruption in check
High	High	Low	General feeling of underpayment—promotes corruption
High	Low	High	Public officials have a demoralizing feeling of undeserved high payment
High	Low	Low	Chances are high that someone in society will try to initiate a case of corruption
Low	Low	Low	Consensus—restrains corruption
Low	Low	High	General feeling of overpayment—works demoralizing and fosters corruption
Low	High	Low	Public officials think they do not get paid enough, which works demoralizing, but society at large does not agree with them
Low	High	High	Cynicism in society with regard to overpayment—promotes corruption

Source: Hoetjes (1982, p. 94).

A distinction has to be made between sanctions imposed inside and those imposed outside the government organization. Sanctions within the organization focus on lowering career perspectives or even, in extreme cases, on dismissal. Sanctions outside the organization often imply criminal prosecution.

It is important that the law concerning corruption reflects a marginal costs approach. In many countries this is not so. If corruption is detected, a more or less uniform sanction is applied. This sanction is to a large extent independent of the degree of corruption. Therefore, if a public official has been corrupt in the past, from a judicial point of view no marginal costs are involved in rendering another corrupt service. This is one of the more important reasons why corruption corrupts. It might be a good idea to change this threshold structure of the law.

Supervision

Corruption can be fought by designing uniform administrative and financial procedures. Publicity and controllability of the actions of a public servant will increase the chances of corruption being discovered and thus increase the expected costs of corruption for the individual public servant. Sometimes it can be advisable to hire an independent controller. Technically skilled accountants and controllers, for example, can check builders' estimates and building plans in the construction industry. It can also be sensible to have more than one public servant work on one task. In this way, the chances of discovery are bigger.

Organizational Changes

The possibility for public servants to collude in corruptive acts forms an argument in favor of open organizational structures. Some studies suggest that once corruption occurs in an organization, a chain reaction is brought about that will lead a growing part of the organization to become involved in corruptive activities.

Activities that are secret by their nature—for instance, police activities—have bigger chances of collusive development of corruption and are therefore more vulnerable. The necessary openness can be achieved by job rotation or by a project-based organizational model with members from different branches working together.

Moral Values

Although it is very difficult for governments to steer the development in moral values within a society, they can try to change the reigning moral values by awareness programs and ads. This way, the psychological costs for public servants increase, and corruption will occur less often.

Apart from trying to achieve behavioral changes in the bureaucracy, a government can also try to influence the behavior of the third party. There is, however, one extra area: in many countries it is still legal to state bribes on a tax return as business costs. And although this is especially focused on foreign markets, it is a bad signal to individual bureaucrats and citizens.

Selection

Another policy instrument is a better screening of individuals when they enter public service. Psychological tests might be effective in identifying persons with strong feelings against corruption. One could fight corruption by hiring such personnel. Intensified research on antecedents can have the same result.

Conclusions

In this chapter we discussed an economic approach to the study of corruption. We believe that such an approach makes it possible discuss the causes of and the fight against corruption. It can also be used to address the question why some governmental organizations are more susceptible to corruption than others. The framework adopted in this article may also shed some light on the apparent sensitivity of the real estate business to corruption.

Corruption might be ineradicable, but it can be pushed back to a low level. Corruption can be fought, but it is expensive to do so. The costs and benefits of fighting corruption must be weighed against one another. Politicians will have to decide what level of corruption can be tolerated. When only the direct costs of corruption are allowed for, it might seem justifiable to tolerate a certain level of corruption. However, when indirect costs are also considered, the tolerable level of corruption is much lower.

Governments can use several instruments to fight corruption. These instruments are aimed at influencing the decision-making process of the individual public servant who weighs benefits against costs. The fight against corruption can however also have undesirable consequences: a more strict selection can lead to not hiring otherwise excellent candidates, changing punishment and wage structures can lead to legal insecurity. Intensifying supervision and changes in organizational structures can cause the efficiency of government actions to decrease, while a governmental policy trying to change moral values can easily lead to indoctrination.

It is necessary to look at the costs of both corruption and of the use of instruments to fight it. However, one should be very careful in deciding on a tolerable level of corruption merely based on the postulate of economic efficiency. Politicians and economists who try to decide under which circumstances corruption might be efficient should never forget what Anthony Downs observed in 1967 (p. 232): "Most democratic and many nondemocratic societies are based upon the ethical premise that men are of inherently equal value in some ultimate sense. Therefore, such societies seek to create systems of law and order that apply a single set of rules impartially to everyone. However, markets respond to money signals given to them by potential buyers and sellers, and money is very unequally distributed in almost every society. Therefore, systems of law and order cannot be based upon markets if they are to treat all citizens as equal before the law." To be more precise, an economic system in which corruption plays a positive role is by definition nondurable because large parts of the population will consider it unjust.

It is probably sensible to fight corruption. However, one should never believe that one can totally stamp out this social phenomenon. Corruption will occur again and again, because, as Alexis de Toqueville observed in 1835, "to pillage the public purse and to sell the favors of the state are arts that the meanest villain can understand and hope to practice in turn." (De Toqueville, 1990, p. 226).

Notes

1. In the literature on corruption, the definitions used are in most cases more or less similar to the one used here. In some articles a broader definition is used, in which corruption is not limited to public officials but corruption in politics and firms is also discussed. In this chapter we limit ourselves chiefly to the analysis of corruption as it occurs in the executive branches of government. However, we believe that, from an analytical point of view, there is no significant distinction between political and bureaucratic corruption and that the model we use can be applied to both forms.

2. For simplicity's sake we have decided to use the male form only. However, whenever we do so, we always also include female public servants or other actors.

3. A good example of such an organization is the police force. The nature of police work makes this organization especially vulnerable for corruption. Individual policemen often have

much leeway in their daily duties, while they are exposed to many temptations. A former Dutch superintendent of police once mentioned seven detonators that can ignite corruption in a police force. Those seven iron D's, as he called them, were: dames, drinks, dimes, drugs, discounts, dice, and dirty tricks (Blauw, 1991). Apart from those temptations, police officers tend to be in contact with individuals or groups who do not think the world of public morality, (Hoetjes, 1982, 99).

4. This process is known as *rent-seeking*. See, for instance, Mueller (1989, pp. 229–246), and also Brooks and Heijdra (1991).

References

Andvig, J.C., and K.O. Moene. (1990). "How Corruption May Corrupt." *Journal of Economic Behavior and Organization* 13: 63–76.

Becker, G.S., and G.J. Stigler. (1974). "Law Enforcement, Malfeasance, and the Compensation of Enforcers." *Journal of Legal Studies* 3: 1–8.

Besley, T., and J. McLaren. (1993). "Taxes and Bribery: The Role of Wage Incentives." *Economic Journal* 103: 119–141.

Blauw, J.A. (1991). "Een Corrupte Diender is de Pest voor het Hele Korps." *Justitiële Verkenningen* 17(4): 36 (in Dutch).

Broeders, J.H.N., and J. Hakfoort. (1994). "Een Steekpenning Bederft het Hart." *Economisch-Statistische Berichten* 3952: 212–216 (in Dutch).

Brooks, M.A., and B.J. Heijdra. (1991). *Dividing the Spoils: Markets, Governments and Corruption*. West Perth: Australian Institute for Public Policy.

Daalder, H., and H. Daudt. (1993). "De Legitimiteit van de Overheid." In J. Bressers, J. Thomassen, and F. van Vught (eds.), *Politicologie en Openbaar Bestuur* (pp. 152–165). Alphen aan den Rijn: Samsom Tjeenk Willink.

Dahl, R.A. (1976). *Modern Political Analysis*. Englewood Cliffs, NJ: Prentice-Hall.

De Tocqueville, A. (1990). *Democracy in America* (vol. 1). Vintage Books: New York.

Downs, A. (1967). *Inside Bureaucracy*. Boston: Little Brown.

Genthe, F. (1994). Containing Corruption in International Transactions: The Challenge of the 1990s. Paper prepared for the Commission on Global Governance by Transparency International, disseminated by the Transparency International (www.transparency.de) Internet discussion list on March 25.

Gould, D.J. (1983). *The Effects of Corruption on Administrative Performance*. Washington, DC: World Bank.

Hoetjes, B.J.S. (1982). *Corruptie bij de Overheid; een bestuurlijk en politiek probleem, sociaal-wetenschappelijk beschouwd*. Den Haag: VUGA-Uitgeverij (in Dutch).

Huntington, S. (1968). *Political Order in Changing Societies*. New Haven: Yale University Press.

Ichniowski, C., and A. Preston. (1989). "The Persistence of Organized Crime in New York City Construction: An Economic Perspective." *Industrial and Labor Relations Review* 42(4): 549–565.

Klitgaard, R. (1988). *Controlling Corruption*. Berkeley: University of California Press.

Leff, N.H. (1964). "Economic Development Through Bureaucratic Corruption." *American Behavioral Scientist* 8–14.

Levy, P.B. (1989). "The Waterfront Commission of the Port of New York: A History and Appraisal." *Industrial and Labor Relations Review* 42(4): 508–521.

Mueller, D.C. (1989). *Public Choice II: A Revised Edition of Public Choice*. Cambridge: Cambridge University Press.

Riggs, F.W. (1964). *Administration in Developing Countries: The Theory of Prismatic Society*. Boston: Little, Brown.

Rose-Ackerman, S. (1978). *Corruption: A Study in Political Economy*. New York: Academic Press.

Sexton, J. (1989). "Controlling Corruption in the Construction Industry: The Quebec Approach." *Industrial and Labor Relations Review* 42(4): 524–535.

Shleifer, A., and R.W. Vishny. (1993). "Corruption." *Quarterly Journal of Economics* 108: 606–607.

6 ETHICS IN REAL ESTATE
Does the German Real Estate Industry Need a Code of Conduct to Support the Implementation of Ethics?

Klaus Homann

Akademie der Immobilienwlrtschaft (ADI) GmbH
Stuttgart, Germany

Abstract

This examination of deficiencies of an ethical nature in the German real estate industry offers examples of unethical practices. Based on the prisoner's dilemma, paradigm, the author identifies the lack of a system of mutual expectations in the German real estate industry as a reason for breaches of ethical behavior. The development of a binding system of rules and regulations—a code of conduct—is therefore suggested as a suitable solution for abolishing these deficiencies. In pursuing this solution, the author discusses existing codes of conduct in Germany and in Great Britain and concludes that there is a need to develop and enforce a binding system of rules and regulations in the German real estate industry.

Introduction

Ethical questions in science evolve from the growing interest in the ethical aspects of doing business—when conflicts arise between economic prosperity (development, wealth, progress) and the resulting negative developments, such as the excessive consumption of nonreplenishable resources and the irrevocable deterioration of ecological systems (Meadows, Meadows, Zahn, and Milling, 1972).

Aside from these relative basic economic and social aspects on the macro level, problematic ethical situations can extend from the meso level (the actions of institutions) up to the individual's field of responsibility (micro level). Each individual pursues his own personal maximization of benefits (a classic example of this behavior is profit optimization). In this pursuit, the repercussions of profit-oriented decisions often clash with the interests of other members of the society. Generally speaking, as a result of these conflicts of interest the legitimation and correctness of companies' and individuals' actions in nearly all sectors of an economy are being questioned more and more.

An initial surface examination of the general characteristics of the German real estate industry reveals the following facts:

- The German real estate industry is a highly regulated sector, especially concerning the development of property.
- The real estate industry has a dubious reputation in certain areas (such as real estate agencies).[1]
- Economic scandals seem to occur with regularity in the real estate industry.

To analyze the reasons for these characteristics, it can be assumed that they may be evidence of a real estate industry in Germany that is fraught with conflicts of interest. Those conflicts of interest may result from ethical deficiencies in this industry. This assumption is based on a thesis by F.R. Hrubi (1993a) concerning the workable conditions of a social system.[2]

In his thesis Hrubi asserts that, in the long run, a social system can exist only under a set of commonly accepted workable conditions. These workable conditions entail that market participants and economic entities rely on and trust each other. Furthermore, Hrubi states that a workable social system—and in our case an economic system—depends greatly on people's trust in those occupational groups or individuals who are empowered with special authority within such an economic system. This reliance and trust refers to the expectations that the given authority be put to use with the corresponding degree of responsibility (Hrubi, 1993a). I.V. Oddy (Chalkley, 1994, foreword) the honorary secretary of the Royal Institution of Chartered Surveyors, confirmed the application of this thesis to the real estate industry, when he stated, "Professions are largely a creature of public demand. They remain in existence because of the continuing recourse by the public to them; and they can only survive if the public has confidence in them. The fact that the professions can command public confidence rests on two essential elements, professional knowledge and ethical conduct."

In summing up the thesis, a *system of mutual expectations* is seen as a foundation of economic activity. Relating the thesis to the real estate industry in Germany, we can note that the assertions of authority and of the specific sphere of influence of market players, as well as their respective responsibility, apply in this context. This conclusion of applicability is based on the following facts, which imply authority, sphere of influence, and responsibility of market players in real estate:

- As Table 6.1 reveals, the real estate industry is a sector of significant economic importance. Irresponsible, negligent, or reckless behavior of market players can potentially result in a decrease of economic welfare.
- Supplied goods and services from the real estate industry are a substantial factor in everyday life (in social functions of real estate, like housing or sheltering) and in the realm of economic activity (in the production of goods and services). Real estate is omnipresent in modern societies (Schulte, 1992, p. 231). Again, irresponsible, negligent, or reckless behavior of market players will have a direct impact on public and economic welfare.
- The specific qualities of property—high asset value, immovability, and singularity (Eekhoff, 1987, pp. 2–3)—lead to the unique characteristics of the real estate market and its functions.[3] The asymmetrical distribution of information as one of those market characteristics bears a considerable potential for improper use, (Dubben and Sayce, 1991, p. 27; Harvey, 1987, p. 23).[4]

The above-mentioned facts underline the extent of influence and simultaneously the exceptional responsibility that practicing professionals in the real estate industry bear. Since far-reaching social and economic conse-

Table 6.1. German real estate–related economic data

Real Estate–Related Economic Data	Volume (in billion DM)
Total assets of private households (1993)	8,850.0
Total assets of private households in real estate (1993)	6,590.0
Construction volume (1996)	573.0
Gross national product (1993)	3,541.5
Real estate transactions (1993)	302.0
Total real estate assets of institutional investors (1996)	302.0

quences can result from the behavior of industry members, one could assume that, from an ideal standpoint, the involvement in this industry should be oriented toward certain criteria of efficiency to ensure the attainment of an almost perfect social and economical benefit.

However, market characteristics such as a high degree of market regulation, dubious reputation of professional groups, or a considerable number of scandals hint toward the possibility that the German real estate industry experiences

- A lack of reliance and trust in its market players, since market-external forces imposed regulations on the industry;
- A lack of responsibility and moral behavior of some market players, since professional groups have dubious reputations and there are considerable scandals in the industry;
- A lack of a system of mutual expectations, as is verified in the following discussion.

Although professional associations have intensified the discussion of ethics in the German real estate industry and have attempted to enforce ethical behavior in their membership, a systematic and comprehensive analysis of the topic has not taken place, and literature on this specific topic in Germany is scant.

As business ethics represent the theoretical foundation for the following discussion, it is necessary to give a concise definition of terms and a brief explanation of the disciplines of social sciences.

Theoretical Foundation

Definition and Differentiation of the Terms Ethos, Morality, and Ethics

The terms *ethos*, *morality*, and *ethics* are often used synonymously—and erroneously—in colloquial speech. To clarify and create a standard of orientation, it is necessary to provide a brief explanation of their meaning.[5]

Ethos. The etymological roots of the term *ethos* lie in the Greek language. It originally signified "practice, tradition, custom, or habit." The scientific description of ethos is the inherent obligation to comply with certain norms, such as following the Ten Commandments or adhering to a class ethos, like the physician's code of conduct.

Morality. The term *morality* describes the practiced or customary behavior of individuals or societies that is considered the typical way of acting for that specific culture. Expressions of individual or social morals reflect the individual or collective transformation of ethos, such as the transformation of the commandment not to steal into the belief in modern societies that violating the property rights of others is highly immoral. This is even enhanced in the transformation of ethos into legislation.

Ethics. *Ethics* is considered the scientific reflection about ethos. It is, with metaphysics and social philosophy, a division of philosophy. As a science ethics—the study of morality—deals with morality and moral phenomena. It is directed toward the coexistence of people—their attitudes and their behavior. Ethics examines how individuals should react and seeks to explain what they should do in situations of uncertainty.

Business Ethics

Business ethics is an interdisciplinary and application-oriented science that reflects on the problems and behavioral patterns inherent in business practices. Its main objective lies in detecting and applying a link between the business world and the moral world (Ulrich, 1987, pp. 123–124). From the point of view of economic theory, business ethics is seen as the resurrection of a normative orientation in a noneconomical sense. This, however, does not imply that this discipline aims to develop broad concepts of frameworks in the form of social aims or the indefinite analysis of social structures. Rather, it is meant to emphasize the expansion of the economic perspectives by incorporating economically relevant elements of social practice, which have so far been largely neglected by economic theory. In this endeavor the idea is not to implement ethics into the business world from external sources, which tend to be critical and admonishing. Instead, ethics should be implemented into economic thinking and acting through an evolutionary process of transformation of business theory[6] in order to ensure an overall acceptance by all who may be concerned.

The discipline of business ethics is essentially considered to be an interdisciplinary endeavor containing a strong empirical component. Rather than to gain theoretical insight and knowledge, the objective of business ethics is to reach an optimal result for economic activity (in an ethical sense) and to discover the corresponding consequences for management (Hrubi, 1993b, pp. 14–16). The priorities of the discipline lie in the application of ethical structures. For this reason, business ethics can be seen as an appropriate theoretical foundation for the following discussion of ethical deficiencies in the German real estate industry and the proposal for solution.

From this theoretical background and based on Hrubi's thesis on workable social systems, this study analyzes the phenomena of market behavior and market performance in the German real estate industry. Examples of the market behavior of market participants will be given, and a game theory–based approach will explain the rationale behind this behavior.

Problems of an Ethical Nature That Arise in the Real Estate Market

The Behavior of Market Participants in the Real Estate Market

Following Hrubi's thesis on workable social systems, it can be assumed that members of the real estate industry act according to their own individual self-interest and that it is in their interest to be honest and reliable, since only this behavior will maintain the reliance and trust of the general public in them. Only the public's reliance and trust in practicing professionals secures their permanent participation in the market. Those practicing professionals who decide to engage in "short games"—or in other words, who earn profit through unscrupulous and unethical business practices—will damage the reliance and trust of the public with the effect that, in the long run, they will be discredited and eventually driven out of the market by its inherent self-regulating forces in order to secure workable conditions of the social system.

Unfortunately, the regulation that takes place in the real estate market hampers the unrestrained maturation of the market and the attainment of a pareto-perfect equilibrium, in which all members of society are provided with the means to effectuate their plans and fulfill their wishes. The framework of the market is so narrowly designed that market participants try to attain their individual objectives (profit and benefit maximization) by ignoring rules and regulations, effecting a breach of trust, or by living with elementary conflicts of interest. At the same time, discreditation and adjustment within the market cannot take place due to the lack of liberty and the nonexistence of a self-regulating mechanism inherent in the market.

The following examples are given to demonstrate market misconduct and not to discriminate against any particular group of market participants. Their justifiable place and function in the market should by no means be contested. The intention lies more in advocating a critical view of behavioral patterns that exist.

One occupational group, real estate brokers, are often mentioned in connection with suspicious moral conduct and unscrupulous behavior. The clientele that brokers cater to is normally composed of leasers and sellers of property. It is a typical practice in the German real estate market that the broker is compensated for his services in the form of a commission paid by the tenant or buyer and not by the actual client. In some cases, depending on the region, cases turn up where a double compensation takes places—in other words, both parties effectuate a payment. In any case, the broker experiences a definite conflict of interest, since it is not clear whose interest he or she can represent most effectively. Additionally, the practice of broker compensation depends on the particular market segment (residential or commercial property) and on the overall economic situation with the effect that, now and then, the role of the compensating party can change.

In general, this practice of payment creates confusion in the customer since the professionalism and performance of the service rendered is not controlled. The extent of compensation of the broker is determined by the market—the rent and sale prices—and legal clauses. Often, this mode of compensation for service does not comply with verifiable objective criteria, so that it is perceived by outsiders that at the slightest effort, the broker is given the right to charge a fee.

In this context, we can observe another business practice of some brokers that provokes a negative impression and disapproval from other players—offering property to the market and billing without authorization. This creates the general impression that some brokers randomly violate the property rights of others.

But the behavior of others in the real estate market—building contractors, project developers, real estate service providers, or even public authorities—also contributes to the lack of trust and confidence in this sector. As far as building contractors go, one can cite the examples of dubious eviction practices (the contractor does this with the help of a real estate service provider) or violations of laws pertaining to the protection of monuments. A further example is cheating subcontracted craftsmen out of the full amount due (by retaining a certain amount of the claim) by claiming defective workmanship, although the workmanship corresponds to the contract. The intention of the building contractor is to delay payment in order to gain a period of interim financing. It is a well-known fact in Germany that it will take the subcontractor approximately two years from bringing such a dispute to court to receiving the outstanding amount. In times of recessive markets such behavior can bring small companies close to financial ruin or even actually ruin them.

In another practice, as an attempt to improve the sales potential of owner-occupied apartments, building contractors often take over condominium management for the investor. Aside from being a marketing instrument (comprehensive service even after the investment), an ulterior motive appears when this administrative service is offered only for the duration of five years. After five years the building contractor's condominium management turns down the mandate, and a different condominium manager takes over. This practice becomes suspicious if we consider that the five years exactly fulfill the warranty period dictated by German civil law. The contractor who offers this service (condominium management) is able to hide any defects of the building, only to turn over the role of administrator to another party in the next period.

In conjunction with this behavior we have to see another unscrupulous practice of building contractors—promising and guaranteeing unrealistic rents. Again, as a marketing instrument, it is a common habit of building contractors in the field of condominiums to offer a guarantee for the rents for a limited period of time with the intention of increasing the marketability of overpriced condominiums. The guarantor is either a subsidiary of the building contractor or an independent company. In the past many of such guarantors went bankrupt or just disappeared. At this moment or at the end of the guarantee period (five years), the investor will face real market rents and realize this unscrupulous practice.

In the context of condominium management the following unscrupulous behavior has to be mentioned. By law,[7] owners of condominiums have to build up a sufficient fund for maintenance and repairs. This fund is managed in trust by the condominium manager.[8] Depending on the building, such funds can collect a considerable amount of money. Unfortunately, quite a few condominium managers disappear every year, and so do the funds.

In Germany, the 1994 scandal involving the project developer Schneider together with often heard rumors involving other well-known established project developers have contributed to the bad reputation of developers.

The increasing corruption on different levels of the administrative body has also contributed to diminishing public confidence in these institutions. Especially in the new states of Germany, more and more cases have become known in which administrative bodies were openly bribed into speeding up construction applications.

A general weakness common to all service providers in the German real estate industry lies in the lack of market entry barriers—for example, in the form of a proof of qualification. Practically anyone can offer real estate–related services as a real estate broker, condominium manager, or facility manager. The only necessity is to register the company as a real estate service provider. The promise of remunerative opportunities, depending on the market situation, entices individuals of diverse backgrounds and without any specific qualifications to enter the market, resulting in sinking levels of professionalism in the industry.

The following theoretical model explains in a somewhat abstract way the observed market behavior of some players and the resulting market performance of such behavior. At the same time, this model should clarify how mutual trust between players can lead to better market performance.

Explanation of Market Behavior Based on Game Theory

The following explanation uses the prisoner's dilemma taken from the fundamentals of game theory (see Figure 6.1).[9] The premises necessary for the game are the following:

- It is a *single-turn game* with two participants, which makes the model a static one.
- The participants do not have any knowledge about each other's behavior.
- Both participants are replicas of *homo economicus* (maximize self-interest) and have therefore no inclination in the slightest toward virtuous or righteous behavior.

The two players in the real estate market (in this case two brokers, A and B) are active in the market completely independently and have no knowledge of the character, morals, or lack of morality of their competitor. Additionally, there are only two alternative behaviors possible—moral (doing the right thing) and immoral (doing the wrong thing)—and both parties aim at survival in the market. Exiting the market is not considered. The environmental conditions, the only basis for decision making that both have in common, is the expected behavior of the opponent. Depending on the other's actions, different market outcomes, as shown in the graph, will result.

At first broker A assumes that broker B will act immorally. An example for an immoral action of broker B would be not to disclose a conflict of interest and not to turn down a mandate, although it will be the necessary action to protect the client's legitimate interest. If A decides to act differently and so morally correctly (meaning turning down the mandate to avoid

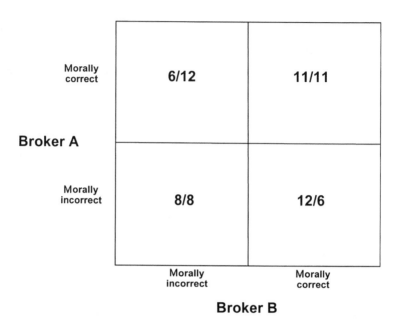

Figure 6.1.   Game results

the conflict of interest and to protect the client's legitimate interest), he can earn only six profit units. B, on the other hand, will gain an excess profit of 12 as he will continue to practice in the cases of conflicts of interest. So that if A follows B's behavior and decides to act immorally, both will make the same or similar profits—thus a higher profit results for A than in the first alternative. However, this result will not be twelve for both but instead only eight profit units. The reason for this result is that the market—in this case, the brokers' clients—react to the morally incorrect behavior by decreasing their demand for the brokers' services. An example in Germany for such clients' reactions are the increasing sales of residential property from one private entity to another. Another reaction of the market, more and more often noticed, is that brokers are cheated out of their commission (Breiholdt, 1996, p. 41). Due to their behavior and the resulting reactions of the market, brokers will face fewer business opportunities and will remain in a performance situation marked as eight/eight. Anyhow, the conclusion of this first decisive situation is that A's dominant strategy would be to behave immorally as he gains a higher profit or benefit level than by acting morally correct.

If A assumes the opposite—that B will act morally correctly—then A will be able to achieve excess profit of twelve by being the one to act unscrupulously. If A decides to act morally correctly, both brokers will be able to achieve a profit level, marked as eleven/eleven. Compared to the individual results of twelve that the brokers can achieve when acting unscrupulously, this result represents a profit for the individual broker slightly below the maximum. The rationale behind this is that the broker in the case of conflicting interest would have to turn down the mandate and, at this point, would advise his client to consult one of his colleagues. This assumption may seem unrealistic, however, as the example of the code of conduct of the Royal Institution of Chartered Surveyors in the next section will show, it can be a standard of practice. Coming back to the decision problem of A, in this situation immoral conduct remains the dominant strategy for A, as he is able to gain twelve profit units instead of eleven.

Turning the decision problem to B, the same pattern will apply to him as to A. Also for B, acting morally incorrectly will be the dominant strategy. The result is that both will inevitably react immorally, hoping to reach a better result in the end. These strategies, however, lead to the market performance of eight/eight. The reason for this economically less favorable benefit level is that neither A nor B can rely on each other. Expressed differently, a system in any particular form generating mutual expectations for the market players does not exist. However, in order to reach higher profit levels or benefit levels for the entire economy, a system of mutual expectations is necessary.

In this context a possible solution can be seen in the development of a binding system of rules and regulations. One approach in pursuing this solution can be to superposition such a system of norms independently from market occurrence. This, however, implies that economic conditions, as well as characteristics and needs of the real estate industry, are neglected. To proceed in this way would again give way to viewing the economic world as being separate from the world of morality.

Solving the problem with the help of government regulations is just as questionable. Since additional regulations will not be able to cover all cases of economic events and the variety of market behavior, such a system will need to be complemented by morality. The actual situation in the German real estate industry, which is marked by a high degree of market regulation, endeavors to persuade different professional associations to implement ethical behavior in their practicing professionals but at the same time is marked by dubious reputation and scandals.

If market coordination, central government directive policy, or other external market forces can only deliver less favorable results, it is essential to identify the missing factor that enables the creation of such a binding system of rules and regulations. A possible solution can be seen in the creation of a code of ethics valid throughout the industry and manifested in a code of conduct. An industrywide accepted code of ethics for real estate can be a significant contribution to ensuring the prevention of negative behavior within the real estate industry through a collective self-commitment to a control system of mutual expectations. This control system must develop from within the industry and cannot be forced on it from outside. The industry itself must include its needs in the development of the system of norms and participate in defining its functions. Only the involvement of the industry in the process of defining a system of norms will ensure a high level of acceptance and comprehension of its legitimation.

The real estate industry has already formed rules of conduct such as the ones of two brokers' associations in Germany (The Ring Deutscher Makler RDM and The Verband Deutscher Makler VDM) or the Royal Institution of Chartered Surveyors RICS in Great Britain on European level.

After a brief discussion of the essential conditions and the functioning of codes of conduct, the following section discusses the suitability of examples of existing codes of conduct.

Code of Conduct: Essential Conditions and Effects

A code of conduct should not only regulate behavioral patterns within an industry, but it should also be concerned with the relations for external interest groups (stakeholders), since a sensible application demands that it should encompass the entire industry. A code of conduct valid only in certain points or branches would incessantly lead to situations similar to the one previously described in which market players immorally violate regulations to gain a competitive advantage. A standard of conduct that applies for all industry segments would therefore be an effective solution and choice to eliminate and prevent the existence of free-riders in the market place.

The development and continuous improvement of a code of conduct can be achieved and implemented only by an institution composed and supported by representatives of the entire industry. By such a system, a high identification of market segments with a control system can be ensured. Through an institutionalization of the code of conduct, the structures within the industry can be set up to enable the necessary adaptation and interpretation of the code of conduct. At the same time such an institution must be equipped with ample authority to enforce the code. Otherwise, it would remain only a superficial facade (Bowie, 1992, p. 341). The existence of effective enforcement and possible sanctions are essential in upholding moral behavior that can ensure maximum prosperity for the real estate industry.

On the one hand, the code of conduct provides a level of confidence in the predictability of the behavior of others. On the other hand, the membership in such an institution and the profession of loyalty to its ethical standards should be rewarded with competitive advantages.

Such competitive advantages can occur when the market—clients or other players—expects the membership in such an institution of those who participate in market transactions. This would be even more the case if high standards of education and permanent training were demanded by the code of conduct in order to secure a high level of competence. Simultaneously, in this way market entry barriers are created since a specific degree of qualification is required, and therefore service quality in the industry can be improved.

The following core criteria summarize what specific conditions a code of conduct must fulfill if it is to control market performance effectively:

- Validity for the entire industry,
- Support by an institution,
- Equipment with a control and sanctioning structure,
- Direct competitive advantage for the members through an improved market position and high standards of qualification,
- Indirect advantage through increased market attractiveness.

Figure 6.2 visualizes again this process of thought.

The development and establishment of a real estate code of conduct also entails other aspects than the competitive advantages mentioned above. Other diverse effects range from motivation to common awareness. The following is a list of such possible effects (Bowie, 1992, p. 337):

- *Motivational effect* The code of conduct creates pressure on the members of an industry—a form of peer pressure brought about by the expectations of colleagues. Such a system of mutual expectations motivates members to fulfill standards and demands.
- *Permanence and invariability* The institutionalization of a code makes it objective and independent from individual persons. The development of the code lies in the hands of the institution, which includes representatives of the entire industry. The equal representation of groups secures that interests of the groups are safeguarded

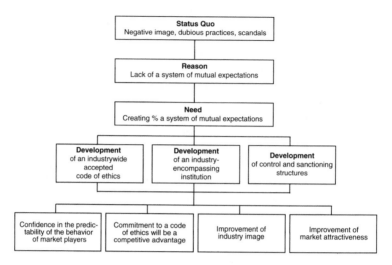

Figure 6.2.   Process of determining the value of a real estate code of conduct

equally. Invariability and constancy are ensured. Constant and
enduring guidelines differentiate between wrong and correct.

- *Orientation and guidance* In situations of ethical ambiguity, a
code can give direction. It guides employees since they have a moral
code to consult as a basis in situations of conflicting interest, which
in turn can limit the power of employers and their ability to misuse
their influence.

- *Understanding and recognition* The social responsibility particular
to a given industry can be defined with the help of a code, which in
turn simplifies the fulfillment of the responsibility since the industry
is informed about its obligations.

- *Self-interest* Summing up, it can be said that the development and
establishment of an encompassing code of conduct for the entire
industry should be in its very own self-interest and advantage. The
code, beyond governmental regulation, discloses the opportunities
that lie in applying the industry's own core competence and in
advocating elevated ethical standards. Thus, the necessity for
external intervention by enforcing more regulations will be
reduced significantly.

After the discussion of the theoretical background of codes of conduct and
the possible effects of applying a code of conduct to the German real estate

industry, it is necessary to analyze the existence and the functioning of such codes in Germany.

Codes of Conduct in the Real Estate Market

Industry Regulations of Brokers' Associations in Germany

In its draft of May 1, 1986, the RDM (Ring Deutscher Makler) published the rules and regulations that apply to brokers and property managers active in the German market. Aside from the preamble, this code of conduct covers three paragraphs that briefly list ten duties, seven examples of unethical conduct, and the possible sanctions for derelict behavior.

A further code was developed by the VDM (Verband Deutscher Makler). The VDM limits itself to recounting laws and legal regulations. This association sees itself and acts purely as a representative of real estate agents and does not necessarily make specific demands of moral integrity on its members.

With the development of the codes of conduct of the two brokers' associations, first attempts at the creation of a control system have been made. However, the existing bodies do not fulfill the criteria needed to implement an effective class ethic by far. Both organizations represent only a small part of the German real estate industry (brokers, condominium managers, and small developers). Consequently, they lack an industrywide recognition, and therefore a comprehensive identification of market participants with these standards cannot be expected. Thus, the essential conditions of an encompassing validity are not given. Additionally, this will not lead to the development of the necessary structures to control and enforce the code in the industry, since it will not be possible to effectuate sanctioning measures in the case of breach of the standards.

In their contents, the two codes focus only on establishing a set of minimum standards rather than on leading prevailing business morality in real estate. (Pivar, 1989, p. 5). Their emphasis lies in classifying actions into legal and illegal actions. However, practicing professionals in real estate are not only expected to meet minimum acceptable standards but also to act in a morally correct manner (Pivar, 1989, p. 4). Furthermore, the codes of the two associations do not lay down standards of qualification. They do not define demands concerning the specific expertise or proficiency of potential players before they enter the market.

Due to the above-mentioned deficiencies of the existing codes in the German real estate industry, the positive effects of a code of conduct will not be realizable. At this point, it is necessary to look beyond national boundaries in search of a possible equivalent. The Royal Institution of Chartered Surveyors (RICS) in Great Britain can be seen as a pioneer in working out a profession-specific ethical norm that is embodied in the Institution's rules of conduct.

The Rules of Conduct of the Royal Institution of Chartered Surveyors

The roots of the RICS go back to the year 1868, when three professional associations (the Surveyors' Club of 1792, the Land Surveyors' Club of 1834, and the Surveyors' Association of 1864) joined together and formed the Institution of Surveyors. In 1881, Queen Victoria awarded the Royal Charter to the Institution, entrusting it with the task to institutionalize the standards of education, formation, and training for the real estate professions in Great Britain. In 1946 the name of the institution was changed into the Royal Institution of Chartered Surveyors. Today, with more than 70,000 professional members and more than 21,000 members in training (students and probationers), the Institution is the most important association uniting the different professions in real estate in Great Britain. The Institution comprises all areas of the real estate industry including the public sector and is devided into seven divisions:

1. General practice
2. Planning and development
3. Building surveying
4. Quantity surveying
5. Land and hydrographical surveying
6. Minerals surveying
7. Land agency and agriculture

The status and the principles of the RICS make it the commonly recognized authority in all areas of valuation, use, development, and management of real estate in Great Britain. The RICS also attempts to extend this recognition to other countries. The founding of the European Society of Chartered Surveyors (ESCS) and many other national associations like the Deutscher Verband Chartered Surveyors (DVCS) in Germany, are the first achievements in this context.

The RICS regards the profession of chartered surveyors as the "property profession." The term *profession* explains the self-understanding of the

RICS. A *profession* distinguishes itself from simple economic interaction (the delivery of goods) by providing sound and confident advice to the best of the professional's knowledge and proficiency. The combination of applied sciences and comprehensive experience in practice characterizes the profession of chartered surveyors.

The maintenance of high standards of qualification of its members and the observance of proper behavior to the real estate industry are explicit goals of the RICS. In order to reach these goals, the RICS has developed structures to improve and to control real estate–related educational programs (undergraduate and postgraduate programs) at universities and polytechnics. Furthermore, the observance of industry behavior is based on the enforcement of a code of conduct—the so-called Rules of Professional Conduct, which are given in *The Chartered Surveyors' Rule Book* (Royal Institution of Chartered Surveyors, 1993). This *Rule Book* consists of the Royal Charter, the Bye-Laws (statutes) as principles of the Institution, and the Rules of Professional Conduct, which specify the predicates of the Bye-Laws. For example, Bye-Law 24(3) and Regulation 8 of the Rules of Professional Conduct instruct members of the RICS in the case of (possible) conflicts of interest to disclose promptly to the client the relevant facts; inform the client that neither the chartered surveyor personally nor his firm or company can act or continue to act for him unless requested to do so after having advised the client to obtain independent professional advice; and confirm to the client the position in writing.

The Rules of Conduct are completed by a multilevel control system. This control system consists of a complaints division, an inquiry commission, and an arbitration authority, which examine the observance of the rules and take sanctioning measures in case of violation or breach of the code. The RICS investigates the observance of the code if complaints are brought to its attention and at random. Should members of the RICS be faced with questions concerning proper behavior in their daily practice, a consulting division of the RICS provides advise on how to act in compliance with the Institution's standards.

The sanctioning system is divided into three bodies, which can exercise different sanctions against members according to the gravity of their misbehavior. These can range from a formal warning to a permanent expulsion from the Institution. This can have tremendous consequences since sanctions are published not only in different media within the RICS (which are read throughout the industry) but also in the local and national press.

In contrast to the previously described situation in the German real estate industry, the Rules of Conduct of the RICS in Great Britain represent a code, which first covers the interest of all stakeholders in the British real estate industry. Second, the code is backed by an institution, which covers all sectors of the real estate industry in an economy. On the other hand, this institution is based on an industrywide acknowledgment. Third, the code is well-known throughout the groups of stakeholders of the industry.

In the majority of all real estate–related issues in Great Britain, the membership in the Institution and the observance of its code of conduct are the prerequisites of participation. In other words, within the British real estate industry a considerable portion of all interactions and transactions is based on the chartered surveying profession, since this basis guarantees a high degree of professionalism and the observance of certain standards, leading to the dominance of the profession of chartered surveyors in all areas related to the British real estate market. Membership in this profession can be regarded as a seal of quality, which is more and more indispensable for market success. Forfeiting the title through sanctions inevitably leads to the loss of market advantages.

Referring to the theoretical explanations of behavioral codes, it can be said that the Rules of Conduct of the RICS comply very well with the criteria of codes. In this way, the example of the Rules of Conduct of the RICS supports the assumption that a code of conduct can create and maintain a system of mutual expectations.

Outlook on the German Real Estate Market

The discussion on market behavior in the German real estate industry has revealed considerable deficiencies concerning the general conditions for economic activity in this industry. A high degree of market regulation on the one hand narrows the economic room to maneuver for everybody in the course of fulfilling individual business plans. On the other, the high degree of regulation prevents the development of self-regulating mechanisms within the market in order to sanction unscrupulous and immoral behavior (short games) of market players. Furthermore, the German real estate industry lacks market entry barriers in the form of proof of professional qualification with the consequence of a decreasing level of professionalism in some areas of the real estate industry.

The findings of the application of the model from game theory support the assertion that also a decline in trust and confidence within the different professional groups of the industry and its stakeholders can be assumed. This phenomenon can be explained by the lack of a system of mutual expectations. As the model reveals, mutual expectations in the market can lead to a better performance. A binding system of rules and regulations—a code of conduct—can be a possible solution to creating mutual expectations in the industry. As the example of the Rules of Conduct of the RICS shows, professionalism in the industry can be improved as well.

Referring to the examples of breaches of ethical behavior in the German real estate markets, the development and enforcement of a code of conduct may have the effects listed in Table 6.2.[10]

Summary and Conclusion

To sum up the findings in the discussion, it can be stated that the deficiencies in the German real estate industry result, to a considerable degree, from the lack of a binding system of rules and regulations. Based on the example of the Rules of Conduct of the RICS in the Anglo-Saxon realm, it can be assumed that a similar system could potentially improve the current situation in the German real estate industry. In addition, Germany lacks a professional association that represents the industry as a whole and that would be the basis for the successful development and enforcement of a code of conduct.

In conclusion, if an institution is established that will represent the German real estate industry as a whole, the development of a code of conduct will be an important contribution toward the necessary abolition of the above-mentioned market deficiencies. Pursuing this idea, it is important to accept the fact that such a code of conduct cannot just be copied from an existing example (the Rules of Conduct of the RICS) or even be imposed. The process of developing a code of conduct must be based on consensus between all groups involveds to ensure its recognition and acknowledgment throughout the whole industry. The process of the development (and its continuous development) is visualized in Figure 6.3.

In the context of a heightened awareness concerning ethical behavior in the real estate industry, a system of mutual expectations, based on a code of conduct, developes within the industry. Control and sanctioning structures are provided by an industry encompassing institutions or professional associations, representing all suppliers of real estate–related goods and services. Customers and stakeholders in the real estate industry are aware of the existence of this institution and of its code of conduct. They rely on the commitment of the members of the institution to the code of conduct as well as on their qualifications and professionalism.

Table 6.2. Breaches of ethical behavior and effects of a code of conduct

Breach of Ethical Behavior	Contents of a Code of Conduct	Consequences
Conflicts of interest in the brokers' case	The client's ethical and legitimate interest must be maintained under any circumstances.	Disclosure of the conflict of interest (informing the client) and the possibility of turning down the mandate
Brokers' compensation	The client's ethical and legitimate interest can be maintained only if the broker is compensated by his client only. There must be a clear definition of the relationship between contractor and client.	Contractor compensated by his client only
Brokers offering property and billing without authorization; building contractors' dubious eviction practices and cheating of subcontracted craftsmen; misappropriation of funds managed in trust by condominium managers; corruption	These forms of misconduct represent violations of property rights or even criminal offenses, on which a code of conduct will impose with severe sanctions. A code of conduct will not be able to eliminate criminal potential but at least may raise market entry barriers high enough to make it more difficult for these elements to establish themselves in the market.	Expulsion from an association; (loss of competitive advantages)
Dubious condominium management practices and dubious rent guarantees	Such behavior will be considered to be unbefitting conduct or even misappropriation and receive severe sanctions.	Expulsion from an association (loss of competitive advantages)
Unqualified participants	Definition of qualification standards	Denial of competitive advantages, as players will not gain the seal of quality in the form of the membership in a professional association

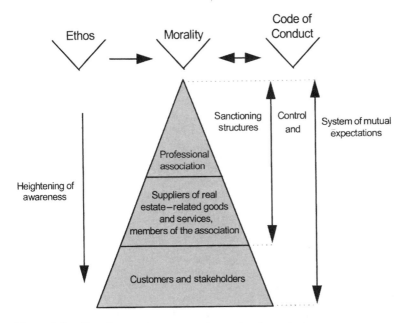

Figure 6.3. Development process of a code of conduct

A binding system of rules and regulations in the German real estate industry will never be able to avoid unethical behavior completely. Scandals or misconduct do also occur in Great Britain, as well as in other countries where codes of conduct have been developed, like the Code of Ethics and Standards of Practice of the National Association of Realtors®, the BOMI Institute Code of Professional Ethics and Conduct, or the Code of Ethics of the National Association of Real Estate Brokers in the United States. However, considering the increased attention in Germany to ethics in the real estate business, the development of an industry-encompassing code of conduct will be an important contribution toward the necessary abolition of the current ethical deficiencies.

Furthermore, it has to be considered that it is virtually impossible to cover all ethical situations in real estate practice by a binding system of rules and regulations. Therefore, it will still be necessary to consider the consequences of actions in respect of one's individual ethics of responsibility (Göbel, 1992, p. 86).

Notes

1. In 1995 a study revealed the overall negative image of the German real estate industry. Following the findings of this study, especially dubious practices of real estate brokers contributed significantly to this negative image (Weyer, 1995, p. 71; Heuer, 1995, p. 3).

2. In his thesis F.R. Hrubi (1993a) implies that an economy can be understood as a system and that the processes occurring within an economy have are social character. In this way an economy is understood as a social system.

3. For a further discussion of the specific economic characteristics of real estate, see Fraser (1984, p. 118) and Ferguson and Heizer (1990, p. 3).

For an in-depth discussion of the unique characteristics of the real estate market and its functions, see Pyhrr et al. (1989, p. 9), Fraser (1984, p. 120), Harvey (1987, p. 23), Ruggles and Walsh (1983, p. 190), and Greer and Farrell (1988, p. 44).

4. In this context Fraser (1984, p. 12) states that "Lack of detailed knowledge is endemic to the property market."

5. For a detailed discussion, see Lorenzen (1991, pp. 38–40).

6. The implementation of ethics into economic thinking and acting through the transformation of business theory is the major requirement of Ulrich (1986).

7. Section 21, p. 5, No. 4, Wohnungseigentumsgesetz (WEG).

8. Section 27, p. 1, Wohnungseigentumsgesetz (WEG).

9. For a detailed discussion of the principles of the game theory and the prisoner's dilemma, refer to the relevant microeconomic literature.

10. The suggested contents of a code of conduct and the listed consequences refer to the regulations of the Rules of Conduct of the RICS (Royal Institution of Chartered Surveyors, 1993, pp. VIII: 1 to VIII: 12).

References

Bowie, N.E. (1992). "Unternehmensethikkodizes: können sie eine Lösung sein?" In H. Lenk and M. Maring (eds.), *Wirtschaft und Ethik* (pp. 337–349). Ditzingen: Reclam.

Breiholdt, P. (1996). "Umstrittene Maklerprovision." *Frankfurter Allgemeine Zeitung*, March 1, p. 41.

Chalkley, R. (1994). *Professional Conduct: A Handbook for Chartered Surveyors* (2nd ed.). London: RICS.

Dubben, N., and S. Sayce. (1991). *Property Portfolio Management: An Introduction.* London: Routledge.

Eekhoff, J. (1987). *Wohnungs- und Bodenmarkt.* Tübingen: Mohr.

Ferguson, J., and J. Heizer. (1990) *Real Estate Investment Analysis.* Boston: Gllyn and Bacon.

Fraser, W.D. (1984). *Principles of Property Investment and Pricing.* Basingstoke: Macmillian.

Göbel, E. (1992). *Das Management der sozialen Verantwortung.* Berlin: Duncker und Homblot.

Greer, G.E., and M.D. Farrell. (1988). *Investment Analysis for Real Estate Decisions* (2nd ed.). Chicago: Dryden.

Harvey, J. (1987). *Urban Land Economics* (2nd ed.). Basingstoke: Macmillian.

Heuer, B. (1995). "Freiwillige Selbstkontrolle." *Immobilien Manager*, 7 + 8.

Hrubi, F.R. (1993a). "Management und Moral." In F. Hrubi and M. Karmasin (eds.), *Wirtschaftsethik* (pp. 78–83). Vienna: Suriptenuerlag der Hochschölerschaft der Wirtschaftsoniversitat.

Hrubi, F.R. (1993b). "Philosophische Fragen im Umkreis der Wirtschaftswissenschaften." In F. Hrubi and M. Karmasin, M. (eds.), *Wirtschaftsethik* (pp. 11–20). Vienna: Suriptenuerlag der Hochschölerschaft der Wirtschaftsoniversitat.

Lorenzen, P. (1991). "Philosophische Fundierungsprobleme einer Wirtschafts- und Unternehmensethik." In H. Steinmann and A. Löhr (eds.), *Unternehmensethik* (pp. 35–67). Stuttgart: Poeschel.

Meadows, D., D. Meadows, E. Zahn, and P. Milling. (1972). *Die Grenzen des Wachstums, Bericht des Club of Rome zur Lage der Menschheit.* Stuttgart: Deutsche Verlagsanstalt.

Pfarr, H. (1988). *Trends, Fehlentwicklungen und Delikte in der Bauwirtschaft.* Berlin: Springer.

Pivar, W.H. (1989). *Real Estate Ethics* (2nd ed.). Real Estate Education Comp.

Pyhrr, S.A., J.R. Cooper, L.E. Wofford, S.D. Kapplin, and P.D. Lapides. (1989). *Real Estate Investment: Strategy, Analysis, Decisions* (2nd ed.). New York: Wiley.

Royal Institution of Chartered Surveyors. (1993). *The Chartered Surveyors' Rule Book: Rules of Professional Conduct for Chartered Surveyors.* London: RICS.

Ruggles, R.K. and J. J. Walsh. (1983). "Demand and the Nature of Value." *Appraisal Journal* 51(2): 190–201.

Schasching, J. (1993). "Keine Wirtschaft ohne Ethik." In F. Hrubi and M. Karmasin (eds.), *Wirtschaftsethik* (pp. 64–68). Vienna: Suriptenuerlag der Hochschölerschaft der Wirtschaftsoniversitat.

Schulte, K.-W. (1992). "Immobilienökonomie als Wissenschaft." In O. Bronner (ed.), *Immobilien in Europa II—Märkte in Bewegung* (pp. 231–235). Vienna: Bronner.

Smith, A. (1776/1905). *An Inquiry into the Nature and Causes of the Wealth of Nations.* Routledge.

Ulrich, P. (1986). *Transformation der ökonomischen Vernunft.* Bern: Haupt.

Ulrich, P. (1987). "Die Weiterentwicklung der ökonomischen Rationalität—Zur Grundlegung der Ethik der Unternehmung." In B. Biervert and M. Held (eds.), *Ökonomische Theorie und Ethik* (pp. 122–149). Frankfurt/m.: Campus.

Weyer, P. (1995). "Miese Noten für Makler." *Immobilien Manager*, 7 + 8: 71.

7 ETHICS AS ECONOMICALLY INFLUENCED: A PRELIMINARY TEST

Norman G. Miller

Department of Finance
College of Business Administration
University of Cincinnati

Abstract

It is argued here that, independent of a priori attitudes toward ethics, economic circumstances influence the tendency of industry professionals to behave unethically. In a preliminary test of this theory, real estate sales are compared to license suspensions over a ten-year period with the results indicating an inverse correlation—that is, license suspensions increase as sales decrease. Further tests in the real estate and other industries are suggested in order to reveal just how much of a role economic circumstances play in decisions to behave ethically.

Introduction

Ethics can be viewed as the paradigm of *just, equitable, and good behavior* in a setting of human interdependency. It is easy to explain ethics in the context of religion, family traditions, and culture. The challenge is to explain the genesis of ethics in the absence of religious faith and cultural momentum.

If ethics are not arbitrary in the temporal sense, then they must be based on innate values of goodness, right, and wrong.[1] But where do such values come from? Theology and historically notable books such as the Torah, Old or New Testaments, and the Koran generally offer faith-based rewards as inducements to prescribed good and ethical behavior or punishments for evil or sinful behavior. Faith in such rewards or punishments do not require a logic-based explanation for evil or unethical behavioral of one person toward another. But in the absence of faith, ethical behavior must depend on notions of good and just behaviors that are based on other explanations.

One alternative explanation for the evolution and need for a set of pre-scribed behaviors or ethics, such as those inscribed in a professional code of conduct, as well as those expected within a given business culture, is based on simple economic theory.

Ethics can arise in the context of developing rules that will minimize the work necessary for a world of numerous humans to survive at a given stan-dard of living. As more people crowd into the same-sized world, more rules are necessary to ensure cooperation and to minimize conflicts. In a society that puts a high value on individual rights, rules on rules evolve to protect smaller and smaller minorities.

Game theory and other cooperative repeat experiments can be used to help explain how ethics encourage expected behaviors to create greater market efficiency. Proofs that repeat play and game theory can help to explain the development of ethics are beyond the scope of this article. It is enough to know that whether innate, culturally derived, or economi-cally influenced by repeat play, a set of ethical behaviors can be described that apply to a given industry at a given point in time.[2] The focus of this chapter is the influence of economic circumstances on violations of such ethical standards, however such standards might have arisen. The hypothesis is quite straight forward:

Hypothesis 1: *Humans seek to maintain current and future expected wealth. Circumstances that increase the difficulty of maintaining current or expected wealth increase the probability of individuals violating common ethical standards.*

A simple and preliminary test indicates support for this hypothesis, but many further tests are needed to better understand the degree of influence of economic circumstances on a person's tendency to behave unethically.

Humans Seek to Maintain Wealth and Fear Change

A basic premise of rational economics is that more wealth is preferred to less. Wealth can be decreased in many ways, and over time many of the par-ticipants in any society will find that their share of resources (wealth) will change. *Wealth* here includes possessions or physical resources as well as human capital resources such as skills and valuable knowledge.

Several examples can illustrate how factors affect wealth over time or influence the ability to maintain wealth. Consider technological changes that make certain types of skills or labor obsolete. Imagine a secretary in the twenty-one century who does not use a computer, even though the computer was at one time a threat to secretarial wealth because it made old skills obsolete, forced new investments in skills, and caused a change in process. Low-wealth immigrants willing to provide the same labor at lower wages are another example of a threat to wealth. A larger retail grocery store, such as those that first replaced the corner grocer and found economies of scale in purchasing goods for less money was at one time a threat to the wealth of many smaller retailers. Cheap foreign rice is a threat to Japanese farmers. There are winners and losers in any society that continues to test new ideas in the production of goods and services and seeks to raise its standard of living on the basis of open-market-based competition.

It does not matter how far beyond basic needs this wealth has become. A particular society or nation could live at the highest standard of living ever attained in the world, where each household owns several luxuries that can rarely be attained in other nations. All that matters is that this wealth is uncontrollably declining. Any time humans perceive a threat to their wealth, they have two choices—concede to the trend and compete or resist. Resistance can take many forms, such as lobbying for trade tariffs, a strike by a union, or lobbying for new laws that forbid a certain process or activity. But aside from legal forms of resistance, illegal forms of resistance may also be tried. The strength of these approaches will probably depend on just how many people are affected and how much cultural contempt is directed at those who may be perceived rightly or wrongly as responsible for the threatening changes.[3]

It seems that humans can act just as evil whether the decrease in resources is at basic survival levels (such as in Somalia), or from a grand height of relative richness, (such as in the deep south USA prior to the civil war). All that matters is that the direction of the change in wealth is negative.

Economic Events Affecting the Real Estate Industry and Implications for Ethical Behaviors

Humans can be viewed as simple animals with simple objectives—to increase wealth and decrease work relative to attaining wealth, thereby maximizing wealth in terms of possessions and in terms of discretionary time. Some of these same humans can and will violate most presumptions of ethical behavior when the risk of being caught for an ethical indiscretion is near zero or when the consequences are minimal.

Illustrations are numerous of situations where we will cheat, steal, take advantage of others less powerful, and more or less exploit others for our own benefit.[4] The savings and loan bailout illustrates how the consequences of risky lending decisions could not be brought back to directly affect most of the decision makers. How many elderly have been taken advantage of by investment advisors who had gained the trust of people who clearly did not understand the risks (or costs) of what was being done with their money? How many times has the due diligence required by consultants been a little less diligent when they knew the deal was already unofficially approved? How many times has an appraiser developed a report with extreme bias on the low side of the probable value distribution when involved in representing a client in a property tax appeal case or almost as easily prepared an appraisal biased on the high side of such a value distribution in anticipation of a client's mortgage application? These are rhetorical questions, based on human observation. Such less than totally honest behaviors are often a part of a business strategy that errs in the direction favored by a client or does the minimum work necessary for some projects in order to subsidize the increased work necessary on other projects relative to fees. Are such practices unethical? If one requires absolute honesty within the guidelines of ethical business behavior, then surely ethical violations run rampant.

When Are Real Estate Professionals Likely to Be Disbonest?

There are several circumstances when real estate business ethics are important to the participants. These ethical guidelines provide expectations for behavior for a particular kind of job or work, as well as the expected behaviors for those requesting the work. Anytime a person depends on another person to appraise, develop a market analysis, represent, negotiate in behalf of, perform certain duties that are prerequisite to a deal, all in anticipation of investing, buying, selling, developing, leasing, lending, or taking on oneself or one's firm any financial risks, there is the potential for violations of ethics in terms of expected behavior.

In the mid- to late 1980s, when an oversupply of real estate in most markets drove down occupancy rates and rents, many developers found themselves unable to refinance existing construction loans. A few such developers went to their lenders and told the truth about the short-term market prospects for increasing occupancy rates or rents and the low probability of securing enough credit elsewhere to pay off the existing construction loan. Most developers, however, would have found it easy in the early stages of an oversupplied market to mislead the lender about current negotiations with numerous or large potential tenants and to therefore buy some more time on the current loans. Many of these developers knew the market was getting worse. Many of the lenders also suspected the market was getting worse but failed to question a trusted client. Dishonesty for the developer was less painful than the thought of going out of business or letting numerous employees of. The ethical dilemma was the struggle between conflicting feelings of loyalty—to employees and subcontractors and to the lender. This same type of ethical dilemma affected everyone in the money food chain, from tenants or buyers to appraisers, leasing agents, and lenders.

Now consider taking the illustration one step further. Assume that the troubled developer has to eliminate overhead and cut down on costs by severing ties with a few leasing representatives. The leasing agents know that the developer is in a bind. The leasing agent is faced with telling the developer the truth about current tenant negotiations or providing an overly optimistic projection of current deals, in the hopes that other leasing representatives will be let go who may have fewer soon-to-sign tenant prospects. The leasing agent's dilemma sets a concern for family, car payments, school payments, or worse yet, medical payments and food, against a sense of loyalty and culturally embedded honesty to the developer. Numerous illustrations can be provided where competing loyalties provide incentives to stray away from the edge of honesty and ethical behavior.

Because society has learned that professionals will cheat and lie, especially when there is a downturn within their industry, it seeks to impose rules on them. Congress in our behalf requires certification of appraisers, who must now take training courses in ethics among other topics. Real estate brokers are required to learn about civil rights by most states that license brokers. Insurance and security sales agents must pass licensing exams that require the memorization of ethical standards of disclosure rules to clients (blue-sky laws). But can such rules do any good?

The answer is that whenever the industry is prosperous or at least stable, most people will find it in their best interest to exhibit the highest code of conduct within their field of work. Whenever an industry is in a long-term contraction and times are rough, no rules of ethics will matter, nor will the typical professional in an industry maintain the same degree of ethical behavior practiced during prosperous times. Stored wealth will allow the majority of players in a moderately successful industry to remain honest, but extreme ethical violations will be observed at the margin among those more desperate to maintain income and wealth.

A Simple Empirical Investigation of the Economic Influence on Ethics in the Real Estate Brokerage Industry

Hypothesis and Data

Using ten years' worth of residential sales data within the state of Ohio derived from both the Ohio Association of Realtors and Amerestate, Inc.[5] along with data on sales suspensions from the Ohio Division of Real Estate, a simple empirical test can proceed. The hypothesis is as follows:

Hypothesis 2: *As sales decrease, more ethical violations should occur, resulting in a greater number of permanent license suspensions, or as sales increase there should be fewer suspensions as a result of ethical violations.*

This test is admittedly crude in several ways. First, many ethical violations and disputes between principals (home buyers or sellers) and sales agents or brokers never end up in front of the appropriate licensing authority with the power to revoke or permanently suspend a license. Arbitration attempts occur at many local Realtor boards, and settlements between parties for dishonest or fraudulent acts may result in avoiding a formal court hearing or an appearance in front of a licensing board. Second, revocation of a license is only an extreme measurement of unethical behavior. Most ethical violations result in temporary suspensions, yet this data was not available to the author. Relative to the number of licenses in the state, the number of annual license revocations is extremely small and never runs more than sixty-five per year, which is less than two-tenths of 1 percent of all licensees. This low sample number can easily result in a fair amount of random variation and noise in the data set that could bias results. Also, there is a time lag in weeks or months that can be expected, from the time of the violation to the time where a complaint is filed and a decision made that could result in license revocation. Using annual data helps to mitigate this last problem; however, some bias can occur in the tail end of each year that might lower statistical correlations. Given all these problems and a very short time period over which the data is available (from 1987 through 1996), a simple correlation and regression is applied to the data.

Results

The data is graphed in Figure 7.1. The correlation statistic is a negative .51694 between contemporaneous real estate sales and permanent suspensions as hypothesized. Shifting the data by one year does not improve the results. Quarterly data, tested both contemporaneously and lagged, contains so much noise that the correlation results declined slightly as did the fit of the regression model. The simple regression—with suspensions LS as the dependent variable and sales S as the independent variable—has the correct sign and is moderately significant.

$$LS = 117.188 - .0007(S) \qquad F = 2.77225 \qquad t = 2.938$$

The Need for Further Tests

While the results above are promising, they fall woefully short of being able to predict the strength and consistency of the relationship between changing economic circumstances or market conditions and the tendency of real estate market participants to violate ethical standards. Data from other states—such as the number of Board arbitration hearings relative to the number of agents or Realtor members in the state over time and in comparison to the number of total sales—might be a better measurement of ethical behavior trends. Other measurements to indicate individual incomes or to provide an indication of market conditions might be developed.

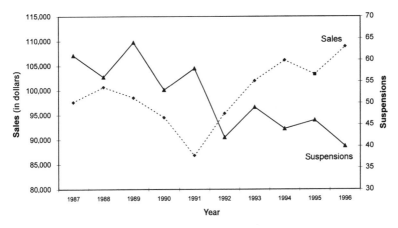

Figure 7.1.   Sales versus license suspensions, 1987 to 1996

Studies across time in various sectors of the real estate industry and various geographic regions would provide insight into the price elasticity of ethical violations at the margin or at least which states have more effective enforcement systems. This author hopes that others might repeat this or improved tests of the relationship between market conditions and ethical violations in order to improve our understanding of when we are more likely to observe an ethical and professional real estate industry.

Conclusions and Summary

Ethics can arise in the context of minimizing work through harmonious coexistence, thereby maximizing welfare relative to work requirements. Ethics evolve into numerous rules of appropriate behavior with infinitely greater detail that seek to clearly communicate loyalties and expectations of behavior for work or services to be rendered. These rules are seen in most trade association codes of conduct. Both an increasing population density within urban areas, as well as the greater complexities of a highly specialized production society, can explain the increase in the number of rules of behavior placed on society today and the general cry for more efforts to teach ethics in business schools.

Preliminary explorations within the real estate industry indicate that sales agents are more likely to be ethical when economic times are good and less likely to be ethical when markets are in decline. Most of us can afford the luxury of high ethical standards and complicated rules during times when we are relatively well off. Future research is needed to better understand the strength of the relationship between market conditions and ethical violations.

Acknowledgments

The author would like to thank Abdullah Yavas, David Geltner, and Timmothy Riddiough for comments on prior drafts along with anonymous reviewers.

Notes

1. The question of whether humans are innately good or bad has been debated for centuries. *Good* here is defined in the altruistic sense, *bad* in the selfish and potentially harmful

and dishonest sense. Often the presumption is made that at some deep level humans are either good or bad and that over the long run the survival of the species will depend on the answer to this all important question. If good intentions toward our fellow humans were on one scale, and bad intentions were on another scale, both sides might be weighty indeed. Yet if the good within humans outweighs the bad by even a small degree, then perhaps there is hope for the long-run survival of the species based on the law of averages and the probability that humans will tend to be led by or choose (even if a random occurrence) to follow good people more often than bad people. This statistics-based outcome was certainly sufficient when people were organized in small groups, tribes, and nations, that lacked the ability to create mass destruction. Today, the proportion of good people must be relatively even weightier than before since such a small group can create so much devastation on the larger group. Thus, we feel a great need to be able to classify others by a single generalizable label of good or evil, ethical or unethical, for many philosophical reasons. We also feel the need to regulate bad behavior and potential for destruction on others such as weapon possession, since such a small minority can inflict such great damage on many others.

2. In Chapter 12 within this issue, titled "Ethical Codes of Conduct for Business Simplified: The Case of the National Association of Realtors," readers can find a discussion of typical ethical concerns and current ethical standards as developed by the largest trade association in the real estate industry.

3. Cultural-based contempt can arise toward specific groups because of ignorance about certain peoples, as well as the ingrained fear and hatred of others who are different. While prejudicial views may be taught by schools and government, they often come from parents who have received there attitudes from prior generations. The current rise of neo-Nazi behaviors in Germany is likely based on both the recent and current threats to wealth from cheaper foreign help and any lingering cultural seeds of hatred toward those said to be less justified in seeking wealth than indigenous Germans.

4. For those readers who may claim that they are above such behaviors, the author is claiming that your cultural conditioning during a time of bountiful resources is sufficient for you to know that harmonious living requires that maintenance of certain behaviors. If you really believed that life was going to get much harder—that you might lose your house, your job, or your honor—you might easily consider violating your ethical foundations, especially when your instincts for survival lead you to consider the consequences as irrelevant or minimal.

5. Amerestate, Inc. is based in Cincinnati, Ohio, and is a real estate data and information firm that tracks real estate sales throughout the state. It is located at 8160 Corporate Park Drive, Cincinnati. OH 45242, telephone number 513-489-7300.

8 "WAR IS WHEN THEY KILL YOUR CHILDREN"

Ethics and Modern Property Development

Michael Benfield

Centre for Research in European Urban
Environments (CREUE)
University of Newcastle upon Tyne

Abstract

Drawing on recent European research (a thirty-two-case project inquiring into the decision processes surrounding permits for major private European development projects—Czech Republic two, England eleven, France five, Germany two, Hungary two, Italy five, Netherlands five) this article confronts the values, choices, and conduct seen as being involved in land and resource development. Viewing progressive changes in government, business, and social mores as unwittingly encouraging an operating environment of unexpected and unjustified license, it prompts real estate professionals to consider how the emerging imperative of sustainability[1] will affect ethical standards and, through them, development practices. Conceiving development processes as driven by accountancy economics, (an economics primarily concerned with profit and loss and balance sheet calculation rather than wider capital considerations), it argues that these are prone to overlook many other forms of capital. Often masked by the common pursuit of cash profits, jobs, and monetary wealth, these include social, welfare, community, cultural, and various forms of resource, capital.

By definition, planning is concerned with futures. By default it appears to have become little more than a cipher for short-term political goals. Regulatory regimes, designed to protect rights and freedoms, are regularly being overridden[2] and (notional) open local government replaced by covert, elitist decision-making practices. Placing democracy and due process under threat, a form of municipal entrepreneurialism may be emerging. This shows Yiftachel's (1996) dark side of development control to facilitate not just social engineering but private profiteering. With no one to speak for the environment, Agenda 21 sustainability and subsidiarity (the principle

adopted by the European Union that decision all should be taken at the lowest possible level)
seem only of interest to cities if they serve the same ends. In the face of this, it is argued, real
estate professionals have a moral obligation to protect land and resources for the benefit
of countless future generations. To ignore this duty may prejudice the existence of both. Thus,
with current ethics in the property industry seen as a sham, a means to replace or renew them
is suggested.

"Ethics is bunk," said the Green futurologist,[3] only to state a little later, "Of course, we do have a duty to do the best we can for the earth, although not for people"! His first point was simple. Ongoing change causes shifts in attitude, relevance, and meaning. More particularly, the speed of change undermines the stability that was once associated with moral mores, making society feel confused, uncertain, and threatened. For example, fifty years ago abortion was generally illegal, thirty years ago it was legalized, in certain circumstances, today it seems acceptable to abort one twin while the other lives. While this extreme case may prove a watershed for medical ethics, it encompasses the dilemmas that increasingly confront people everywhere. Their old, trusted, reliable standards are undermined by the advancement of science. The distinctions between right and wrong concepts, good and bad conducts are no longer certain even within religious ministries. Yet how old and trusted these standards are may itself be questionable. Not so long ago, for example, it was not unusual for Eskimos to kill one twins at birth.

His second point is perhaps more difficult for mere mortals to take on board, let alone swallow. In geological time, humankind has occupied the earth for but an instant. More pointedly, in Lovelock's (1979) Gaia hypothesis (the idea that the earth is a self-healing, self-regulating organism), the importance of human life is questionable. Yet with new evidence reinforcing the concept and convincing the skeptics, the new science of geophysiology is rapidly being adopted. Dick Holland, professor of geochemistry at Harvard University, for example, is a founder member of the newly formed Geophysical Society. Brian Goodwin of the United Kingdom's Open University attaches the concept of superorganism—the state of order that emerges from complex interactions between myriad components—to the Gaian (Earth) complex of regulatory feedbacks. He suggests that each superorganism manifests a boundary and its own dynamics but still reflects the chaos from which it arose (Tickell, 1996). Thus, with the entire Earth seemingly alive or at least having lifelike properties, the rapid growth of human life and its destructive activities may equate with a cancerous growth. What matters to our futurologist is the Earth, not people, since after us a more intelligent, respectful life form may arise or colonize the planet.

The Ethics of Real Estate Development

What has such bunkum got to do with the noble art of real estate development and those honorable professions that serve its cause? If the way people view their world influences their principles or standards of conduct—their ethics or morals—then the mere fact that attitudes are changing implies a potential shift in the way they approach real estate. Since historically such shifts are discernible, present trends and the extrapolations of futurologists may help identify some of the challenges the property industry will have to face as we turn the millennium.

As with any industry, real estate involves two sorts of people—producers and consumers. But in real estate perhaps a wider range of people is involved on the production side than in many other industries. Besides the craft workers in the extraction, component, and construction processes, these include a wide range of service professions—from surveyors, architects, planners, and engineers to lawyers, marketers, advertisers, financiers, and managers. While for most their professional conduct may be governed by codes of ethical behavior, they are also all consumers in one way or another and, as members of society at large, interact with and modify their views as social attitudes change. Thus, the way people involved with real estate development interpret and apply their personal and professional codes may vary. Such interpretations may or may not reflect the draftsperson's intent. Here some of vagaries, doubt, and license intimated above can already be seen creeping in.

To protect against this, most countries independently regulate the use and development of land and property. At least in part they do so to uphold certain standards, as is the case with planning and development control systems. Seen as ethical constraints, a huge part of the justification for them is that they resolve competing claims over the use of resources, attempt to balance an uneven distribution of power, and protect the interests of weaker groups (Kivell, 1993, p. 8). However, such regulation may itself fall subject to interpretation.

How robust are these systems and how can one tell, particularly when the use and objectives of their rules (the combination of legal plans, legal regulation, and formally declines land use and development policy) may change, both over time and with conflict within and between countries. As shown by Table 8.1, they may also reflect ideological persuasion. For example, the New Right of the 1980s continually argued that government support of property markets and private enterprise led to a level of market-based redistribution, betterment, and the promotion of social values.

Table 8.1. Objectives of different national development control rules

Redistribute betterments	Support land and property market
Social values	Promote private enterprise
Containment	Expansion
Sustainable development	Creation and growth of settlements
Balanced communities	European spatial development
Protection of natural resources	Control of natural resources
Development according to local community interests	Development according to general public interests
Neighborhood protection	Communications
Healthy neighborhood	Political interests in responding to various crises
Environmental quality	Reconstruction
Ecology and landscape	Rational organization of human settlements
Quality of life and environment	Compete with European cities

Given that calls for improved environmental quality may necessitate reconstruction and that ecological and landscape concerns may also depend on rationalization in the organization of human settlements, a the admonition goes, "Don't listen to what they say. Watch what they do!" In part, this is the aim of this article.

English Versus Continental European Development Control System

Several of the concepts in the simple expression *real estate* require at least passing consideration. To avoid boring readers with lengthy definitions, here the term is taken to mean "legal interests in land, other natural resources, and all immovable property attached to them." In this, *property* describes any object or right that can be owned, and *ownership* involves, first and foremost, possession (ownership and possession have separate legal constructs). In modern societies, this implies the rights to use, prevent others from using, and dispose of property, such rights being legally protected. While in this context *development* is taken to mean the laying out and construction of infrastructure, services, and building, the more generic term *development*, meaning "to grow or evolve from latency to or toward fulfilment" may serve as a useful signpost for this consideration.

In theory, then, rights to own property and to use or withhold its use in or from development should be protected and exercised fairly. Interests in real estate development should be moderated both by regulatory systems and by the rules governing the conduct of those professionals involved. All should deliver equity, although the way in which they attempt to do this may vary.

To return to planning and development control legislation, for example, there are major differences between the way U.K. and continental planning systems approach this task, not the least being that all mainland countries follow written constitutions, whereas no such document exists in the United Kingdom. These differences and the related permit decision practices are shown diagrammatically in Figure 8.1. Simplistically, in the United Kingdom planning and building regulations are addressed separately by different municipal departments. It is the duty of professional planning officers to give effective *de novo* planning consideration to each application—to mediate (Healey et al., 1988) between interests and advise political decision takers on the balance of these as they affect individual cases. Rough justice is accepted as part of the cost of such judgmental discretion. On the mainland, land-use allocation is seen as taking place when impartial professionals make the plans. It is they who weigh and determine all considerations. Technical officers should merely assess applications for development for conformance with these plans along with the building regulations. Only those that comply with all requirements should receive permits—at least in theory.

However, the research on which this article draws suggests that, whatever the intention, the way in which rules are used may be changing. It points up many ethical concerns and struggles with Mammon. Given Europe's two distinct planning and development control systems, two heuristic models of the permit decision process were conceived for this research. The English, policy-led, discretionary decision and the Continental, preplanned, conformance decision. Additionally, following the work of Goodchild and Munton (1985) a third, latent, negotiative model was envisaged for England.

European Permit Decisions in Practice

In fact seven decision making practices were identified across Europe. Overall they suggest that might is right, that Hobbes'[4] war is extant, and that Nietzche's Übermensch[5] is the reality. Although most permit decision processes appear to follow a mix rather than a single model, contrary to

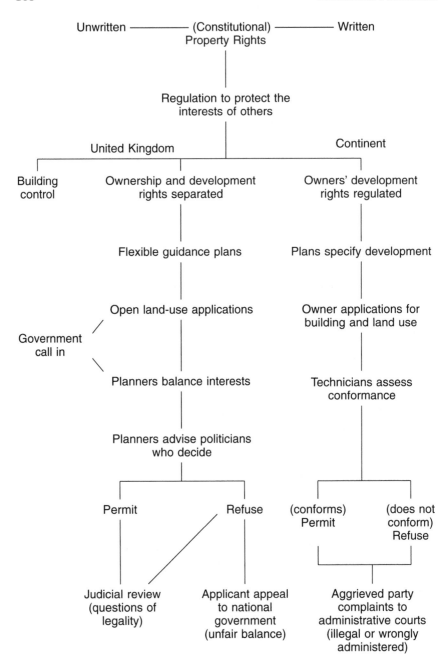

Figure 8.1.   United Kingdom and continental development control in theory

theoretical expectations, negotiation or deal making emerged as the most important. Indeed, informal negotiation appears to be a well established and accepted practice on the mainland. Overall, more than 82 percent[6] of case decisions were seen as negotiated in one way or another. The vast majority being either straightforward negotiation (41 percent) or involving a mix of policy and negotiation (41 percent). The number of cases in each category is represented graphically in Figures 8.2 and 8.3. One of the most significant findings was the identification of two new hybrid forms of the permit decision process. Similar in form, each emphasizes the entrepreneurial and exclusive nature of such decisions when major private projects are concerned.

Although large for its type, the study contains too few cases for these to be considered representative. However, what it does suggest is that throughout Europe a major shift may be in process—a shift a way from the observance or legal enforcement of predetermined plans and toward the elite, corporatist negotiation of permits. In general, rules seem freely interpreted, manipulated, disregarded, or used as a screen to avoid responsibility. Seldom do they protect or address rights and interests equitably.

Case findings were supported by evidence from expert witnesses—that is, informants not associated with any case. In Holland, for example, a

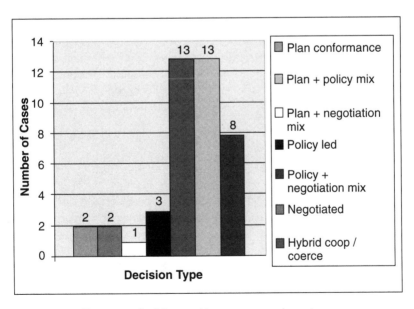

Figure 8.2. European decision-making processes by category

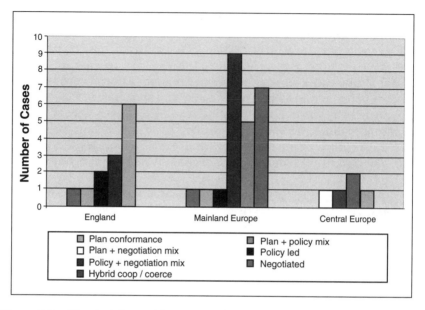

Figure 8.3.   The decision-making process by number of cases per country group

national planning inspector had found that "75 percent of developments . . . do not accord with the plans," and the director of a national
development company asserted that "The DRO [municipal planning
office] 'massage' the regulations so that wanted developments can
proceed." In Germany a chief building officer confided that (decision
takers) "close their eyes to the B-plan and regulations and permit the new
development regardless."

Everywhere it seems that, in Europe's new ethos of competition, ad hoc
development policies are being determined on the hoof. While ideology and
party politics appear to engage more at higher than local levels of government, land-use planning is viewed as lacking purpose. As an English case
planning officer explained, "Local plans in general are overridden or cir-
cumvented because of market pressures in favour of development." A
French maire agrees, stating that "Regulations can always be led astray. The
only true constraints are financial ones. The market is the limit." Here, the
opinion of a German professor is telling. In his view, "All the rules are bent.
That is not what is important. The important thing is that everyone should
get equal treatment under them." Unfortunately, if the research is a fair
reflection, this seldom occurs.

It might be argued that such wide spread aberrations undermine conventionally accepted standards of ethical behavior. But a case may also exist for seeing them as society's response to wrong and bad regulatory limitations imposed in the past that have resulted, or are resulting, in both improper constraints on liberal freedoms and unequally favoring an insensitive form of democracy. If so, then what is happening may be legally wrong but morally good in terms of the collective search for a higher natural justice in the cooperative good. But this is a long process during which many wrongs may arise, unless both Curran's *vigilance*[7] and Bennett's *publicity*[8] admonishments are heeded.

The Self-serving Nature of Ethics

What is also seen through the research is that the degree to which different actors and agencies need to become involved in particular developments depends very much on the substitutes available to them. Additionally, their behavior and response to risk may vary according to their interests and objectives. For example, those whose interests revolve around redevelopment (Watson, 1992) may act very differently from those with a wide range of economic interests who may look completely outside development for other opportunities (Gore and Nicholson, 1991). But, as Crenson (1971, p. 34) notes, "the stimulus response conception of power fails to account for the way in which men define their own interests and the way in which others perceive and respond to those interests."

If the conflicts observed by the research between decisions and rules are linked to endemic change driven by market forces, it is perhaps not surprising to find developers devising strategies and tactics to capitalize on these—or that the nonelected, business domination of local government has led, for example, to left-wing councils anxious to promote their own local economies, courting business interests, and attempting to demonstrate not only their responsible management but also their desire to work in partnership with the private sector. As Brouillon asserts (Newell, 1995, p. 19), "What Governments (i.e. politicians) want is to stay in power and to stay in power they have to please voters and to please voters there has to be jobs and growth and in that sense the way governments go is the way we go because development is the goal."

In the same way that the skeptic may disparage political and business ethics, he or she may also view professional ethics merely as a form of protectionism, a hangover from the guilds. To widen the scope of this discussion with an example from the United States, take opinion Number 15 of the Ethics Committee of the Mississippi State Bar on Rule 27 governing rules of professional conduct.[9] In essence, this states that, when additionally qualified as, say, an accountant, insurer, or realtor, a lawyer may not advertise such services from the same premises. To do so might serve as a feeder for their lawyer's practice and could lead to suspicions of unethical conduct since "Direct or indirect advertising or solicitation is unacceptable in any size of community." On reading this the skeptic might think that the concern of the esteemed Ethics Committee was with protecting, first, those lesser qualified (and able?) lawyers from the (unfair) competition of their brethren and, second, the image of the profession. Little regard seems shown for the quality and convenience of service delivered or, more important, the duty and responsibility of trust, care, and attention to clients' affairs. Whose interests does such an *ethical* opinion serve?

Again, the skeptic may see lawyers the world over as enjoying the sinecure of legislative protection. Only those qualified and licensed to practice may do so. In many countries this extends to other professions. For instance, in mainland Europe architects and engineers enjoy similar privileges, and in most such countries they are the only people allowed to prepare town plans. In contrast, since the late 1970s English solicitors have lost various protections, like conveyancing. But, as if to compensate, their governing Law Society now permits them to operate as estate agents, a much longer-standing practice in Scotland.

In addition to the general protections noted above and despite the niceties of legal wrappings, the detail of construction and property regulation may also serve as a feeder for professional work. To take another U.S. example, Philadelphia's department of licenses and inspections issues over 160 kinds of license. While not specifically spelled out, this effectively requires proprietors and owners to engage the services of a range of professionals, including now electricians and plumbers, to make (acceptable) applications for property construction, alteration, and use (DLI, 1996). Likewise, the codified regulations of many continental European countries imply, if not apply, similar controls and certainly support professional practices. In England, too, a "creeping codification" via "back-door"[10] statutes, is creating a "certainty" to replace the vagaries of discretionary, common-law-style judgments that progressively is achieving the same end.

To take a jaundiced view, whatever their original intent, ethics, as part of the rules that govern society and its professional servants, have become part of a rhetoric to direct and kid the punters. As Lukes (1974, p. 24) identified, rules and institutional practices may indeed be used to systematically bias the operation and outcomes of the social system in favor of some issues (and interests) and against others. If so, ethics may indeed be bunk.

The Immorality Surrounding Property Development

In themselves, neither property development nor the rules that attempt to control it are either good or bad. Their morality lies in the way in which they are implemented. Like the gun lobby's argument, what matters is whose finger is on the trigger. And increasingly the motives that lead to it being squeezed are becoming suspect.

For example, Europe may have adopted different approaches to development control (see above) but reached the same end. Supported by expert evidence (from planning and property development professionals providing information as noncase informants), what the research indicates is that a *culture of cooptation* is emerging in which dissident voices are bought off, persuaded not to rock the boat, are silenced, or simply are ignored.[11] Whether or not they are important or relevant, their *interests* are just not strong enough to count. Yet the lobbying, prenegotiation, and hidden agendas, found by the research, and the deliberate delays and noncooperation also noted by Newell (1995) can all be expected of a process that encourages use of the media to project a good, competitive image.

Westra (1994, ch. 3) observes that, "If we demonstrate that a social system is unfair, disrespectful, there is no obligation to respect the system's integrity or protect its future." To judge from the research findings, this is exactly what is happening in real estate. If the indications from Europe are anything to go by, if professional ethics follow the U.S. example, and if codified regulations are being used to reinforce professional exclusivity, then those rules that supposedly govern land use and development have been reduced to being mere bargaining chips for elite-circle deal making.

In this, the dominant actors of the 1980s (Thatcher, Reagan, Mitterand, and Delors) now appear to have been mere sycophants of a much wider movement, pawns in a larger game—a game in which Goldsmith's (1993, p. 76) description of the shift in British local government from the welfare-state model toward an economic-development model, also appears typical of the continent Short-term, profit-and-loss, finance economics (a narrow definition of economics concerned primarily with finances—revenue, profits, losses, balancing budgets, returns on investment, and the expertise needed to address these) is now a demigod. Where this prejudices the long-term interests of other forms of capital, it may also be considered unethical. Competition, the touchstone of the Thatcher and Reagan years (Thornley, 1991), has given rise to precisely the kind of growth coalitions described in the U.S. literature. However, in mainland Europe they are often led by the public, rather than private, sector. Competition has resulted in a new urban corporatism (Dunleavy and King, 1990, and others) in which reliance on outside agencies may "compel local planning authorities to incorporate production interests into the plan-making process" (Simmie and French, 1989, p. 18). Municipal resources (rules, land, and personnel) are effectively placed at the disposal of commercial enterprises to lure whatever ventures will aid a town's other policies. Additionally, many obligations in texts are sufficiently ambiguous to enable powerful industry groups to press upon governments interpretations beneficial to their interests (Newell, 1995, in his consideration of the fossil-fuel lobbies).

This highlights the bargaining power of actors, based on the control of resources and information. It also helps explain why financial institutions usually take the lowest risk of all (Gore and Nicholson, 1991), since those on whose resources the success of the development process most depends are likely to be in the position of greatest bargaining strength. Thus, to find that allocation of land for private developments turns more on decisions made on applications than on inclusion of land within a development plan, with agreement to grant a permit negotiated in advance, should not be surprising, nor should the lack of interest in planning systems and rules. Although not the same as there being no interests at stake, with few people really knowing much about these frameworks and the chance that, as an Italian professor recognized, "they have been copied from somewhere else—badly" it is hardly surprising that, as in Italy, "Planning law has no influence on the PRG [Pianno Regolatore Generale] or any subsequent amendments" and that. "there are no planning justifications for design . . . no strategic overview of the problems of a town."[12] Although plan-making activities might normally be expected to take place well before permit decisions come to be negotiated, they may actually be concurrent. For example, in one Italian case the promoter appeared to simultaneously negotiate the permit while organizing national legislation to help him do this.

There is an apparent commercial collusion between political leaders, private organizations, and officers. Arguably, this makes the fundamental question of how robust any development control system is in balancing interests at the point of decision, a nonsequitur. Concentration on competition is at the expense of all else, most markedly local communities and the environment. Yet in competing for jobs, cities are actually trying to export their unemployment elsewhere. And where is the morality in this? As Van der Krabben (1995, p. 232) asks, should we "favour a property system that incites local authorities . . . to compete with each other in their efforts to attract companies to their respective municipalities?" while "the environment dies in silence"[13] (Kramer, 1995)?

A further danger, potentially enhanced in systems that permit ad hoc policy decisions and protect private property values, is that private gains from land conversion (from one use to another) are so great that they introduce possibilities for corruption. Although bribes were observed in only one (Italian) case, potential for favors and obligations to influence planning decisions was noted in all countries. These seem always linked with policy instruments. It matters not who the actors are, whether from the local aristocratic family, business, politics, or simply the local Mr. Big, fringing on the mafiosi.[14] For, as one Italian informant explained, it is more the pattern of patronage in which "men of honour" are responsible to whomsoever they owe fealty for position and protection and must discharge "obligations" whenever they are called upon to do so, even to the extent of "killing another person" (sic).

Here the concern is not just that strict morality is marred by impropriety that design competitions are often a sham device, that municipalities undertake work on behalf of developers, or that the developers themselves are certain that corruption is present everywhere. Nor is it that, according to a Dutch planning inspector, the whole claim to need more and more houses is "a lie" designed to create work for major development companies.[15] What is more important is that environmental concerns are overridden and that costs and prices are increased as both landowners, contractors, and developers fight to secure the necessary margins to make their payoffs. Often this means maximizing short-term profits at the expense of long-term impacts.

Not infrequently it turns out that open government is more about insider dealing, that the protections afforded by regulatory systems are traded away, and that, through economic competition, the planning and development game (Healey, 1983) is in process of being transformed back into Hobbes's war of all against all. As Habermas (1975) explains in his theory about the colonization of civil society, both the monetarization and bureaucratization of social relations have created a set of social benefits and securities at the cost of creating a new range of dependencies, while destroying or severely atrophying existing solidarities. This destructive process has served to undermine people's capacities for self-help and cooperative forms of horizontal communication for resolving problems at the base of societies—in civic communities.

To judge from the research evidence, collectively we may be witnessing a greater immorality. As the Green futurologist might argue, the immorality of a war not to defend and protect life but against life itself. As tools in the hands of increasingly desperate politicians, our systems of planning and urban design have created a world that grows far beyond the capacity of the environment to sustain life into the future.[16] Thus it is sustainability that holds the challenges of the new millennium.[17]

The Costs of This War

Presently the real estate industry seems driven by the self-serving ethics of competition, profits, and growth. Instead of honoring the principles of nature, it violates them, producing waste and harm regardless of purported intent. As architect William McDonough (1993) argues, as we destroy more topsoil, build over more habitats, destroy more forests, burn more coal, produce more toxic and radioactive wastes, dam more rivers, drift-net more fish, poison more insects, bleach more paper, and burn more garbage in order to build, furnish, light, and heat property, feed, educate, and entertain people, and then clean up after them, we create a vast industrial machine. Increasingly, reports of death and disease linked to environmental pollution, industrial and traffic accidents, ozone depletion, and so on depict this world as a place not for living in but for dying in. It is a war, to be sure—a war that only a few more generations can surely survive.

Referring to the glass, plastics, synthetics, electrics, and so forth of modern constructions, McDonough (1993) describes his team's search for materials that won't make people sick when placed inside buildings. They discovered that today's entire system of building construction is essentially toxic. They also learned how, 350 years ago, when the oaks were cut to build one of the English Oxford Colleges, the architect specified that a grove of trees be planted and maintained to replace the ceiling beams when needed. He then explains how one of their office designs in Poland guaranteed the building a long life by making it convertible to other uses when its office utility was no longer. Then, after calculating the energy cost to build the structure and the energy cost to run and maintain it—6,400 acres of new forest were needed—they required the clients to plant 10 square miles of forest to offset the building's effect on climate change. The cost to plant these trees in Poland was equivalent to a small part of the firm's advertising budget.

Today's consumption may be seen as a form of rake's progress. Nature operates on current income. It does not mine or extract energy from the past. It does not use its capital reserves. And it does not borrow from the future. In contrast, our resources, work, effort, and other contributions are measured by paper currency and gross national product. Yet as McDonough (1993) asks, "What are we really measuring? If we have not put natural resources on the asset side of the ledger, then what are they? Does a forest really become more valuable when it is cut down? Do we really prosper when wild salmon are completely removed from a river?" Today mass systems of production for the capitalist marketplace, the economic sphere, dominate society and kinship relations. Not the family but the impersonal corporation is the dominant institution of production (Carr, 1996).

Similar sentiments can be found over and over again among first nations (the preferred term for underdeveloped countries with a high proportion of endogenous peoples). In a report written by a team of first nation people the authors describe why, in native traditions, respect for people and for the earth is linked together in order for people to survive and care for at least the next seven generations. When we begin to separate ourselves from what sustains us, we immediately open up the possibility of losing understanding of our responsibility and our kinship to the earth. When we view the world simply through the eyes of human beings, we create further distance between our world and ourselves. When the perceived needs of one *spirit being* is held above all others, equality disappears (Clarkson, Morisette, and Regallet, 1992).

In fact, the costs of development's war of attrition against nature are potentially much greater. McDonough (1993) illustrates this well. When he worked on the master plan for the Jordan Valley for King Hussain, he was walking through a village that had been flattened by tanks and saw a child's skeleton squashed into the adobe block. He was horrified. The king looked at him and asked "Don't you know what war is?" McDonough said he guessed he didn't. And the king replied, "War is when they kill your children." In the same way as, for example, the rise in asthma in our young appears related to modern development practices, failure to call a truce and seek sustainability in all our development may prejudice the lives of our children even beyond seven generations.

Higher Natural Justice

What the research indicates is that society now uses a narrow definition of *economic* and plays by negotiable rules. Progressively it is being conditioned to accept the domination of market competition in which there are losers as well as winners.[18] In Healey's (1992, p. 159) terms there is a "naive belief in the power of democratic discussions, while the forces of global capitalism ever more cleverly conceal the ways they oppress us." Equity, it seems, has been usurped by competition around which elite groups form. Yet acceptance that rational persuasion will not work on the masses does not require surrender to either present or alternate elites. Instead, through an improved understanding of how they behave, it demands that the conditions for sustainability be identified and to then require *all* elites to justify how their (intended) actions will satisfy these conditions. It requires a return to equity in moral philosophy (ethics)—a search for and a reliance on a higher order of natural justice. Like McDonough, we have to recognize that to live within the laws of nature means to express our human intention as an *interdependent* species, aware and grateful that we are at the mercy of forces larger than we are. It also means that we obey these laws in order to honor each other and all things. We must come to peace with and accept our place in the natural world.

However, issues of the environment and interdependence are complex and long term. They entail a far more radical critique of industrial societies than, say, Marxism (Orr, 1992, p. 69). But politicians who talk about complex issues and difficult choices don't win elections. What appears to be needed is the separation of long-term planning from short-term politics. Unfortunately, since there is no political gain in surrendering control over resources, while contemporary politics concentrates on immediate issues, like jobs and crime, and government partners business to secure development, the prospects for truly meaningful new legislation seem slim.

Happily, released from the ossification of political and economic evolution imposed by the capitalist-communist ideological standoff of the cold-war years, a long overdue rethink of many issues has commenced. The growing volume of literature on, for example, Green politics,[19] alternative economics,[20] direct democracy,[21] and so forth evidences this, with planners being seen as potential champions of community (Poulton, 1995, p. 12) and environmental (Benfield, 1994; Kramer, 1995) interests. New concepts for planning and development are emerging. For Albrechts (1991), these will involve a shift from planning for capital to planning for society. The danger, as Ophuls (1977, p. 163) warns, is that ecological scarcity will create "overwhelming pressures toward political systems that are frankly authoritarian."

Ideas for limiting this danger are increasingly presented for evaluation.[22] Many of these endorse the principle of *sustainability* adopted at the Rio de Janeiro Earth Summit of 1992 and currently exercising the collective planning consciousness. Together with *subsidiarity*, this faces all concerned with land-use planning and development with the potential emergence of a new morality (Benfield, 1995). But switching to a new paradigm for development involves seeing the world differently (Harper and Stein, 1995, 4). It involves such radical change in the standards of measurement, in the range of questions and answers, and in the lexical structure of the perceived world that those with different paradigms literally live in different worlds (Ross, 1995). As Kuhn (1970) states, "we are prisoners caught in the framework of our theories, our language." On this extreme view, different paradigms become unintelligible to those who have not *converted* to them (Harper and Stein, 1995, 9–10).

In attempting to bridge this gulf, Westra, (1994, ch. 6) proposes that urban centers should be guided by the principle of integrity. She asks how much urban culture is the minimum we can live with and at the same time the maximum the earth can tolerate. She argues that whatever we choose as morally right, this must not conflict with the way nature functions. Linking with geophysiology and the Gaia concept, she suggests this requires all actors and agencies to consider humankind's place in the universe. It means that they—we—must address the ethical dimensions and qualitative limits of our interaction with the environment, the scale within which we operate for quantitatively morally defensible interactions with the environment, and the scale, size, and quality of disturbances (to which duration may be added). Invoking Ophul's authoritarian fears, she recommends the use of ecological eyes that choose laws and regulations according to an ideal good rather than voter preference and that supersede individual states and countries as the final arbiters for choosing these laws and regulations.

The Cooperative Consciousness

Opposed to Thomas Hobbes's concept of ruthless and unremitting struggle as the basic law of nature, Kropotkin,[23] among others asserts, that survival of species is furthered by mutual aid. Humans, he argues, have attained primacy among animals in the course of evolution through their capacity for cooperation.[24] And cooperation, it is suggested here, introduces the need for fairness and the quality of being just. This springs from an individual inner sense of delivering what is properly due or merited. As David Hume (1711–1776) (in *Essays Moral and Political* (1741–1742) and Adam Smith (1723–1790) in *Theory of Moral Sentiments* (1759) recognized, it draws on the feelings of sympathy that people bear to one another even when not bound by kinship or direct ties. Ultimately, it leads to Immannel Kant's (1724–1804) categorical imperative to "Act as if the principle on which your action is based were to become by your will a universal law of nature". It also invokes Jeremy Bentham's (1748–1832) universal, hedonistic utilitarianism, in which the highest good is the greatest happiness of the greatest number of people.[25]

But to appeal above temporal considerations to some universal law of nature is surely unrealistic. It requires empathetic human beings to seek mutual aid through a cooperative order that protects individual freedoms, liberty, and choice to secure greatest utility (e.g. John Dewey, 1959–1952).[26]

As Moore (1873–1958),[27] might argue, it requires good, moral behavior to take on an unanalyzable, emotional quality in which equity subsumes justice, even-handedness, fairness, and impartiality.

Surprisingly, and to confound the doubters, recent evidence suggests that this *cooperative consciousness* may be wakening. According to EDK (1996), survey and focus groups have found a growing number of Americans believing that greed, rather than competitiveness, is motivating large corporations. Besides being angry with government, their anger is now mounting over corporate behavior. They don't begrudge big profits but are angry that these aren't shared with the workers. They're not angry at huge CEO salaries but because these salaries come from making thousands redundant, using temps instead of permanent staff, and using low, cost youngsters to replace older workers. They still admire large corporations that play by the old rules, perceived as an unwritten social contract between workers and management. But when an organization is profitable and breaks this, they get angry. This is the same for all age groups, races, educational backgrounds, income groups, and political parties. Seeing this as a greater problem than government corruption, waste, and inefficiency, EDK suggest the findings show that, increasingly, objectors are ready to support intervention to curb these excesses.

Although the imperatives of sustainability are not yet widely understood, this is changing rapidly. If the public makes a link between their great-great-grandchildren's inheritance, past and present consumption, and what they perceive as corporate greed, then their anger may boil over. Were this to happen, political and regulatory systems that can take account of the very long term may emerge. If so, then the real estate industry will be on the battle's front line.

Rights and the Good Earth

By any definition, *planning* is future orientated. In the same way, rights, understood as interests, are always future orientated. One inevitable consequence of property rights theories that rely on ethical justifications is the acceptance of some kind of Lockean proviso that provides all generations with a chance to acquire some previously unowned property. This presents planning and therefore development with a major difficulty, since one near universally accepted limit on property rights is that their use must not constitute force. However, a close analogy can be made between the relationship that present society has with beings in the future to one of force. Consequently, if the same criteria that apply among contemporaries are applied to the property rights of earth's future inhabitants, then, as Fairweather (1992) asserts, substantial obligations to protect natural resources are inevitable.

Yet how can nonexistent future beings who might have such rights and that would require the environment to be protected now have rights now (Attfield, 1991, p. 92)? If, as Beatley (1994) contends, the present generation has "no absolute right . . . to use or develop land or to reap high profits from its use where significant environmental destruction is the outcome, then where such activities fundamentally change the natural character of the land, the presumption must be against allowing extensive development."[28] This argument adopts both Baier's (1984, p. 227) belief that "future persons interests can be determinate even when the persons themselves are not yet determinate" and Rawls's (1971) just savings principle—that rational individuals deciding on the principles of social justice (and under a veil of ignorance) would acknowledge certain obligations to their immediate descendants.

If the earth is our common heritage, then land, like other natural resources, may be considered a common, rather than individual, possession (George, 1937, 1947, 1953). Contrary to the Lockesian[29] tenet, this suggests that land should be managed in the common interest. It contrasts with Plato et al's[30] notions of proportional distribution and limitation on holdings, giving all interests a voice in its use and a share in its produce. Such view sees land being held and managed for the common good, its use regarded as a privilege, not a right, with change being evolutionary, small, and slow (Leopold, 1949). This position argues for *environmental rights* to be respected even where they are not socially efficient or optimal under a utilitarian model. They may involve rights *to* things, such as rights of access to mountains and rivers and beaches, or rights to be *free from*, for example, excessive levels of pollution. But they face theoretical and practical differences in determining their extent and whether they can legitimately vary from one country, region, or culture to the next (Beatley, 1994, pp. 20–21). If systems for development were based in equity, (meaning justice, fairness, and impartiality), then fair treatment of interests, issues, and power between stakeholders in land-use decisions might form a central platform in land-use planning and development systems, possibly revisiting Geddes's theory of planning. As summarized by Ferraro (1995, p. 13), this is presented in Table 8.2.

Summary: The Battle Lines

This chapter has not just been about ethics in real estate but about their role in setting new agendas. Using the academic research of practical

Table 8.2. Geddes's theory of planning as seen by Ferraro (1995)

- Planning cannot be based on authority. It mainly requires cooperation.
- Cooperation within each generation is an attitude of respect and conservation, of care of the life and the earth, while cooperating among different generations is an attitude of openness toward the future.
- The plan must develop as a game, and the planner needs to keep the game open to new (now unforeseeable) interpretations and the future aspirations to come[a]
- The work of the planner is mainly communicative: his words and his action (the appeals he makes and the incentives he distributes) do not directly build objects, but they are intended to stimulate interpretations and "moves" from people and to persuade people (through appeals and incentives) to cooperate.

a. *Town Planning in Balrampur: A Report to the* Honble Mahanaja Bahadar, Murnay's London Printing Press, Lucknow, 1917 (cited by Ferraro, 1995, p. 13).

decision making across European countries, it has shown how the interventionary use of land-use planning and property development has shifted from concern with the improvement of living conditions, through economic competition, to the cultural manipulation of social groups in the battle for municipal entrepreneurial supremacy. Seeing sectional ethics and legislative protections as, in the main, tools for promoting the self-interests of those elitist cadres that are party to land-use permit decisions, it has suggested that, where major private developments are concerned, regulatory systems provide merely a negotiating framework—that, as deals are agreed, allows regulatory protections to be bargained away, that can be hidden behind to avoid responsibility, and that enables both earth and citizen to be robbed of access and voice.

This trend is attributed to a growing global, amoral, economic juggernaut, whose progress is distorting not just democratic systems, rights, and freedoms but fundamental truths and values. Pointing to myopic politics, land and property greed, and the destruction, rather than creation, of sustainability, this chapter has argued for real, long-term wealth creation. This involves social, welfare, community, cultural, and various forms of resource capital—assets that are often masked by the common pursuit of cash profits and jobs. By drawing attention to the looming crisis and mismatch between world resource stocks, renewability, and demand, the article highlights the need for centennial if not millennial time spans to be used when evaluating land and natural resource issues. This requires appropriate recycling and conservation approaches in planning, design, construction, and all other aspects of real estate development. Its pursuit is enormously complicated, resource intensive, time consuming, and knowledge demanding, and its outputs, together with the thought, imagination, and effort expended on them, represent real wealth, which should be invested not just for present society but for coming generations over the very long term.

Four things seem clear. First, with the function and discipline of planning and development control seen as lacking purpose, regulatory regimes appear widely manipulated, if not ignored. Second, with plans superseded by individual, ad hoc, negotiated decisions, planning's rationalist project has failed. Third, with access to decision processes reserved for key resource holders, planning's participation and mediation objectives may be thwarted. Fourth, with the new imperatives of sustainability and subsidiarity increasingly being recognized, there is an urgent need for all those concerned with land-use and property development to devise and adopt a new ethic, a new moral philosophy, in their tasks, duties, and responsibilities. These will face the real estate industry with hard decisions over, for example, ownership, property rights, durability, and renewability. The property development industry will be forced to consider earth's latent potential rather than its rampant exploitation.

The proposition here is that it must find ways to transcend society's presently distorted economic goals. It must take on concern for intergenerational equity. And, as the Green futurologist might argue, it must give the earth a major voice at the negotiating table. In presenting this challenge to the whole property development industry, it addresses those professional bodies concerned with the regulation and conduct of members behavior in particular. If their ethical codes were redrawn and subsequently enforced to ensure that members did not transgress the principles outlined above, then they could *de facto* move land and resource issues out of the short-term political arena. In doing so they would strike a bold blow for long-term sustainability and limit the excesses of latter-day economic myopia.

As a wider recognition of earth's geophysiology dawns, as we ponder the prospect of alternative occupants for our planet, as the first skirmishes herald the onset of war for the future of our next seven generations, which side are *you* fighting on?

Notes

1. United Nations Earth Summit, Rio de Janeiro, 1992. For the principles underlying sustainable development, see *International Journal of Sustainable Development and World Ecology* 2: 104–123.

2. Although large for a study of its type, the number of cases involved is too small to be considered a sample.

3. Personal communication with Keith Hudson, The Job Society.

4. Thomas Hobbes (1588–1679) assigns greatest importance to organised society and political power. He argues that human life in the "state of nature" (apart from or before the institution of the civil state) is "solitary, poor, nasty, brutish, and short" and that it is "a war of all against all." Consequently, people seek security by entering into a "social contract" in which each person's original power is yielded to a sovereign, who regulates conduct.

5. Friedrich Nietzche's (1844–1900) startling but logical elaboration of the Darwinian thesis—that survival of the fittest is a basic law of nature—holds that so-called moral conduct is necessary only for the weak. Moral conduct—especially such as was advocated in Jewish and Christian ethics, which in his view are slave ethic—tends to allow the weak to inhibit the self-realization of the strong. According to Nietzche, every action should be directed toward the development of the superior individual, or *Übermensch* ("superman"), who will be able to realise the noblest possibilities of life.

6. Where percentages are given, these have been rounded up or down to the nearest whole number. However, these are merely a device to aid comprehension. They do not give a quantitative scale and should be treated with circumspection. Comparisons are of patterns between cases and cannot be generalized to all cases possible.

7. "The condition upon which God hath given liberty to man is eternal vigilance", Speech of John Philpot Curran (1750–1817) on the right of election of the Lord Mayor of Dublin, July 10, 1790.

8. "The price of justice is eternal publicity," Arnold Bennett (1867–1931), *Things That Have Interested Me* (2nd series, 1923), "Secret Trials."

9. Cited in Newell (1995, p. 19).

10. L. Whittaker LIB, 1995, personal communication.

11. The related statements are all taken from case findings.

12. As for planning laws, the engineering schools are more conservative and teach more of these than the architects. With reform of the architecture schools they have a big restriction on the area of planning. Only 300 hours out of 4,500 hours allocated to this (6.6 percent) (I-B/AB).

13. Author's note from conference proceedings.

14. Mafiosi are local power structures, not to be confused with organized crime Mafia. This is often resisted, although increasingly it seems this is gaining control of the local structures, mainly as a result of drug trafficking.

15. Elsewhere many Europeans question the real need for much demolition and replacement and the overall efficacy and social justice of, for example, out-of-town shopping malls and greenfield industries.

16. Such arguments have been increasingly promoted since limits to growth (Meadows, 1974) appeared over thirty years ago.

17. Numerous discussion groups have formed around this issue, such as the Internet Sustainable Cities Network (SCN-discuss@mailbase.ac.uk).

18. Cheshire (1991) has identified numerous European cities that have done badly as well as improved.

19. See, for example, Ash (1992), Brown (1993), Deblonde (1995), Dobson and Lucandie (1993), Gibbs (1993), Jacobs (1991), and Lundmark (1995).

20. See, for example. Chichilnisky (1994), Clark, Burrall, and Roberts (1993), Douthwaite (1992), Jacobs (1993), Robertson (1974), Robinson (1995), and Strong (1995).

21. See, for example, Cadogan (1974), Hoggett (1995), Horrocks and Webb (1994), and Will (1993).

22. See, for example, Bailey (1995), Benfield (1994, 1995), and Carta (1993).

23. Prince Pyotr Alekseyevich, Kropotkin 1842–1921, Russian geographer and foremost theorist of the anarchist movement. Principle works include *Memoirs of a Revolutionist* (1885; trans. 1899), *Fields, Factories, and Workshops* (1899), *Terror in Russia* (1909); and *Ethics, Origin and Development* (1924).

24. "Mutual Aid; A Factor in Evolution" (1890–1902) and "Ethics, Origin and Development" (posthumously published, 1924).

25. *Principles of Morals and Legislation* (1789).

26. According to Dewey, the good is what is chosen after reflecting on both the means and the probable consequences of realising the good.

27. In *Principia Ethica*, Moore argues that ethical terms are definable in terms of the word *good*, whereas *good* is undefinable. This is so because goodness is a simple, unanalyzable quality.

28. This principle has been perhaps more eloquently articulated by the Wisconsin Supreme Court in its landmark decision *Just v. Marinette*. The court upheld a local shoreline-zoning ordinance that prevented a landowner from filling and building on a wetland site. The court stated that "An owner of land has no absolute and unlimited right to change the essential character of the land so as to use it for a purpose for which it was unsuited in its natural state and which impairs the rights of others. The exercise of the police power in zoning must be reasonable and we think it was not an unreasonable exercise of that power to prevent harm to public rights by limiting the use of private property to its natural use" (56 Wis. 2d, at 201 N.W.2d, cited in Beatley, 1994, p. 35).

29. John Locke (1632–1704) reflects the British philosophical tradition that possession of property is a fundamental, natural right. The concept of freedom is closely allied to property ownership and the notion of a property-owning democracy (Norton-Taylor, 1982).

30. In *The Republic*, Plato (1955–1987) recommends that landed property be distributed in equal proportions among all citizens of a state. Phaleas of Chalcedon, to whom Plato refers, actually earlier proposed this proposition. In the *Laws* he holds that accumulation should extend to no more than five times the amount owned by any other citizen. Aristotle's *Politics*, in his chapter on Phaleas, refers to Solon who "introduced laws restricting the amount of land which an individual might possess." Other laws forbade the sale of property. No Lucian could sell his property unless he could show beyond all shadow of doubt that he had suffered some grave misfortune. Original allotments of land had to be kept intact (Rose, 1985, p. 8).

References

Albrechts, L. (1991). "Changing Roles and Positions of Planners." *Urban Studies* 28(1):123–137 (cited in Berry and McGreal, 1995, p. 4).

Ash, Maurice. (1992). *The Fabric of the World: Towards a Philosophy of Environment*. Dartington: Green Books.

Attfield, Robin. (1991). *The Ethics of Environmental Concern*. Athens: University of Georgia Press (cited in Fairweather, 1992).

Baier, Annette. (1984). "For the Sake of Future Generations." In T. Regan (ed.), *Earthbound: New Introductory Essays in Environmental Ethics*. Philadelphia: Temple University Press (cited in Fairweather, 1992, p. 14).

Bailey, Sinead. (1995). "The Importance of Local Level participation in the Design and Management of Conservation Development Projects." Paper presented at IRNES Conference, Keele University.

Beatley, Timothy. (1994). "Environmental Ethics and the Field of Planning: Alternative Theories and Middle Range Principles." In H. Thomas, (ed.), *Values in Planning.*

Benfield, Michael. (1994). "Futurology: Plan Makings Missing Element?" Paper presented at Planning for a Broader Europe, Istanbul, Turkey.

Benfield, Michael. (1995). "Forging the New Morality: Will Planners Be Guardians or Ciphers?" *DISP* 121 (April): 25–36.

Brown, G. (1993). "Greening government." *New Ground* (35): 4–7 (cited in Gibbs, 1993).

Cadogan, Peter. (1974). *Direct Democracy: An Appeal to the Professional Classes, to the Politically Disenchanted and to the Deprived.* London: Direct Democracy.

Carr, Mike. (1996). "Social Capital, Civil Society, and the Informal Economy: Moving to Sustainable Society." Paper presented at Local Planning in a Global Environment, July 25–28, Toronto, Canada.

Carta, Maurizio. (1993). "The Territory of Chiron: Museum's Role in the Cultural Planning of the Territory." Paper presented at AESOP Summer School, Lodz, Poland.

Cheshire, Paul C. (1991). "Causal Factors in Western European Patterns of Urban Change, 1971–88." Reading, Eng. Centre for European Property Research, Faculty of Urban and Regional Studies, University of Reading.

Chichilnisky, Graciela. (1994). "Sustainable Development and North-South Trade." *FEEM: Fondazione Eni Enrico Mattei* 3.

Clark, Michael, Paul Burrall, and Peter Roberts. (1993). "A Sustainable Economy." In A. Blowers (ed.), *Planning for a sustainable environment: A Report by the Town and Country Planning Association.* London: Earthscan.

Clarkson, L., V. Morisette, and G. Regallet. (1992). "Our Responsibility to the Seventh Generation: Indigenous Peoples and Sustainable Development." Winnipeg, Man.: International Institute for Sustainable Development (cited in Carr, 1996 #1170, 12).

Crenson, M. (1971). *The Un-Politics of Air Pollution.* Baltimore: John Hopkins University Press.

Deblonde, Marian. (1995). "Environmental Economic Scientists and Politics." Paper presented at IRNES Conference, Keele University.

DLI. (1996). "Licenses and Inspections." *Philadelphia Internet Page* (20 July): 2.

Dobson, Andrew, and Paul Lucardie (eds). (1993). *The Politics of Nature: Explorations in Green Political Theory.* London: Routledge. Reviewed by Ian Thompson, 1994.

Douthwaite, Richard. (1992). *The Growth Illusion.* Dartington, UK: Green Books.

Dunleavy, P., and D. King. (1990). "Middle-Level Cities and Control of Urban Policies." Paper presented at PSA Urban Politics Group, June, London School of Economics.

EDK. (1996). "Corporate Irresponsibility: There Ought to Be Some Laws." New York: EDK.

Fairweather, Ben. (1992). "Deriving Environmental Obligations from Property Rights." Paper presented at IRNES (Interdisciplinary Research Network for Environmental Studies) Conference, Sheffield.

Ferraro, Giovanni. (1995). "A Communicative Planing Theory at Work. Patrick Geddes Planner in India, 1914–1924." Paper presented at ninth AESOP Congress, August, Glasgow.

George, Henry. (1937). *A Perplexed Philosopher*. London: Henry George Foundation of Great Britain.

George, Henry. (1947). *The Condition of Labour: An Open Letter to Pope Leo XIII*. London: Land & Liberty Press.

George, Henry. (1953). *Progress and Poverty*. London: Hogarth Press.

Gibbs, D. (1993). Manchester: *The Green Local Economy. Centre for Local Economic Strategies.*

Goldsmith, Mike. (1993). Local Government: In R. Paddison, B. Lever, and J. Money (eds.) *International Perspectives in Urban Studies 1*. London: Jessica Kingsley.

Goodchild, R., and R. Munton. (1985). *Development and the Landowner: An Analysis of the British Experience*. London: Allen and Unwin.

Gore, T., and D. Nicholson. (1991). "Models of the Land-Development Process: A Critical Review." *Environment and Planning A* 23: 705–730.

Habermas, J. (1975). *Legitimation Crisis*. Boston: Beacon Press (cited in Carr, 1996 #1170, 15).

Harper, Thomas L., and Stanley M. Stein. (1995). "Sustainable Planning: Is a Paradigm Shift Required? "Paper presented at Ninth AESOP Congress, August, Glasgow.

Healey, P. (1983). *Local Plans in British Land Use Planning*. Oxford: Pergamon Press (cited in Gore and Nicholson, 1991).

Healey, Patsy. (1992). "Planning Through Debate: The Communicative Turn in Planning Theory." *Town Planning Review* 63(2):143–162.

Healey, Patsy, Paul McNamara, Martin Elson, and Andrew Doak. (1988). *Land Use Planning and the Mediation of Urban Change: The British Planning System in Practice*. Cambridge: Cambridge University Press.

Hoggett, Paul. (1995). "Does Local Government Want Local Democracy?" *Town and Country Planning* (April 1995): 107–109.

Horrocks, Ivan, and Jeff Webb. (1994). "Electronic Democracy: A Policy Issue for U.K. Local Government?" *Local Government Policy Making* 21(3): 22–29.

Jacobs, Michael. (1991). *The Green Economy: Environment, Sustainable Development and the Politics of the Future*. London: Pluto Press.

Jacobs, M. (1993). "A Green Route out of Recession." *New Ground* (34): 4–5 (cited by Gibbs, 1993, p. 15).

Kivell, Philip. (1993). *Land and the City: Patterns and Processes of Urban Change*. London, Routledge.

Kramer, Ludwig. (1995). "Recent Developments in EC Environmental Law." Paper presented at The Impact of Environmental Law in the United Kingdom, conference, London University, Centre for the Law of the European Union.

Kuhn, T. (1970). "Natural Science and Its Dangers." In Lakatos and Musgrove (eds.), *Criticism and the Growth of Knowledge.* Cambridge: Cambridge University Press (cited in Harper Stein 1995, p. 4).

Leopold, Aldo. (1949). *A Sand County Almanac.*

Lovelock, J. (1979). *Gaia: A New Look at Life on Earth.* Oxford: Oxford University Press (cited in Nijkamp, 1994, p. 13).

Lukes, S. (1974). *Power: A Radical View.* London: Macmillan (cited in Heap, 1993).

Lundmark, Carina. (1995). Green Seeds to Democratic Thought Within Swedish Political Parties." Paper presented at IRNES Conference, Keele University.

McDonough, William. (1993). "Design, Ecology, Ethics and the Making of Things." Paper presented at Centennial Sermon, February 7, Cathedral of St. John the Devine, New York City.

Meadows, Donella H. (1974). *The Limits to Growth.* New York: Universe Books.

Kant, (1785/19). *Principles of the Metagdysies of Ethics.*

Newell, Peter. (1995). "The Fossil Fuel Lobbies and the Politics of Global Warming." Paper presented at IRNES Conference, Keele University.

Norton-Taylor, Richard. (1982). *Whose Land is it Anyway? Agriculture, Planning and Land Use in the British Countryside.* Wellingborough, UK: Turnstone Press.

Ophuls, William. (1977). *Ecology and the Politics of Scarcity* (vol. 3). San Francisco: Freeman (cited in Orr, 1992, p. 68).

Orr, David W. (1992). *Ecological Literacy: Education and the Transition to a Post-modern World.* Albany: State University of New York Press.

Plato. (1955–1987). *The Republic.* (p. 7, bk. VI). Harmandsworth: Penguin (cited by Rose, 1985, p. 8; Stewart, 1992).

Poulton, Michael C. (1995). "The Strange Relationship of Zoning and Planning." Paper presented at the Ninth AESOP Congress, August, Glasgow.

Rawls, J. (1971). *A Theory of Justice.* Cambridge, MA: Harvard University Press (cited by Beatley, 1994, p. 21; Heap, 1992, p. 319).

Robertson, James. (1974). *Profit or People? The New Social Role of Money.* London: Calder & Boyars.

Robinson, Nick. (1995). "The End of the Road for Roads? The Royal Commission on Environmental Pollution as a Spur to Change." Paper presented at IRNES Conference, Keele University.

Rose, Jack. (1985). *The Dynamics of Urban Property Development.* London: E&FN.

Ross, M. (1995). "Goods and Life Forms: Relativism in Charles Taylor's Political Philosophy." *Radical Philosophy* (May-June) (cited in Harper and Stein, 1995, p. 4).

Simmie, J., and S. French. (1989). *Corporatism, Participation and Planning: The Case of London.* Oxford: Pergamon.

Strong, Carolyn. (1995). "The Influence of Children on Family Purchase of Environmentally Friendly Grocery Products. Paper presented at IRNES Conference, at Keele University.

Thornley, Andy. (1991). *Urban Planning Under Thatcherism: The Challenge of the Market*. London: Routledge (cited by Simmie, 1993, p. 10).

Tickell, Oliver. (1996). "Healing the Rift." *The Independent on Sunday Review* (August 4).

Van der Krabben, Erwin. (1995). *Urban Dynamics: A Real Estate Perspective— An Institutional Analysis of the Production of the Built Environment*. Amsterdam: Thesis.

Watson, Glenn. (1992). "Recycling Disused Land in the Black Country: Developing a Model of the Recycling Process. PhD. dissentation, Oxford University.

Westra, Laura. (1994). *An Environmental Ethic Proposal for Ethics: The Principle of Integrity*. Lantham, MD: Rowman & Littlefield.

Will, George F. (1993). *Restoration: Congress—Term Limits and the Recovery of Deliberative Democracy*. New York: Free Press.

Yiftachel, Oran. (1996). "Planning and Social Control: Towards a New Understanding." Paper presented at Local Planning in a Global Environment, July 25–28, Toronto, Canada.

III ENVIRONMENTAL ISSUES

9 GOOD INTENTIONS, POOR EXECUTION: ETHICAL DILEMMAS OF THE SUPERFUND LEGISLATION

Ellen S. Weisbord

Pace University

Abstract

Since their adoption in the late 1970s, the various environmental regulations known collectively as the Superfund laws have given rise to a plethora of compliance problems for owners of commercial and industrial properties. Criticism leveled at the Superfund laws has been based upon the widely held view that existing remediation standards are both economically and logistically indefensible. Such criticism appears valid in light of the actual results of the legislation: exorbitant cleanup costs and minimal cleanup.

In addition to this much publicized imbalance between cost and result, existing environmental laws have spawned unethical and illegal behaviors which are designed to keep property owners away from the scrutiny of governmental oversight agencies. These behaviors can be described in brief as "hide the problem" (don't remove the contamination), "hide the waste" (dump it illegally), and "hide the clean-up" (keep even valid clean-up efforts secret from the government).

This paper argues that the Superfund legislation has cast an inequitable burden upon small firms that do not have the magnitude of resources required to bear the cost of compliance, and that the root of the injustice is a standardized and centralized system of enforcement. The legal and unethical behaviors are a result of this failure of environmental justice. The development of a systematic approach to voluntary environmental compliance, specifically tailored to small commercial and industrial property owners, which would increase equity—and thus compliance—is proposed.

Introduction

Since their adoption in the late 1970s, the various environmental regulations known collectively as the Superfund laws have given rise to a plethora
of compliance problems for owners of polluted commercial and industrial
properties. These problems relate to all environmental media including
air, water, and land and primarily involve processes applicable to waste
generation, handling, treatment, storage, and disposal.

Criticism leveled at the Superfund laws has been based on the widely
held view that existing remediation standards are both economically and
logistically indefensible. Compliance procedures under existing laws are so
costly and so cumbersome that they reduce funds available for actual
cleanup and may be perceived as devices to line the pockets of specialized
lawyers and consultants. Most unfortunately, existing regulation serves
to cause otherwise moral people to seek methods of circumvention and
avoidance rather than compliance.

It is the intent of this chapter to discuss the problems of the Superfund
legislation within the specific context of its inequity to small commercial
and industrial property owners. To avoid scrutiny by governmental oversight agencies, property owners engage in unethical[1] and illegal behaviors
that can be described in brief as "hide the problem" (don't remove the contamination), "hide the waste" (dump it illegally), and "hide the cleanup"
(keep even valid cleanup efforts secret from the government). The argument to be presented is that the financial ramifications of environmental
injustice—resulting from (1) the standardized application of regulations
demanding that all waste be cleaned to maximum pristine levels and (2) the
frequent placement of cleanup responsibility on the wrong party—create a
burden that is particularly unjust to small property owners with limited
resources. The legal and unethical behaviors mentioned above are a result
of this failure of environmental justice.

In the sections to follow, both the concept of environmental justice and
the particular inequities to small commercial and industrial property
owners are addressed. First, two views of current management thought concerning the relationship of the organization to the natural environment are
discussed. Stakeholder theory is presented as the normative perspective
underlying the more radical position. Next, the stakeholder perspective is
related to the concept of environmental justice, which is used as an underpinning to explain illegal and unethical behavior. The history of the Superfund legislation is then reviewed and the causes of its inequity examined;
the absence of real and perceived fairness of the distribution of benefits and

burdens is argued to be the result of a centralized and standardized system. Finally, a voluntary environmental compliance program for industrial and commercial property owners based on self-regulation and third-party oversight is proposed as a solution that would increase equity—and thus compliance—and still be protective of the environment.

The Role of the Natural Environment in Organization Studies

Treatment of the natural environment is an important and controversial subject that has evoked tremendous sociopolitical as well as economic interest and that people respond to with considerable passion. Thus, it is not surprising to find a burgeoning interest in this topic by organization theorists—a recent volume of *The Academy of Management* containing a special topic forum on ecologically sustainable organization, a new journal *Organization and Environment*, and a new Academy of Management interest group Organizations and the Natural Environment (ONE). To this group of thinkers, illegal and unethical behaviors would come as no surprise.

A wide range of ideas exists regarding the proper place for the natural environment in a contemporary discussion of business organizations. The most radical approach calls for a full revamping of the management paradigm. Proponents of the need for paradigmatic change argue that management theory is consistent with an *anthropocentric paradigm*, defined as "the belief that there is a clear and morally relevant dividing line between humankind and the rest of nature, that humankind is the only principal source of value or meaning in the world" (Eckersley, 1992, p. 51). They call for a reconceptualization of organizational environment to give centrality to the natural environment, exhorting us to move from understanding the environment from an organizational viewpoint to understanding the organization from an environmental viewpoint (Shrivastava, 1994). The new paradigm would reflect an ecocentric perspective, viewing ecosystems as having worth independent from human value judgments. The *ecocentric responsibility paradigm* (Purser, Park, and Montuori, 1995) is based on efforts to maintain, preserve, or restore the health of ecosystems. The goal is the achievement of sustainable organizational development—that is, organizational development that "meets the needs of the present without compromising the ability of future generations to meet their own needs" (WCED, 1987, p. 43).

At the other end of the spectrum, the approach to the "greening" of organization studies is what the more radical theorists refer to as an "egocentric" orientation (Purser, Park, & Montuori, 1995). Egocentric organizations defend the legitimacy of maximizing shareholder value. Within this rubric, "corporate environmentalism" is concerned with the management of organization problems created by the natural environment. The criticism leveled at this type of environmental management is that concern with the environment is limited to issues that threaten the egocentric identity of the firm (Boje and Dennehy, 1993). The objectives of firms with an egocentric orientation are to protect their reputation; protect themselves from legal liability; improve cost effectiveness, safety, and quality; and satisfy the sense of morality of corporate leaders (Post and Altman, 1994; Brown, Derr, Renn, and White, 1993). Therefore, according to critics, corporate environmentalism will result in policies, standards, and procedures for guarding the environment only when it is in the firm's self-interest.

Clearly, these two views are at considerable odds. One group places the individual and the firm at the center of the universe, while the other would bestow equal rights on all components of a ecological system.

Two traditional perspectives on the primacy of objectives in managerial decision making underlie these two positions. One holds maximization of shareholder wealth to be the appropriate guiding principal of management; therefore, it advocates corporate environmentalism as "an accommodation that addresses some of the worst environmental excesses while deflecting demands for more radical change" (Levy, 1997, p. 129).

The second perspective holds that principled moral reasoning ought to motivate management decisions (Quinn and Jones, 1995); it embraces stakeholder theory, which contends that all stakeholders (those with legitimate interests in the corporation) are of intrinsic value and that each stakeholder group merits consideration for its own sake. Stakeholder theory gives each of the various groups a moral interest, commonly referred to as a *stake*, in the affairs of the corporation (Donaldson and Preston, 1995).

The environmentally oriented proponents of the stakeholder theory—believing that humanity is ethically responsible for the world's ecological integrity and ultimately vulnerable, like all other species, to the harms that humans inflict upon nature (Rosenbaum, 1989)—argue that the natural environment should be treated as a legitimate organizational stakeholder. Indeed, Shrivastava's (1995) assertion that nature (and derivatively, human welfare) is the stakeholder at greatest risk from industrial activities is the basis for his proposal of a new, alternative ecocentric paradigm for management—that of sustainable organizational development.

Environmental Justice

Environmental justice refers to the fairness and equity of environmental regulation. Its foundation is the concept of distributive justice—the fair apportionment of benefits and burdens.[2] The basis of distributive justice is determined by the goal of the regulation (Deutsch, 1985). For example, when the objective is economic productivity, the basis for fairness is often equity; an individual's relative input determines his relative share of the benefits. For social objectives, the intent of fair distribution is usually to create equality. In areas of personal development and welfare, need may serve to determine fairness. The concept of property rights is also based on fundamental ideas of distributive justice. Therefore, it is legitimate for property rights to include restrictions from harmful uses that would impact other stakeholders (Donaldson and Preston, 1995).

According to proponents of environmental justice, the need for environmental protection and the need for social justice can be mutually exclusive and often is (Wenz, 1988). Analysis of data related to U.S. environmental lawsuits concerning Superfund hazardous waste sites have shown that cleanup of toxic Superfund sites takes longer to occur, the level of cleanup is less rigorous in communities of color than in white communities, and those who pollute are likely to pay significantly lower fines if they pollute in communities of color than in white communities (Head, 1995).

Studies further show that race is the most salient demographic characteristic for the siting of commercial hazardous waste facilities. While all socioeconomic groups resent the nearby siting of major facilities, the middle and upper socioeconomic strata possess better resources to effectuate their opposition (Head, 1995). As a result, the current environmental justice movement is rooted in poor and oppressed communities, organized around ecological demands in response to particular corporate offenders, and characterized by a sharp awareness of power relationships in environmental politics (Wallis, 1997).[3]

Theories of distributive justice that underlie environmental justice are not limited to technical environmental matters but are applicable to a broad range of moral issues. Their concern is the manner in which scarce benefits and burdens should be allocated (Wenz, 1988). Thus, while the environmental justice movement has focused on the issues of the poor and underrepresented in matters of environmental safety, it can appropriately be applied to any group in which burdens are unfairly placed. In addition to the victimization of low-income and minority communities that lack the political clout to keep their neighborhoods free of unwelcome waste disposal sites, there are other biases. For example, it is financially disadvantageous for certain businesses to conform to environmental requirements when their competitors (such as foreign companies) do not have to meet the same criteria.

Stakeholder theory unites the academic proponents of the paradigm of sustainable organizational development with the environmental justice movement. The environmental justice movement rejects environmental strategies that marginalize politically weak groups, skewing the distribution of costs and benefits to the powerful (Levy, 1997). In this way, the Superfund scheme has cast an inequitable burden on small firms that do not have the magnitude of resources required to bear the cost of compliance.

Effective enforcement of any regime requires cooperation based on a perception of justice on the part of the governed. In the case of many small commercial and industrial property owners, there is a perception of inequity. As a result, those falling under the jurisdiction of the legislation often do not feel compelled or willing to conform their behavior to the law.

History of the Superfund Laws

For many years following the industrial revolution, dumping toxic waste in commercial landfills and waterways was considered a practical and socially acceptable solution to growing waste-management needs. By the late 1970s, however, abuse of the environment had become cause for alarm. Chemicals once considered helpful were being reevaluated as harmful. The city of Love Canal, New York, had to be evacuated.[4] Public perception embraced the tenet that quality of life and life expectancy were adversely affected by a lack of control over chemicals in the workplace, and state and local governments began to be blamed for doing an inadequate job of protecting the public from industry.

In response to public outcry, the U.S. Congress enacted the Resource Conservation and Recovery Act of 1976 (RCRA) and the Comprehensive Environmental Response, Compensation and Liability Act of 1980 (CERCLA). RCRA imposed cradle to grave responsibility on waste generators, transporters, and persons involved in the treatment, storage, or disposal of hazardous waste. CERCLA (commonly referred to as the Superfund legislation), enacted in 1980 and considerably fortified by the Superfund Amendments and Reauthorization Act of 1986 (SARA), was intended to clean up contaminated property and to develop and enforce uniform standards for identifying, evaluating, using, handling, working with, and disposing of hazardous substances. In addition, the legislation developed a national list of toxic sites and established procedures with the objective to clean them up.

As described in John Pearce and Linda Riesenman's (1995, pp. 3–5) history of the waste management industry,

> [When] the EPA identified the potentially responsible parties (PRPs) of the site contamination, it forced the parties to either perform the remediation or reimburse the Superfund Act trust account for an EPA-contracted cleanup. Under SARA, PRPs were defined as persons who arranged for waste treatment or disposal at a site, persons transporting the waste to a site, present owners and operators of waste disposal facilities, and previous owners and operators of waste disposal facilities. If a PRP refused to perform a remedial action, treble damages could be levied.
>
> In the event that PRPs could not be identified, the cleanup was financed out of the trust account. This account was funded primarily from a feedstock tax on petroleum producers and on manufacturers of certain chemicals. Congress approved an annual Superfund operating budget of $1.8 billion per year through 1995. Although the EPA investigated more than 30,000 hazardous waste sites, only about 1,200 of the most seriously contaminated sites made the EPA's National Priority List.
>
> Accountability of PRPs under SARA was promoted by three standards of liability that relieved the EPA of the burden of proof in most cases: strict liability, joint and several liability, and retroactive liability. To charge a PRP with strict liability, the EPA need not prove that the PRP acted negligently in its handling or disposal of waste. There was no defense to the strict liability provisions of SARA. Under joint and separate liability, the PRP could be held responsible for the entire cleanup even though the PRP's contribution to the waste problem was relatively small. Retroactive liability existed for actions that had occurred before CERCLA was enacted if they continued to present a hazard.
>
> As of 1986, SARA was extended to cover all federal agencies. [More recently, the EPA has shifted the responsibility for administering compliance programs to the states.]

The adoption of environmental protection legislation further raised public consciousness of the dangers presented by hazardous wastes and the necessity of proper procedures for dealing with them. Moreover, an entire industry of hazardous waste management was spawned: consultant services for permit preparation, environmental audits, compliance audits, risk assessment studies, laboratory analyses, and remedial investigations and feasibility studies (RIFS) that define a contamination problem and propose solutions; remediation services that include on-site activities such as incineration and chemical stabilization; and various treatment services that differ based on the specific nature of the hazardous material to be dealt with.

Results of the Legislation: Inequity and Noncompance

Though well intended, existing environmental legislation has effected few positive results. The Superfund costs the government and the private sector $4.14 billion annually (47 percent of which is unrelated to cleanup). In 1993, projections of the program's eventual total costs exceeded $1 trillion, factoring 26,000 identified sites with administrative and transaction costs (primarily legal fees) ranging between $300 to 700 billion (Graves, 1993). The number of sites identified for cleanup is increasing at the rate of 2,000 to 3,000 a year; by 1995 the number was over 30,000 (Shrivastava, 1995). About 1,300 sites are currently listed on the National Priorities List (because they represent active danger to human health), and the number may eventually grow to 3,000 (Grumbly, 1995).

Despite this outpouring of money, actual cleanup has been negligible. The Superfund Reform Coalition reports that only 291 of the identified 1,300 national priority sites have been cleaned to date.

One reason for the minimal scope of cleanup is related to the cleanup process itself. RIFS usually take three to five years to complete, and most cleanups cannot begin before the studies are finished and after the complicated and sophisticated *Record of Decision* has been obtained—almost always involving extensive public participation. The actual site cleanup may then take up to twelve to fifteen years (Lane, 1995).[5]

Exorbitant process costs diminish cleanup efforts as well. The regulatory scheme fosters legal gridlock and incentives to delay compliance and site remediation; litigation can be less costly than cleanup. Rules often make profitable the frustration rather than the accomplishment of cleanup by offending firms, at the same time providing windfalls for the lawyers who slow down the process via litigation.

For example, a firm faced with an assessment of $50 million for a cleanup may well choose to spend $10 million for the fees and costs of a ten-year contest of the assessment rather than to do the cleanup—hoping for a savings of $40 million or, even in the event of loss, avoiding the problem for many years and possibly reducing liability. Moreover, lawyers and insurers for potentially responsible parties will generally hunt for others to share legal and financial responsibility, creating a legal gridlock. Though legal, the ethics of this behavior is arguable.

Other causes underlying the problem and particularly germane to small commercial and industrial property owners stem from the centralized and standardized governance structure of the legislation.

The Problem of a Centralized Administrative Structure

The existing centralized administrative system is ineffective in applying the legislative program to small property owners. It is typical in a bureaucracy for systems, procedures, planning, and bureaucratic momentum to take precedence over leadership and responsiveness (Mintzberg, 1979). The inability to see the big picture and a greater concern for process than outcome are quintessential bureaucratic dysfunctions that in the case of small commercial/industrial property owners have led to haphazard oversight and long delays.

Indeed, the major complaints by small and medium-sized businesses against the federal Environmental Protection Agency (EPA) and state Departments of Environmental Conservation (DEC) pollution-prevention programs and against government and private-sector recycling and waste-reduction audit programs are (1) lack of attention to detail in the compliance measures themselves, especially in the followup how-to of implementation, monitoring, reporting, dealing with haulers, contractors, and suppliers, and many other details, (2) lack of knowledge of the business itself from both technological and financial points of view, and (3) inadequate use of better, cheaper emerging technologies and preventive measures that turn out to have been overlooked (Reaven, 1997).

Because the regulations governing waste generation, handling, treatment, storage, and disposal as well as site cleanups and liability are extremely complex, compliance requires mastery of a vast body of rules, procedures, and technologies. Navigating this regulatory maze requires extensive time and resources, which is particularly cumbersome to small property owners. Truly sustainable development depends on a trend toward decentralization and the distribution of economic power (Miller, 1995). Bureaucracy precludes the type and degree of attention necessary for the small property owner, and so the agencies are perceived to be inconsistent, unreasonable, and unjust.

The Problem of a Standardized, One-size-fits-all Solution

Blame for the perceived environmental injustice of the Superfund laws and consequent lack of success in their enforcement also rests with the standardized structure of the legislation—that is, the application of standard, one-size-fits-all solutions implemented through central federal or state oversight. The current standard of cleanup is pristine-based or carcinogen-based rather than risk-based. That is, regardless of the future use of the property—whether industrial or residential—current regulations demand that cleanup be undertaken to eliminate waste on every property to the extent that groundwater is brought to a drinkable level.

The inherent unfairness is in imposing such a standardized system in widely disparate situations. Site characteristics present a wide variety of business uses and site-specific physical characteristics. Both result in vastly different means and levels of actual and potential contamination. As a result, the levels of cleanliness appropriate to different sites are not the same. It is neither necessary nor realistic for effective waste pollution control to assume that every property needs to be cleaned to a drinkable level. By using a standard cleanliness measure, acceptable preventive activities (activities undertaken to maintain the integrity of property in the day-to-day operations of ongoing businesses) and remedial activities (activities undertaken to accomplish cleanup) are not commensurate with projected risk and the likely impacts to those groundwater resources recharging existing and future drinking water aquifers.

In short, the result of this standardized approach has been the imposition of unduly onerous cleanup costs on many properties. This legal, but unethical, regulation poses particular hardship and injustice to smaller property owners with limited financial flexibility. A more ethical paradigm for cleanup of contaminated sites might result from moving away from the viewpoint of "how to assure cleanup that brings groundwater to pristine levels" and toward "how much contamination can we safely leave in the ground."

A second issue related to standardization is the blanket imposition of strict, joint, and several retroactive liability standards. More than 100,000 potentially responsible parties have been identified at Superfund sites. Often, these are not Fortune 500 companies but small businesses (McKee, 1995). The strict liability standards of the Superfund legislation have caused tremendous hardship to many of these small (and often blameless) property owners.

For example, the owner of a thirty-acre property on Long Island, New York, purchased for commercial redevelopment and use, has spent ten years and $1 million in cleanup costs to remove hazardous contaminants from the property, despite the fact that the U.S. Environmental Protection Agency acknowledged that his company was not at all responsible for creating the polluted conditions. This burden fell on the second-generation owners of a family business who had acquired the site under the management of their father (who suffered an accidental death). Without knowledge of the existence of contamination and without the benefit of an environmental audit when it was purchased (not a requirement at the time), there was no question of blame or of equity (Harris, 1995). To date, the appropriate governing agency has not signed off on the cleanup, and the property remains an identified Superfund site.

The arbitrary imposition of responsibility is further illustrated by the example of an eighty-four-year-old Oregon widow who owned a small commercial building that she bought with the proceeds of a loan in the hope of providing herself with security in her old age. The property site apparently had been contaminated by waste products discarded by its dry cleaner tenants some forty years earlier, who conformed to disposal standards accepted by the community in the 1950s. Faced with full liability for cleanup costs, the widow could attempt to distribute the burden of the environmental cleanup among others, such as the prior owners, the companies that supplied the offending chemicals, and the insurers of the building for periods before environmental hazards were written out of liability coverage. The cost of spreading the burden, primarily attorney fees, would be hers, however, since the property owner remains fully responsible notwithstanding the existence of other, equally responsible, and more culpable parties (Kortge, 1995).

While legal, it is easy to argue that it is unethical for Congress to pass laws that do not fairly place the burden of cleanup on those who caused the problem.

Illegal and Unethical Responses to Inequity

For want of a reasonable process to solve a manageable problem, current laws provide disincentives to legal and ethical behavior on the part of potentially affected parties. Such parties are encouraged to hide contamination conditions (that is, to do no cleanup at all), to hide the illicit waste (by disposing of it illegally), and even to hide the fact that a proper cleanup has been accomplished from the legal system (to avoid potential complications of the agency process).

Disincentive 1: Hide the Problem

The issue of cost is the primary driver behind this breach of legal *and* ethical behavior. The most cost-efficient approach is to hide rather than rectify problems, to do no cleanup at all. While failure to notify the EPA that a problem exists is not legal, the costs incurred in following the protocols required to perform the mandated RIFS are prohibitive, so much so that the cost of the RIFS can be greater than that of the actual cleanup. To avoid incurring this expense, owners maintain a low profile by avoiding involvement with the EPA and thereby avoiding the directive to undertake RIFS.

An added inhibitor of open remediation is the fear of having property publicly listed as a Superfund site. The National Priorities List (NPL) of Superfund sites was developed using, initially, a model (the Mitre model) that selected candidates for the NPL based on available site data. Thus, a site with no available field data would not and could not qualify as a candidate for the list.[6] Further, once a property is involved in an agency (EPA or DEC) action, bureaucratic red tape and, often, issues of agency turf[7] make it very difficult to permanently close the case. At best, the market value of a property designated as a Superfund site is reduced. Worse, property that is contaminated can't be financed or, in some instances, insured. Developers are afraid to touch these *brownfields*. Since an unresolvable liability issue under the Superfund laws would destroy the value of any parcel of real estate, avoiding public disclosure of the condition or of unapproved remediation is clearly in the property owner's best interest.

Disincentive 2: Hide the Waste

Environmental legislation stipulates that contaminated soil must be isolated, dug out, and shipped to a secure landfill, where it is to be put back into the ground or stored in drums. The same legislation further stipulates that even after hazardous material is shipped (legally) from an owner's property to a landfill, the owner retains responsibility for any problem that may occur in connection with that soil forever. Thus, not shipping the contaminated material or not reporting a spill substantially reduces the risk of being held accountable for contamination and reduces concomitant expenditures of time and money.

On the other hand, when the EPA or DEC does become aware of contamination at a site, there are no limits on what they can ask the property owner to do. Failure to comply can result in the levy of heavy fines; continued resistance may lead to the property being listed as a Superfund site. The EPA or DEC could then impose and implement its own testing and cleanup program and hold the owner responsible for all costs.

Disincentive 3: Hide the Cleanup

Responsible behavior by a property owners, short of self-incriminating and wastefully expensive confession to a prosecution-minded governmental agency, results in his criminalization under existing laws. While it is legal to ship regulated substances from one's own property, the property owner is legally bound to report the shipping. In doing so a paper trail is created, potentially bringing the property owner to the attention of the governing agencies. Thus, fear of the consequences of being subjected to the agency process provides an incentive to hide even proper cleanup.

Responsible property owners do exist who are proactive in implementing environmental compliance programs in which qualified inspectors investigate tenant practices to identify and correct environmental problems. These owners hide their efforts, however, for fear of the system. They do not report problems they find or cleanup they accomplish to relevant government agencies; thus they break the law, although they truly behave in an ethical manner.

An Illustration

The following hypothetical story, based on a true case, illustrates some of the issues raised above. In an upscale warehouse complex on Long Island, an environmental compliance team (hired by the property owner) observed a fifty-five gallon drum in the rear doorway of one of the tenant businesses. A hose coming out of the drum was draining liquid into the soil behind the building. Near the drum were open containers of chemicals that had been used to clean metal objects manufactured by the tenant. The team told the tenant-owner of the business that what he was doing was illegal and demanded that he stop dumping immediately. The tenant-owner said the liquid solution was weak and wouldn't hurt anything. The team then took samples of the solution and soil, notified the property owner immediately, and showed her photographs of the illegal spill.

The property owner called an environmental attorney, who advised that if contacted, the EPA or New York State DEC would, in all likelihood, fine the offending tenant $100 and hold the landlord personally responsible for the entire cleanup cost.

The property owner confronted the tenant, whose position was that no one could prove any wrongdoing on his part. The tenant claimed to have personally tested the water in the drum and determined that it was clean. So challenged, the property owner reasoned that the tenant would claim to have never dumped at all, or perhaps just that once, and would assert an inability to afford any further tests and reports. If informed, the DEC would direct the property owner to pay for everything and sue the tenant. A suit would be costly and judgment collection unlikely. If evicted, the tenant might well close shop, relocate, and reopen under a new (and insulated) corporate name. If the tenant were vindictive, chemicals might even be intentionally spilled on his property and reported to the DEC anonymously (the property owner had heard several such stories).

Tests revealed that the contamination was almost six feet deep and extended under the foundation of the building. The tainted soil would have to be removed. Legally, this had to be reported to the New York State Department of Environmental Conservation. The property owner knew that once the DEC was notified, a lengthy and costly series of tests and reports would have to be compiled before any cleanup could begin. The owner estimated that, with the government involved, the cost of cleanup would be increased by a minimum of $30,000 for additional tests, oversight, and legal fees. Instead of one qualified consultant and testing laboratory assessing the problem and supervising the cleanup, the government would require an investigation done in triplicate. Additional consultants and testing laboratories would be needed to oversee and double check the entire process. A thick technical report following a government format would have to be prepared at the property owner's expense and analyzed by the agency before any solutions could even be proposed. All things considered, the cost of cleaning under DEC regulations could exceed the value of the property.

The property owner decided not to report the contamination.

Wanting the contaminated soil removed before rain washed it deeper into the ground, making it harder to clean up, the property owner hired an environmental consultant to clean up the spill following government guidelines. The results of the cleanup were the same as if the government had been involved; however, the process took about forty-five days instead of eighteen months and cost $15,000 instead of $45,000. The tainted soil was excavated and shipped to a legal landfill. This was the proper thing to do but against the law because the government wasn't notified of the spill and didn't grant permission to clean it up.

The tenant's lease will not be renewed. However, the property owner will not sue the true wrongdoer to recover costs because to do so would expose her own illegal acts.

As this tale demonstrates, the Superfund legislation has created strong incentives for unethical and illegal behavior by small property owners with regard to the disposal and cleanup of hazardous wastes. The legislation encourages property owners to hide the problem (take no remedial action at all and let waste stay in the ground), hide the waste (dispose of hazardous material in illegal dumping areas), and even to hide cleanup efforts (cover up proactive steps to maintain a clean property).

Existing Programs and Competitive Disadvantage for Small Property Owners

Large corporations are better able than small ones to both avoid and protect themselves from onerous legislation. For the small commercial or industrial property owners, an important source of the real and perceived inequity in the apportionment of burdens is the prohibitive costs of pollution control, which reduce the ability of all but the deepest pockets to comply with regulations and still be competitive. The motivation to avoid actions that might place smaller, poorer firms at competitive disadvantage encourages defensive behaviors that are illegal and unethical and thwarts progress toward ecological sustainability.

As the mountain of data collected and articles written demonstrates, a great deal of attention has been paid to the problems of the Superfund legislation. Proposals for Superfund reform that are currently circulating through Congress range from a total repeal of retroactive liability for periods prior to 1987 to the provision of tax credits for costs incurred in cleaning up sites. In addition, these proposals address the need to develop generally applicable cleanup standards for commonly found hazardous substances, to define cost-effective, generic remedies for different types of sites, to establish procedures for selecting a remedy at a particular site, to issue a standard protocol for risk assessment, using realistic assumptions, and to allow the parties bearing the economic burden to more fully participate in the remedy selection process (Grumbly, 1995).

Approaches to address the problems have come from both the government and the private sectors. Market-based regulatory approaches such as emissions taxes and government-issued tradable permits, which "instill costs upon firms in proportion to the amount of environmentally harmful outputs they generate," are argued to be far more efficient and effective than the traditional command-and-control regulations (Starik and Rands, 1995) typically employed by government regulatory agencies. Interestingly, these government-issued rights to pollute the environment draw bids not just from big utilities but also from environmental groups that can buy them and retire them, keeping them out of the hands of utilities companies (Taylor and Kansas, 1993).[8]

While some argue that marketable permits programs are a creative approach to controlling aggregate pollution emissions, others are against them on the grounds that the approach will not serve to move pollution out of the neighborhoods that incur the greatest burden.

Another opportunity to reduce disincentives to sustainability-oriented behavior is through peak organizations (Maitland, 1985) such as trade associations and other umbrella organizations. These influential organizations can promote environmentally proactive behavior by creating "sustainability-oriented self-regulatory programs" and by "encouraging and assisting other organizations to simultaneously adopt sustainability-oriented actions and achieve economic success" (Starik and Rands, 1995, p. 924).

Private organizations and governmental agencies can also work together to develop alternative models of self-assessment programs for property owners. One such program is the Risk-Based Corrective Action program (RBCA), an alternative cleanup program limited to oil spills. The genesis of RBCA was the recognition by both the oil industry and the regulatory agencies that the overwhelming number of spill sites, and the costs concomitant with their cleanup under current remediation criteria, warranted a need for alternative cleanup criteria at petroleum release sites. In response to this need, the American Society for Testing and Materials (ASTM)[9] formed a committee to develop a more streamlined risk-based approach to the assessment and remediation of petroleum spills. The committee, which included researchers from various oil companies, consultants, and academics, produced a document entitled "Guide for Risk-Based Corrective Action Applied at Petroleum Release Sites." The ASTM also created a training program aimed at state regulators, whose agencies would benefit from RBCA both economically on their own sites and in prioritizing sites so that their limited resources could be focused on those sites truly needing attention. The New York State DEC required the oil companies to provide several sites for a demonstration project. NYSDEC then used the demonstration sites to calibrate their own guidance documentation, which was a modification of the ASTM standard, using input from the New York State Department of Health.[10]

A more recent sign of government interest in streamlining the rigid pollution framework is a federal pilot program that allows businesses to devise their own pollution control plans—plans that must commit participating companies to exceed existing environmental standards. In return, participants benefit from the opportunity to simplify regulatory requirements and avoid enormous bureaucratic effort and costly regulatory delays. Several companies are currently involved in this Clinton administration initiative, including Intel Corp. and the Minnesota Mining and Manufacturing Corp. (fifty companies in total are expected to participate in the project) ("U.S. Seeking Options," 1996).

These pilot programs offer a way out of the regulatory maze but only for large companies. Although the development of compliance plans take a considerable amount of time, having a legally binding agreement in place with the EPA provides businesses with a competitive edge by saving even more time, as when, for example, manufacturing processes change and approval for new processes would otherwise have to be sought from the government. However, it is only the largest companies that have the resources to develop their own unique plans. Therefore, although the basic principles are much the same, a different approach is needed to address the regulatory issues faced by many owners and operators of commercial and industrial properties.

A Proposed Program

A comprehensive environmental compliance program specifically developed for commercial or industrial property owners and operators, decentralized through the use of third-party certification, and specifying specific waste-disposal methodology based on site category, is proposed as a viable solution to the legal and ethical quagmire that has been the result of the Superfund legislation for this stakeholder group. This proposal is for a unified program for environmental auditing, monitoring, reporting, permitting, pollution prevention, waste minimization, recycling, and so on that would be tailored, implemented, and evaluated for each commercial or industrial participant.

In the envisioned program, written guides would be prepared for participating participants. Protocols would be arranged with EPA and DEC. Auditing of compliance would be handled by properly licensed, bonded environmental consultants, much the way towns use fire marshals and building inspectors. The program would thus have three components— technical (engineering solutions for maintenance and cleanup procedures), administrative (the practical details of costs, work duties, training, contracts with haulers, accounting, and just general hand holding of participants), and regulatory and legal (third-party certification and oversight mechanisms).

Such a program should minimize waste emissions to the air, water, and land. It should make legal compliance easier and more agreeable than illegal and unethical hiding behaviors by allowing for the prevention and correction of existing environmental problems with a minimum of agency red tape and cost.

To assess the benefits of decentralization in terms of the issues raised earlier in this chapter, we can look at the extent to which each of the three unethical and illegal behaviors would be affected by the proposed compliance program.

Hide the Problem

The issue of cost was identified as the primary driver of this behavior. A streamlined process free of undue bureaucratic red tape would be more equitable in terms of cost. For one, there would be less time and money spent in completing the protocols currently necessary before even getting to the actual cleanup. For another, a clear and user-friendly system would enable property owners to avoid excessive attorney and consultant fees. A more streamlined and less expensive system would also reduce the property owner's need to look for other PRPs with whom to share the financial burden, reducing legal fees even further. As a result of all this, the costs attached to cleanup of contamination could be brought in line with what would be considered fair and reasonable, generating a perception of equity on the part of property owners and resulting in a greater willingness to assume what costs there are rather than hide the problem.

Hide the Waste

Clearly, the relationship between the EPA and the small property owner is an antagonistic one: the EPA does not trust the property owner to take proper steps in protecting the environment, and the risk of being held accountable for contamination and subject to EPA or DEC directives motivates the property owner to illegally dispose of waste. A less bureaucratic, more decentralized system might motivate property owners to operate their businesses in an environmentally sound manner. Establishing qualification standards for private environmental consultants and establishing a framework within which they can supervise property owners' compliance programs—absent the huge costs generally associated with agency cleanup—should thus encourage legitimate methods of compliance.

In an added benefit, shifting the bulk of the workload to the private sector will reduce agencies' monitoring and enforcement costs and free up the agencies to focus on the most serious sites.

Hide the Cleanup

The current system stymies self-regulated compliance because of the complex nature of environmental laws that are difficult to decipher, often involve overlapping jurisdiction of several layers of government, and waste economic resources on remedies that are not site-specific. Providing commercial and industrial owners the tools to meet and exceed regulatory requirements at a savings from current costs of compliance will foster a compliance environment in which property owners are not reluctant to identify minor problems that might be caused by an occupant *before* they become a major expense. This will allow environmentally conscious behavior in which maintenance is addressed proactively and problems are corrected sooner. Moreover, by maintaining the cleanliness of their properties, cost savings will be generated by avoiding problems altogether.

Conclusion

America has a long tradition of wealth creation through the production of goods and services without regard for the effects of production technology on the environment. For decades, however, the public has shown an increasing sensitivity to the protection of the ecosystem. According to a 1984 public opinion poll by the U.S. Department of Justice, industrial criminal polluters are considered to be worse in the public eye than armed robbers, ranking in seventh place after murder but ahead of heroin smuggling. Commitment to environmental protection is no longer the exclusive domain of a small environmental protection movement. Today, public concern for environmental quality has reached an all-time high, with a majority of the public identifying themselves as environmentalists (Dunlap and Rik, 1991). There has been a change in both the intended and actual behavior of Americans, who are increasingly responsive to environmental protection.

The rising tide of concern about the environment has led to government intervention in the form of environmental regulations meant to repair damage caused by past transgressions and to prohibit future destruction of ecosystems. Unfortunately, the execution of these legislative remedies has been seriously flawed. Legislation has been particularly neglectful of small commercial and industrial properties, although this sector is a significant contributor to society's overall environmental problems.

Although tenants and operators may want to do what is right for the environment, many are simply not aware of the proper procedures for the storage and disposal of both hazardous and flammable materials.

Typically, when an inspector from an environmental agency visits a facility, all communications are between the tenant or operator and the agency. Often, it is not until a notice of violation is issued that the property owner is made aware of an environmental problem at the property—a problem that the property owner may be responsible for correcting. Out of fear of the regulatory maze of environmental requirements that currently exists, owners of commercial property, even those businesses that attempt to comply with applicable regulations, are rarely in full compliance with the law. Laws that should serve to protect the environment instead impose regulatory burdens that make criminals of ordinary citizens.

I have argued in this chapter that effective enforcement of the Superfund laws has been unsuccessful mainly due to the inherent unfairness of imposing a standardized, centralized system on widely disparate situations. Numerous property owners lease property to tenant-operators—from electronics manufacturers and defense contractors to everyday neighborhood businesses, such as dry cleaners, printers, and photographic processors—that store, use, and dispose of a variety of hazardous materials. Regardless of the size and the complexity of the operation, there are a variety of environmental regulations that companies in all of these industries are required to follow. Because the laws are perceived to be unfair, as well as unwieldy, property owners fail to comply with them.

The remedy proposed is the move toward programs that are decentralized and that take a risk-based rather than standardized approach, matching cleanliness levels with land use. Effecting a change from a centralized program that relies on government oversight to a decentralized program that includes private-sector monitors will result in a far more efficient system. Tailoring maintenance and cleanup methodology to specific land-use conditions will result in a system that is far more environmentally just. Under a fair and efficient system of user-friendly environmental compliance, property owners will be motivated to undertake voluntary self-maintenance and to behave lawfully and ethically.

The struggle to repair damage caused by years of misguided disposal of hazardous waste has been largely ineffective, and attempts to prevent future damage equally weak. Public sentiment demands a strong fight against environmental abuse.

Notes

1. There are many ethical theories, including theories with specific application to business (see, for example, Beauchamp and Bowie, 1993; Donaldson and Werhane, 1993). It is beyond the scope of this chapter to present a comprehensive discussion of this topic. Instead, the discussion of ethics here rests on the core principles recognized in most moral philosophy, which include avoiding harm to others, respecting the autonomy of others, avoiding lying, and honoring agreements (Quinn and Jones, 1995).

2. Justice takes two forms in our society, distributive and retributive. Retributive justice is punishment for disobeying the law. Retributive justice is inadequate to enforce environmental legislation because those who profit from environmental abuse may be far removed, in both

proximity and time, from their victims. The concept of environmental justice must be based, therefore, on principles of distributive justice.

3. In 1994, President Clinton signed an executive order to "ensure that all communities and persons across this nation live in a safe and healthful environment." The order called for federal agencies to include an analysis of environmental justice—the fairness of the distribution of burden—in all future federal regulations. That mandate reflects the frustration that has come from inequities in the apportionment of burden in environmental legislation.

4. In 1942, the Hooker Chemicals and Plastics Corp. (corporate predecessor to Occidental Chemical Corp.) leased a site in the city of Love Canal, New York, and began dumping 25,000 tons of industrial waste into an old canal bed and adjacent pits. When the site was graded over and sold in 1953 to the Niagara Falls School Board, there was little public awareness of the potential health hazards (though the deed did acknowledge that the waste was buried there). An elementary school and hundreds of homes were built over the buried chemicals. The toxic waste that had leached into the groundwater and soil over a period of twenty-five years contaminated much of the city, resulting in a disproportionately high number of birth defects and miscarriages among the residents. A settlement between the federal government and the Occidental Chemical Corp. (for $129 million) did not occur until 1995.

5. Once the EPA or DEC becomes aware of contamination at a site, there are no limits on what they can ask the property owner to do, such as requiring the property owner to sample the soil behind every tenant's door and in every storm drain in the parking lot and to check the ground water at a variety of places on and off the property. Failure to comply can result in the levy of heavy fines; continued resistance may well lead to the property being listed as a Superfund site. The EPA or DEC could then impose and implement its own testing and cleanup program and hold the owner responsible for all costs.

6. This has resulted in an NPL that fails to include certain sites with serious problems, including instead sites with less serious problems, as well as many large and complex defense sites that can't realistically be cleaned up cost effectively with current technology.

7. For example, in the case of the Long Island property owner, a RIF was conducted according to a New York State DEC directive; just after it was finished, the EPA requested one of its own.

8. Further, since companies can either use their permits to comply with clean-air laws or they can clean up their operations and sell their unused permits to other utilities, pollution-rights auctions effectively turn the right to pollute into a commodity to be traded like grain or pork bellies.

9. The ASTM is an independent group that developed the national standard for Phase I of the Environmental Site Assessment, a due-diligence standard for transfer of property, refinancing, and so on established under CERCLA to allow owners to qualify for the use of the innocent-land-owner defense. The ASTM is currently working on developing the standard for Phase II of the Environmental Site Assessment.

10. The use of risk-based corrective action and the ASTM standards has been supported by the EPA's Office of Solid Waste and Emergency Response (OSWER) in the case of underground storage tank (UST) release sites. A recent policy statement sent to state managers of UST corrective action programs, "Directive 9610.17: Use of Risk-Based Decision-Making in UST Corrective Action Programs," stated as its purpose "to encourage the use of risk-based decision-making as an integral part of the corrective action process at sites where leaking underground storage tank (UST) systems have released petroleum products into the environment and thus created risks to human health and the environment" (OSWER Directive, p. 1.)

References

Beauchamp, I., and N.E. Bowie. (1993). "Ethical Theory and Business Practice." In T. Beauchamp and N.E. Bowie (eds.), *Ethical Theory and Business* (pp. 1–48): Englewood Cliffs, NJ: Prentice-Hall.

Biblow, C., C. Niemcyzk, C.A. Rich, and E. Weisbord. (1996). "Cleanup Cures for Risk-Based Environmental Sites: A Voluntary Environmental Compliance Program for the Nineties." *Proceedings from World Workplace '96*, 1: 103–111.

Boje, D., and R. Dennehy. (1993). *Management in a Postmodern World*. Dubuque, IA: Kendall-Hunt.

Brown, H.S., R. Derr, O. Renn, and A.L. White. (1993). *Corporate Environmentalism in a Global Economy: Societal Values in International Technology Transfer*. Westport, CT: Quorum.

Cushman, J.H. Jr. (1996a). "Many States Give Polluting Firms New Protection." *New York Times*, April 6, sect. 1, pp. 5, 16.

Cushman, J.H. Jr. (1996b). "U.S. Seeking Options on Pollution Rules." *New York Times* May 27, p. 11.

Deutsch, Morton. (1985). *Distributive Justice*. New Haven: Yale University Press.

Donaldson, T., and L.E. Preston. (1995). "The Stakeholder Theory of the Corporation: Concepts, Evidence, and Implications." *Academy of Management Review*, 20: 65–91.

Donaldson, T., and P.H. Werhane. (1993). "Introduction to Ethical Reasoning." In Thomas Donaldson and Patricia Hogue Werhane (eds.), *Ethical Issues in Business: A Philosophical Approach* (pp. 5–17). Englewood Cliffs, NJ: Prentice-Hall.

Dunlap, R.E., and S. Rik. (1991). "Trends: Environmental Problems and Protection." *Public Opinion Quarterly* 55: 651–672.

Eckersley, R. (1992). *Environmentalism and Political Theory*. Albany: State University of New York Press.

GAO Report. (1995). "Superfund: Legal Expenses for Cleanup-Related Activities of Major U.S. Corporations." *GAO/RCED-95-46* (March 13).

Graves, T.J. (1993). "Clean Up Superfund's Legal Problems." *Legal Backgrounder* 8(39).

Grumbly, T.P. (1995). "Lessons from Superfund." *Environment* 37(2): 33.

Harris, R. (1995). "Liberty: Its Past, Present and Future." *Farmingdale Observer* 35(23) (February 17).

Head, R. (1995). "Environmental Equity Justice Centers." In B. Bryant (ed.), *Environmental Justice: Issues, Policies and Solutions* pp. 57–66. Washington, DC: Island Press.

Jennings, P.D., and P.A. Zandbergen. (1995). "Ecologically Sustainable Organizations: An Institutional Approach." *Academy of Management Review* 20: 1015–1052.

Kortge, C.S. (1995). "Taken to the Cleaners." *Newsweek* (Oct. 23), p. 16.

Lane, E. (1995). "Superfund Peril: New Danger Seen in Overhaul Bill." *Newsday*, Nov. 5, sect. A, pp. 7, 53.

Levy, D.L. (1997). "Environmental Management as Political Sustainability." *Organization and Environment* 10: 126–147.

Maitland, I. (1995). "The Limits of Business Self-Regulation." *California Management Review* 27(3): 132–147.

McKee, K.C. (1995). "Testimony November 08, 1995 Kathryn McKee Legislative Representative National Federation of Independent Business; Before: Subcommittee on Water Resources and Environment House Committee on Transportation and Infrastructure; Subject: Superfund Reform." *Capitol Hill Hearing Testimony*, Federal Document Clearing House.

Miller, M.A. (1995). *The Third World in Global Environmental Politics*. Boulder, CO: Lynne Rienner.

Mintzberg, H. (1979). *The Structure of Organizations*. Englewood Cliffs, NJ: Prentice-Hall.

Pearce, J.A., and R. Robinson. (1995). "Note on the Hazardous Waste Management Industry." In J.A. Pearce and R. Robinson (eds.), *An Industry Approach to Cases in Strategic Management* (2nd ed.). Chicago: Irwin.

Post, J., and B. Altman. (1994). "Managing the Environmental Change Process: Barriers and Opportunities." *Journal of Organizational Change Management* 7: 64–81.

Purser, R.E., C. Park, and A. Montuori. (1995). "Limits to Anthropocentrism: Toward an Ecocentric Organization Paradigm?" *Academy of Management Review* 20: 1053–1089.

Quinn, D.P., and T.M. Jones. (1995). "An Agent Morality View of Business Policy." *Academy of Management Review* 20: 22–42.

Reaven, S.J. (1997). *Stony Brook Environmental Compliance Project for Business and Industry*. Stony Brook: State University of New York at Stony Brook.

Rosenbaum, W.A. (1989). "The Bureaucracy and Environmental Policy." In J.P. Lester (ed.), *Environmental Politics and Policy: Theories and Evidence*. Durham: Duke University Press.

Shrivastava, P. (1994). "Castrated Environment: Greening Organizational Studies." *Organization Studies* 15(5): 705–726.

Shrivastava, P. (1995). "Ecocentric Management for a Risk Society." *Academy of Management Review* 20(1): 118–137.

Starik, M., and G.P. Rands. (1995). "Weaving an Integrated Web: Multilevel and Multisystem Perspectives of Ecologically Sustainable Organizations." *Academy of Management Review* 20(4): 908–935.

Taylor, J., and K. Kansas. (1993). "Environmentalists Vie for Right to Pollute." *Wall Street Journal*, March 26, p. C1, C14.

U.S. Department of Justice. (1984). "Use of Risk-Based Decision-Making in IST Corrective Action Programs." *Bureau of Justice Statistics Bulletin, OSWER Directive 9610.17.*

"U.S. Seeking Options on Pollution Rules." (1996). *New York Times*, May 27, p. 11.

Wallis, V. (1997). "Lester Brown, the Worldwatch Institute, and the Dilemmas of Technocratic Revolution." *Organization and Environment* 10: 109–125.

Wenz, Peter. (1988). *Environmental Justice*. Albany: State University of New York Press.

World Commission on Environment and Development (WCED). (1987). *Our Common Future*. Oxford: Oxford University Press.

10 "BROWNFIELDS": ARE THEY AN ETHICAL SOLUTION TO A MAJOR URBAN POLLUTION PROBLEM?

Robert J. Shedlarz

Department of Finance College of Business University of Akron

Karen Eilers Lahey

Department of Finance College of Business University of Akron

Abstract

"Brownfields" are unused urban manufacturing sites that are not being recycled because the potential costs of environmental cleanup may vastly exceed their current market value. This chapter addresses the ethical issues involved in recently legislated state solutions to this environmental problem. It posits the following question: If "greenfields" are unattainable and "deadfields" are unacceptable, are state certified "brownfields" a reasonable and ethical compromise?

Introduction

Environmental issues have had a significant impact on real estate transfers since the passage of the Comprehensive Environmental Response, Compensation, and Liability Act of 1980 (CERCLA),[1] with environmental liability for owners and lenders under federal law continuing to evolve. While this has made it difficult and costly to sell and redevelop old manufacturing and commercial sites in major urban areas, at least a partial solution to the allocation of environmental liability has emerged under state law with the passage of "brownfields" legislation.[2] With an accompanying federal program[3] to bolster the concept, the ethical ramifications of this environmental remediation forms the subject of this chapter.

Ethical Questions

When faced with the cost of an environmental survey and cleanup of urban property, should the seller or the buyer be responsible? To what extent should the government dictate or influence this decision? If parties other than the immediate transferor and transferee are to share these expenses, how should this be determined? To what extent should the government dictate or influence this additional liability and in what format?

Ultimately, as these various costs are distributed in time and space the ethics of the allocation devices and ultimate results must be considered. Who should bear them on an interim basis: government, business, or individuals? Do the ethics of capitalist economics dictate the interim financial benefits by restoring commercial properties to the tax rolls that ultimately "trickle down" to local residents who have to trade off increased government solvency for slightly "dirty" commercial neighbors? What environmental sacrifices should be made so that business profits translate into jobs? These are all questions that have a moral basis.

As the environmental effects of industrial development have been ignored for most of our history, an answer has been provided for the allocation of the burden of industrial waste and toxic by-products of this system. Everyone pays, but those who benefit most from the industrial development pay the least, and those who benefit least pay the most. This no longer appears to be a satisfactory ethical solution to the problem of pollution.

Creation of the Problem

This traditional response to pollution was directly embodied in the classical method of transferring real property. It is expressed in the Latin doctrine *caveat emptor* or "let the buyer beware." The seller had no incentive to provide for environmental safety as the doctrine shifted ownership of the property to a buyer who was solely responsible for the problem. The cycle continued, and the property became more and more contaminated. Eventually this contamination migrated from the site to adjacent properties. Historically, remedies were unavailable, since the legal system presented a Catch 22 response based on the common law of nuisance. Private-sector nuisance suits were not allowed as the eventual pollution problem degraded a group of properties. On the other hand, public-sector nuisance suits were not available since there were no laws putting the government in the pollution control business. As a result, the legalities actually ignored industrial pollution, and we had the ethical quandary of allowing business to profit at the expense of individuals who were harmed by the pollution.

In this primitive state of affairs, dilution was the only solution to pollution. As the toxic effects of a polluted environment became well known, this was no longer a satisfactory resolution. Reduction of the generating of environmental hazards, pretreatment, and cleanup of past toxic wastes became the solution to pollution.

Seller Disclosure of Information

Given this change in the nature of responsibility, how are mechanisms devised to deal with the reality of today? If the *caveat emptor* basis for real estate transfers might still have some credence, then it is ethically important for the buyer to be informed. The necessary information can be provided by the seller.

If it is in the seller's best interest to provide the disclosure, then it can be done without the coercion of governmental sanctions (Roulac, 1993).[4] One way is to provide a statute or judicial decision that states that the general "as is" implications of a real estate transfer do not apply to environmental problems.

If a seller wants to preserve the allocation of the environmental risk to the buyer, then the seller must provide more disclosure than the traditional, boilerplate expressions, either expressed or implied, of "as is," "where is," or "with all faults". A disclosure by the seller to the buyer will also encourage the buyer to conduct further investigations of the property to determine the extent of the environmental problem and the cleanup costs.

An example of a deed transferring a gas station could contain the following language:

> And grantee has carefully inspected the premises and acknowledges that the premises has been used as a service station or related purpose for the storage, sale, transfer, and distribution of motor vehicle fuel, petroleum products, or derivatives containing hydrocarbons, and that such fuel, products, or derivatives may have been spilled, leaked, or otherwise discharged into the premises and accepts conveyance.

For prior uses other than a service station, appropriate variations in this language could be used. It can be effective in providing for the traditions of the real estate transfer, while additionally ensuring that there is no unfair advantage taken of the buyer in terms of what otherwise could be a very expensive cleanup.

For example, In the mid-1980s, a buyer was purchasing a service station that had been used for retail sales of gasoline. Since this was before the state insurance funds for underground storage tanks had become available in the particular state where this property was located, there was little if any direct governmental oversight with regard to this transfer of property. It was generally known in the petroleum industry that a certain amount of cumulative contamination from spillage was normal and to be expected. However, a purchaser who had no knowledge of this contamination and who also expected to change the use of the site would purchase such property at their peril.

In this instance, as an ethical requirement, although not at the time a legal one, the seller informed the buyer of the environmental condition of the property and clearly indicated that the buyer was assuming the risk of any required remediation of the premises. Not only was the language used here to exonerate the seller from any liability to the buyer for contamination and remediation costs, but the parties discussed the potential costs, and the purchase price was negotiated with this contingency in mind. When the buyer took title and demolished the exiting service station structure, it then excavated for the concrete pad for its new building to be used as a fast-food take-out facility. Contamination was indeed encountered, and a degree of remediation was required, which was done by the buyer at its own expense.

In this instance, two parties dealing with an environmental problem effectively paid for a substantial portion of the remediation with funds that represented a negotiated reduction of the original proposed purchase price. A fully informed buyer made a proper choice as to the purchase of the property, and a seller avoided potential litigation once the contamination was discovered.

Seller Assumes Responsibliity for Cost

There are circumstances, however, where placing the burden of environmental problems on the buyer may be inappropriate. While a moral obligation certainly exists to inform the buyer of the potential pollution risks in the property purchase, the remediation cost should not be shifted to a buyer who is unable to financially assume the cleanup costs. Based on federal law, if the buyer's obligation to remediate cannot be fulfilled, the seller remains liable anyway.

This presents a more complicated set of problems with a more definite set of parameters to describe the various options to be undertaken and the pollution problems that might appear. In this more intensive investigation, the parties must deal with both the requirement of some sort of environmental assessment and the allocation of the risks that the assessment reveals through language providing for an environmental indemnity. Since these issues must be addressed at the beginning of the real estate transaction, language for providing for them would appropriately appear in the purchase agreement of the parties. Dealing first with the environmental assessment situation, a purchase agreement could contain the following language:

> ENVIRONMENTAL ASSESSMENT: Seller will, at Seller's expense, perform or cause to be performed an environmental assessment of the premises, with a Phase I assessment being the minimum requirement, along with whatever additional tests and procedures such Phase I assessment reveals as necessary or advisable. The results of such tests, procedures, and assessments should be within acceptable limits, as provided for by law or regulations or as generally accepted in the industry, whichever limits are most strict. Such test results, in documented form will be provided by the Seller to the Buyer immediately on their availability. In the event that this environmental assessment reveals contamination requiring remediation, then the Seller or Buyer may immediately cancel this Agreement. In the event that contamination requiring remediation is revealed and the parties mutually agree to proceed with this Agreement, then the Seller, at the Seller's sole expense, shall cause the premises to be remediated. Such remediation shall proceed until a "no further action letter" or its equivalent is received from the appropriate governmental authority.

This language provides a very definite set of parameters for the parties to agree on and, as an ethical proposition, describes who owes what to whom with great clarity. By making the seller responsible for the remediation, the seller retains control over the situation and can thus ensure that past contamination is remediated and does not come back at some distant time in the future. At the same time, the ethical consideration of responsibility for cleanup is placed where it ought to be—with the seller—and the buyer is assured that the remediation will be done at the seller's expense.

Since the advent of various laws dealing with strict liability for cleanup costs incurred by the government that relate back to prior owners in the chain of title, it is in the seller's best interest to ensure that any needed remediation is discovered and taken care of at the time of transfer. In this manner a seller may be able to exonerate itself for future financial claims by the government for remediation costs. Any future contamination will be done by someone other than the seller or its predecessors in title. Thus, it would not be ethical for a seller to be required to contribute to future remediation costs if the site was free of contamination when it left the seller's ownership and control. If the seller takes charge of remediation, it has a way to prove that it should not be held liable for future discoveries of contamination.

Alternatively, the wording can be used if the seller wished to retain control of remediation because the cost of such cleanup is being financed, at least to a significant extent, by insurance available in the private sector or with some available state assurance cleanup fund. Such third-party insurance funds are for the seller's benefit, and it is important to make sure that they provide the protection that the seller's insurance premiums covered.

Buyer Responsibility for Costs

Conversely, a variation of this language can place the risk and cost of remediation on the buyer when special circumstances dictate this direction. For example, if the seller is in the process of liquidating a Chapter 11 proceeding, it makes no sense to allocate the cost to the seller since it has no money to pay for this work and in any case the bankruptcy judge and Chapter 11 trustee would be very unlikely to approve any setting aside of scarce funds for such an undertaking.

Indeed, the bankruptcy situation may require the buyer to assume the risk of remediation with any state assurance fund assistance available to the buyer only if this type of language is used in the purchase agreement and included in some fashion in the order of the bankruptcy court approving the property transfer. In this fashion, the property can feasibly be sold, and the proceeds can then be divided among the seller's creditors in as fair a manner as bankruptcy law will allow.

Environmental Indemnity

To make sure that the seller lives up to its responsibilities for a cleanup, there should be further language in the purchase agreement to continue the seller's liability for the environmental problems through the use of an environmental indemnity provided in the agreement:

ENVIRONMENTAL INDEMNITY: Seller shall indemnify and hold Buyer harmless from and against any and all claims, damages fines, judgments, penalties, costs, liabilities, or losses (including, without limitation, any and all sums paid for settlement of claims, attorney's fees, consultant fees, and expert fees) arising as a result of hazardous substances that were present in, on, or about the Premises prior to the date of closing, that were placed or released in, on, or about the Premises by Seller or Seller's predecessor in title, or that may have migrated onto the Premises from adjacent property, prior to closing. This indemnity shall survive the closing and remain binding on the Seller.

As used herein, the term "hazardous substances" shall mean, without limitation, any substance, material, or waste defined as "hazardous substances," "hazardous materials," or "toxic substances" in the Comprehensive Environmental Response, Compensation, and Liability Act of 1980, as amended, 42 U.S.C.A. sec. 9601 *et seq.*; the Hazardous Materials Transportation Act, as amended, 49 U.S.C.A. sec. 1801 *et seq.*; the Resource Conservation and Recovery Act of 1976, as amended, 42 U.S.C.A. sec. 6901 *et seq.*; the Federal Water Pollution Control Act Amendments of 1972, as amended, 33 U.S.C.A. sec. 1251 *et seq.*; the Toxic Substances Control Act of 1976, as amended, 15 U.S.C.A. see. 2601 *et seq.*; the Safe Drinking Water act of 1974, as amended 42 U.S.C.A. sec. 300f *et seq.*; and any comparable, analogous, or related provisions of federal law or the laws of any state, and all rules or publications adopted or promulgated pursuant to any of the preceding laws, codes, regulations, rules, or statutes.

This certainly encourages the seller to "take care of business" when it comes to environmental issues of potential environmental risks.

Technological Difficulties

Comprehensively shifting the environmental risks and costs to the seller and providing for notice to the buyer of this arrangement will work only as long as technology provides the appropriate data for a site assessment. If a clean standard is demanded, then science must provide the assessment mechanisms, the cleanup techniques, and objectively measurable standards to judge when both have been accomplished. With regard to many types of environmental problems, the demand is more than technology can effectively deliver.

As noted earlier, the technology for generating pollution is as old as the industrial revolution; the technology for cleaning up the environment is in its infancy. Since the knowledge embodied in science proceeds to a significant extent on a linear basis, there is a significant amount of "catchup" that cleanup must undertake. Science has, at present, a great deal of difficulty delivering solutions to pollution.

In its primitive infancy, the science of pollution control can in most instances accomplish a limited set of goals. It can move pollution to more acceptable areas and package it in more acceptable ways. Pollution management is the best available technology in many situations.

Both sellers and buyers must also contend with the reality of the technology that detects pollution. It is the many instances flawed and thus unreliable. For these reasons many potential buyers are not willing to undertake the risks of purchasing a property that is known to have been previously contaminated. The exact extent of the contamination is often unknown to a significant degree, and thus the cost of cleanup is to the same extent unknown. Even if this has been allocated as a risk and expense to the seller, what if the seller goes out of business? What if the seller goes bankrupt?

The feasibility of providing a cleanup for contaminated sites to a level of no detectable contamination at all can be a daunting enterprise with its own potentially expensive and unreliable results. As a consequence, particularly in areas previously used for industrial enterprises, the incentives to provide any present or future productive reuse would not be provided by any mechanisms indicated so far in this chapter.

"Brownfields" Legislation

In a perfect world, there would only be "greenfields" perpetually unspoiled by the effects of industrialization. In the real world, industrialization has historically generated side effects that degrade the environment. In numerous instances, a cost-versus-benefit analysis indicates to a prospective buyer that the property cannot profitably be restored to its pristine original condition (Simons, 1994).[5]

If the efforts of governmental remediation overwhelm public budgetary constraints, then no cleanup at all occurs, and past urban industrial sites sit unused as the "deadfields" of our cities—dangerous environmentally and a burden economically, since unused industrial sites do not generate property tax revenues. In these instances it is ethical to consider a compromise, and this is embodied in what is known as "brownfields" legislation.

The first state to pass legislation dealing with industrial waste cleanup was New Jersey's Environmental Clean-up Responsibility Act (ECRA),[6] which Gerber (1992, p. 177) states is the "first and most comprehensive state property transfer law." It influenced many other states to pass similar legislation. Unfortunately, the New Jersey system requires government approval before the property transfer closes. The process of an overworked bureaucracy can result in delays lasting months before a government inspector finally reaches a particular property transfer. As a matter of ethics, there is the specter of having the delay result in the cancellation of the commercial development project. "Time of transfer" administrative backlogs can generate costs that are shifted to those who are unwilling to pay them.

Starting in the early 1990s, a few states have passed legislation that attempts to break the log jams created by CERLA and state Superfund legislation such as New Jersey's ECRA. These statutes attempt to make it possible for a voluntary cleanup program that has definite goals, government supervision, lender assurances, and speedier reuse of the property. O'Reilly (1994) discusses legislation passed in Indiana in 1993 and cites legislation passed by Michigan (1993) and Oregon (1991). The discussion in this chapter of "brownfields" legislation is based on the Ohio law passed in July of 1994.[7]

In essence, these laws encourage voluntary cleanup of contaminated property by buyers who plan to reuse these sites for industrial purposes. These buyers are not required to restore these sites to a "greenfields" condition but are to make particularly certain that existing pollution will not migrate offsite. Property tax abatements at the local level can help to finance the cleanup costs, and the state provides a level of certainty in terms of costs by setting standards for site assessments and cleanups and agrees not to sue the buyer for any further cleanup.

As an ethical tradeoff, the property is restored to commercial productivity. When the property tax abatements expire, the site is returned to the local government's tax base. This "brownfields" system equitably allocates the cost of sufficient cleanup to protect the public, based on the monetary incentives present in the capitalist system.

Ethical Considerations

As an ethical proposition, would it be more beneficial to the general population to leave unused, downtown former industrial sites in their present, polluted condition or restore them to their pristine, preindustrial condition of 250 years ago, which isn't going to happen because there is no financial incentive to do this and the technology to accomplish this miracle isn't available. In the less-than-perfect world, would it be ethical instead to have these same properties restored to useful productivity for industrial purposes by having them cleaned up to a degree that the onsite pollution is remediated to a degree and no longer presents a significant risk of migrating offsite and polluting further properties? If so, the idea will work only if the government is willing both to determine who shares the risk between the seller and buyer and intervene by allocating the additional potentially unknown costs to neither the seller nor buyer but the government itself.

The problem with this solution is that the government doesn't have any money other than what it takes from its citizens. This interim shifting of liability to the government is an ultimate shifting of costs to those that the government can tax in order to accomplish these goals. In addition, to stay profitable businesses shift their tax burdens to individuals, and so it is the public at large that ultimately pays for the cleanup. Admittedly, this can present an ethical dilemma: since it is the public that ultimately benefits from the cleanup, shouldn't that same public ultimately bear the financial burden? On the other hand, why should the public pay for a problem that was actually caused by another sector of society? There is only a partial solution to this problem. If the public must ultimately bear the costs, in our capitalist system it is more efficient (and cheaper) for the business sector to bear them initially.

If the seller and buyer allocate the cleanup costs between them initially, with a level of cleanup that can be at times much less perfect, the public ultimately bears the additional risks that are unknown and might occasionally appear later. This shares the entire package of risks and costs in the most equitable manner possible. The public does not wind up with the "greenfields" of the past, but it may be willing to make do with the "brownfields" of the future in order to avoid the "deadfields" of the present.

"Brownfields" Compliance

In this practical and imperfect world, "brownfields" statutes do not provide all the answers and old fashioned due diligence is still necessary in order to avoid costly mistakes. How ethical it may be to protect people from their own ignorance or lack of business sense is an issue at this point. "Brownfields" statutes do not deal with who is responsible for what under federal law; these are state statutes. Therefore, the various devices discussed earlier in this chapter are still relevant and must be recognized since they address liability allocations between seller and buyer that need to be positioned because of U.S. federal governmental intervention in the environmental process.

If the financial solvency of the seller is being relied on to implement the seller's responsibility to the buyer in the future, than no system of documents can guarantee that money will be available to cover this responsibility. The prudent buyer must take into account this possibility.

"Brownfields" compliance is also a shifting of responsibility to the government after the initial cleanup has been completed and the government looks to the buyer to make sure that these initial steps have been accomplished. Just as the purchase of the property is a decision made voluntarily by a buyer, the compliance with a "brownfields" statute is a voluntary undertaking by that same party. The tradeoff is a "covenant not to sue" made by the state government to the buyer if it is determined that contamination has been satisfactorily addressed and cleaned up to the extent required, even though the degree of cleanup may be less than perfection.

Benefits of "Brownfields" Statutes

"Brownfields" statutes do not create a Garden of Eden. They do, however, provide sufficient incentive for the revitalization of urban parcels of real estate. In the Ohio statute, financial incentives such as real property tax abatements for up to ten years and low interest loans are available to help pay for the cleanup. The loan programs include Water Pollution Loans and Economic Development Loans.

These financial incentives are an ethical decision that shifts part of the cleanup cost from the buyer to the local and state taxpayers. In the case of the tax abatements, the increase in value to the property because of the cleanup is abated, which should lead to more property being converted into recycled "brownfields" real estate. An equitable distribution of the tax abatement cost is one that initially saves a business money, which it can spend on environmental remediation. The public receives less return in business taxes and must make up the difference via other tax revenue streams to fund the functions of government. In return, the public receives at least a somewhat cleaner environment and commercial developments provide employment. Thus, a more efficient use is made of available resources, both public and private.

The individual who participates in the voluntary program also avoids the need to obtain multiple permits, licenses, and plan approvals from the Ohio EPA because the legislation provides for a consolidated standards permit. This one-stop approach reduces both the time and costs for the cleanup.

It is also feasible for a present owner to initiate the "brownfields" benefits, since they are transferrable to a buyer in the future. The system operates to first identify the nature of the existing contamination. Within the previously discussed limits, this statutory scheme encourages the best use of technology to identify the nature of the present environmental situation and the proposed standard of cleanup based on commercial or industrial use of the property. Such applicable standards may ultimately restrict the use of this property based on the acceptable level of contamination that remains following remediation.

It is important to note that the "brownfields" scheme may also permit the present owner to seek legal remedies via a civil action against the person who caused the contamination in the past or against those who conducted business on the site and who contributed to the hazards that have been identified. This becomes a critical issue that sellers should address prior to transferring property that may later become eligible for "brownfields" treatment, and the risk allocation and shifting mechanisms detailed earlier in this chapter remain important tools.

By contrast, this liability of prior owners and operators is limited by the "brownfields" mechanism to costs necessary to protect the rest of the environment and the health of the surrounding population; it does not reach so far as to require these prior parties to pay for restoration to residential standards. Therefore, under this arrangement the present owner deals with "brownfields" compliance requirements that the state government expects this person to directly bear, but the present owner may look to past owners and operators involved in this property to recoup at least some of the remediation costs. Costs that are spread tend to be costs that are more equitably allocated, and this is part of the "brownfields" format.

Certification of Cleanup

A provision must be made for the responsibility of certifying that the agreed cleanup has taken place. Since the state basically agrees not to sue the party that undertook the "brownfields" cleanup, it would not be equitable for that same party to certify that the law has been satisfied. Governmental enforcers and inspectors might be a substitute, but since the government is agreeing not to do something (not to sue), the bureaucracy might attempt to enforce the "brownfields" standards too strictly, thus defeating its purpose and negating its benefits.

An ethical compromise is built into the system where a private-sector professional who is certified as such by the public sector must oversee the compliance procedures and certify the success and results. This ethical compromise is probably reasonable because although such a certified professional might be influenced by the owner who is paying for his or her services, the risk of losing professional certification and future livelihood is expected to be adequnte to keep honesty in the system. In addition, the number of certified professionals will rise to the level of the number needed, so that delays in the process due to shortage of oversight personnel will not occur.

This professional is the control person with regard to "brownfields" compliance, covering everything from assessing the present condition of the property to approving remediation techniques and on site machinery, if needed, to control and treat the property in the future. The risk assessments and risk solutions must be scrutinized and approved by this private-sector professional, who then recommends to the appropriate state agency that a covenant not to sue be issued by the state. This entire process must be monitored by appropriate administrative rule making and oversight, which the state government must implement and maintain.

Recording of Environmental Status

In addition, appropriate notice is provided to future purchasers or operators with regard to the property. This is accomplished by recording in the local real estate records the certified professional's "no further action" recommendations to the government and the government's covenant not to sue. These records are discoverable with a standard title search and are disclosed by the title insurance commitment.

Thus, both purchasers and lenders are made aware of the "brownfields" statutes of the property. Lenders in particular are afforded certain protection for their security interest in the "brownfields" arena but should not expect more than what is presently available under recent environmental protection regulations, which do not provide a great level of comfort.

One of the problems with the "brownfields" arrangement is that lenders may not find a sufficient level of security to justify making a mortgage loan with this kind of property as collateral. "Brownfields" is a state law, and the federal law with regard to lender liability is still problematic, despite the recently enacted Asset Conservation Act of 1996. The lender cannot purchase and operate the contaminated property itself and escape environmental liability. And, in any case, because of potential owner liability, the lender may have difficulty finding a buyer, since there is no *bona fide* purchaser protection under federal law. As a matter of degree, however, "brownfields" legislation provides a "covenant not to sue" the party that undertook the remediation. The ethics of protecting a professional lender must be tempered with the willingness to presume that lenders can protect themselves, if the law gives them the opportunity to do so. Not being sued by the state once the lender remediates the property to "brownfields" requirements is an attractive incentive to proceed with the clean up.[8]

Conclusions

As a matter of morality, is the "brownfields" scheme ethical? Considering the alternatives that are available in reality, instead of theory, the ethics are in favor of this arrangement. One of the significant risks of doing nothing is the pollution can migrate offsite and contaminate adjacent properties or reach the groundwater. The contamination of the drinking water supply is a definite hazard, and, indeed, a site is not eligible for a covenant not to sue if the groundwater under or flowing from the property is already contaminated. If the "brownfields" law limits the spread of aquifer contamination, then that alone is a sufficient justification.

From a financial point of view, the urban areas of our country are in need of every advantage; the major cities are in physical and financial difficulty, and devices to help restore them benefit those who live and work there. Restoration of jobs, financial incentives for suppliers to businesses, and more and better products locally available to consumers are all potential benefits to be realized. Also, as a matter of reality, the present system of environmental remediation has done nothing to encourage reuse of urban industrial facilities; it has done exactly the opposite and thus contributed to the longer-term problems of pollution. Pollution control is itself an ethical proposition, and "brownfields" in this imperfect world delivers the greatest good to the greatest number.

Notes

1. 42 U.S.C. sec. 9601–9675 (commonly known as the Environmental Protection Agency Superfund). This legislation had the dual purpose of cleaning up abandoned hazardous waste sites and determining who should pay for the cleanup. During the eighteen years since its passage, billions of dollars have been spent on court cases to determine who should be liable for payment, and very little has been spent on cleanup.

2. The first four states to pass "brownfields" legislation include Michigan (Mich. Comp. Laws sec. 299.614 (Supp. 1993)), Oregon (Or. Rev. Stat. sec. 465.285 (1991)), Indiana (1992 Ind. Legis. Serv. P.L. 87–1992 (S.E.A. 392) (West)), and Ohio (Ohio Rev. Code sec. 3734.30–3746.99). By 1998, all but four states (Nevada, Mississippi, North Dakota, and South Dakota) issue at least limited liability letters for "brownfields."

3. The federal program is known as the Brownfield Project. It started in Cleveland and har authorized programs in Richmond, Virginia, and Bridgeport, Connecticut. The purpose of the program is to bring together the necessary people and resources to redevelop these properties. Contact person at the federal level is Crane Harris at the EPA at (202) 260-9192. Lee A. Chilcote and John J. Gruttadaurio of Hahn-Loeser-Parks in Cleveland, Ohio, have produced a booklet called "Ohio Voluntary Real Estate Reuse and Cleanup Program" that explains the initial information available on the Ohio legislature. They can be contacted at (216) 621-0150.

4. Roulac surveys California developers in 1991 and finds that only 83 percent were aware of a 1987 state law requiring sellers to disclose the existence of hazardous substances on a property.

5. Simons estimates the cleanup costs to prepare "brownfields" sites for residential lots in the city of Cleveland. He estimates that it will cost $14,000 a lot, with the remediation costs the dominant factor. This amount is double that for land that was formerly residential and makes them noncompetitive for residential use.

6. N.J. Stat. Ann. sec 13:1K-6 to 13:1k-14 (West 1991).

7. Ohio Rev. Code sec. 3734.30–3746.99.

8. This concept has become so attractive that the EPA has a "brownfields" website supporting federal and state activities in this area. The website address is http://www.epa.gov/brownfields.

References

Gerber, Ellen JoAnne. (1994). "Industrial Property Transfer Liability: Reality v. Necessity." 40 *Cleveland State Law Review* 177 1992 (West 1994).

O'Reilly, James T. (1994). "Environmental Racism, Site Cleanup and Inner-City Jobs: Indiana's Urban In-Fill Incentives." 11 *Yale Journal on Regulation* 43 (Winter) (West 1994).

Roulac, Stephen E. (1993). "Environmental Due Diligence Information Requirements and Decision Criterial." *Journal of Real Estate Research* (Winter): 139–148.

Simons, Robert. (1994). "How Clean Is Clean?" *Appraisal Journal* (July): 424–438.

IV ETHICAL ISSUES IN THE CONTEXT OF TRANSACTIONS

11 ETHICAL STANDARDS FOR BUYERS AND SELLERS OF REAL ESTATE

Chris Manning

*Department of Finance and
Computer Information Systems
Loyola Marymount University*

Abstract

Much of what has been written and discussed about ethics in business has been in general terms and not specifically helpful to the buyers and sellers of real estate who daily must choose between ethical and unethical behavior in the marketplace. While it is not the buyer or seller's responsibility in any marketplace to protect the capital and wealth of other buyers and sellers, principles can be applied that can provide some general guidelines as to what behavior is unethical.

After discussing a conceptual framework for distinguishing ethical marketplace behavior, illustrations are used to further differentiate unethical behavior. Finally, it is suggested that in some real estate marketplace situations, there is competition to develop a reputation for honesty and compassion and that there are good business reasons, over and above ethical considerations, for being trustworthy and compassionate in these situations.

Introduction

There appears to be no code of conduct or guidelines written down anywhere to assist buyers and sellers of real estate to know what marketplace behavior is unethical or bordering on being unethical. Drawing on my personal market transaction experience and study of religions, refined through observation of corporate executive behavior, this chapter attempts to begin the process of reaching consensus on a written set of ethical guidelines for real estate marketplace participants. Toward this end, a number of unethical market practices, as well as more subtle ethical issues, are suggested. More important, however, a theoretical framework is put forth for differentiating unethical from ethical real estate marketplace behavior. It is believed that without some agreement on a perspective for how to approach differentiating unethical from ethical behavior, the effort encouraged by this chapter will not progress far.

Categorizing behavior in any marketplace as either ethical or unethical is not always easy due to the complexities surrounding both the markets themselves and its participants. Nevertheless, previously practiced acceptable marketplace behavior should not be deemed ethical merely because it has been accepted in the past by convention and practice. Such acceptable marketplace behavior may serve to further cloud determination as to whether the behavior is truly ethical.

This chapter begins by differentiating unethical from ethical marketplace behavior by examining unacceptable behavior within a profession that violates that profession's formalized code of conduct. To facilitate differentiating ethical from unethical behavior, the concepts of spiritual intuition and enlightened conscience are defined in order to serve as helpful guides in identifying unethical behavior. Examples of unethical real estate marketplace behavior are then put forth to illustrate. In conclusion, it is suggested that ethical marketplace behavior is a minimum requirement for fostering long-term business and professional relationships where trust, efficient communication of complex concepts, creativity, and a genuine concern for the other party can better serve participant goals of financial gain and personal health.

Where Can We Look to Distinguish Ethical Behavior?

The underlying teachings of the founders of many world religions (such as Judaism, Christianity, Buddhism, Hinduism, Islam, and so on) are not only similar but also can provide a starting point for distinguishing ethical behavior. Yet application of these ancient teachings to the tremendously complex ethical issues that confront overstressed real estate buyers and sellers today is a formidable challenge. It seems helpful to begin this task by first orienting ourselves to what is both illegal and unprofessional (what is in violation of a profession's formalized code of conduct) along a continuum of higher and more restrictive standards governing social behavior (Wofford, 1983).

At the far left end of this continuum (the end of less strict behavior standards) are the laws passed by a society's legislatures that establish minimal guidelines for limiting destructive social behavior. Such minimal behavior standards afforded by the laws of the land are usually aimed at preventing anarchy and securing a minimum of social justice. At the opposite end of this continuum, to the furthest right, lies the most refined set of guidelines for shaping social behavior (the end of the most limiting behavior standards). Such behavior is usually associated with (1) having genuine compassion for other people, (2) being totally honest with others, and (3) being part of a sheltered social environment (a healthy supportive family, a fraternal organization, or a religious order of brothers or sisters).

As we move to the right along this continuum away from the lower behavior limits of the laws of the land toward stricter guidelines of social behavior, we soon encounter codes of conduct in professions such as medicine, law, accounting, real estate brokerage, and real estate appraisal. Such professional codes of conduct serve to further limit unethical behavior (Wofford, 1983) as well as promote social trust and confidence in that profession. Professional codes of conduct have practical social value in addition to pointing the direction for establishing a framework for a higher, more restrictive, level of ethical behavior guidelines.

It is interesting to note that while many professions have found it to their advantage to establish codes of conduct to constrain their profession's conduct beyond what is legal, marketplace participants have rarely, if ever, done so. As a consequence, recent years have witnessed much government interest in regulating marketplace behavior to promote public trust and confidence. This has been particularly true in the stock market, where public trust is essential for the efficient investment of consumer savings. During the 1980s, government prosecution of insider trading and financial institution fraud were examples of this.

It is suggested herein that there is a zone along this continuum of stricter and stricter guidelines for acceptable social behavior, somewhere between professional codes of conduct on the left and healthy family values and bonafide religious orders on the right, where a set of standards for guiding ethical behavior among the buyers and sellers of real estate could be developed to distinguish unethical behavior. It is also suggested that an enlightened conscience exercised by knowledgeable participants in a marketplace will be valuable to assist in developing consensus and eventually formalizing a set of ethical behavior standards.

While the problem of defining exactly what is meant by *enlightened conscience* will probably remain indefinitely, much can be said to narrow down its meaning. For example, doesn't it stand to reason that knowledge and experience both of buying and selling real estate as well as spiritual intuition[1] are more likely to produce an enlightened conscience in a person than someone who has not participated in real estate markets or developed their spiritual intuition awareness? Thus, neither a spiritual saint of a religious order who is ignorant of marketplace realities, nor a respected real estate investor who has not developed their spiritual intuition skills, would have the enlightened conscience referred to here. Yet it might be said that each would be halfway there if each had the aptitude and chose to develop it.

To illustrate the exercise of enlightened conscience in the context of buyers and sellers of real estate, we can use the ethical issue of lying through omission (a seller failing to disclose information relevant to what a buyer is willing to pay for the property). For example, it is clearly unethical, in addition to being illegal in many states, for a seller of certain real estate (such as single-family detached houses in California) to not disclose known physical property defects to a prospective buyer (such as building structural flaws, geological problems, and so on). Yet in regard to information that is publicly available to a prospective buyer (such as zoning restrictions, neighborhood rents, planned developments, and so on), it is not the ethical responsibility of the seller to do a buyer's normal due diligence investigation for them. Yet between these two extremes of a seller's full disclosure to a prospective buyer lie many situations and types of information pertaining to the sale of real estate where a seller's enlightened conscience would require the disclosure of information that could result in the buyer not wanting to pay as much money for a property.

Illustrations of unethical real estate marketplace behavior

The following are illustrations of buyer behavior suggested as being unethical:

- A buyer who misrepresents their ability or willingness to pay as agreed on a mortgage note obligation given to a seller as partial payment for the purchase of real estate;
- A buyer's *mis*representation of any information to a seller during negotiations to induce the sale of real estate at a more favorable price;
- A buyer's use of purchase contract contingencies as an excuse not to go forward and comply with the spirit as well as the terms of a property purchase agreement;

- A buyer holding back material relevant information during negotiations until the last minute, which if revealed to a seller early in the negotiations would have resulted in the seller breaking off discussions and not wasting their time with this "undesirable buyer" (where a buyer misrepresents early in negotiations that they are able to, or willing to, pay more for a particular property than they really are);
- A buyer's intentional stalling of the completion of their purchase of a property to lull the seller into a compromised position and then take advantage of the seller's compromised situation to further their gain at the seller's expense (for example, the approach of the due date of a large mortgage note on the seller's property when refinancing prospects are unfavorable).

The following are examples of seller behavior suggested as being unethical:

- Intentionally providing a buyer with misleading information about a property's past rental income, expense of operation, environmental problems, financial capability of property tenants, or any other misleading information that might induce a buyer to pay more for a particular property;
- Manipulating the negotiation process through deception in such a way as to either waste the time of a buyer or place the buyer in a weakened negotiating position for their advantage (for example, a company needing to buy a property in a particular area to open a new plant or office as soon as possible).

More Subtle Real Estate Marketplace Ethical Issues

The following are questions concerning buyer and seller behavior that, while probably not considered unethical, should nevertheless cause a person with an enlightened conscience to pause and reflect on just how generous or compassionate they, as a buyer or seller, might wish to be to the other party:

- Is it the responsibility of a buyer or a seller to protect the other party from its own ignorance or failure to do adequate due diligence investigation or analysis during negotiations? (This does not refer to a real estate syndicator selling securities to investors in REITs or limited partnerships that are covered under securities laws.)

- When a distressed seller of real estate overlooks a competing alternative to a transaction or merely a more favorable alternative transaction structure, is it the buyer's responsibility to educate the seller to the overlooked opportunity?

Developing "Enlightened Conscience" in Guiding Ethical Behavior

A test of enlightened conscience might be whether a person looks for loop holes in the written agreement (or even verbal understanding) entered into with the other party to a real estate transaction. To do so suggests excessive interest in one's own position at the expense of the other party and would not meet the test of spiritual intuition discussed above.

Where a person possesses adequate real estate marketplace experience and claims to exercise spiritual intuition, a test of this person's enlightened conscience might be to reflect on a particular ethical issue from the perspective: Would you consider it unfair or unethical if the subject behavior were done to you? The answer to this question needs to be no for a particular behavior to qualify as ethical. It is unlikely that you will find people with significant spiritual intuition becoming defensive and lapsing into rationalizations for their behavior when confronted by the possibility of such an inconsistency.

One's enlightened conscience becomes challenged when people ask themselves: "Would I like it if I were on the other side of this transaction and I had happen to me what is now happening to the other party?" One's spiritual intuition would have compassion for the other party when the answer to this question is no. Yet in such cases, enlightened conscience would need to ask the additional question: "Has this person been placed in a disadvantaged position due to circumstances that I have caused?" If the answer to this second question is also no, then you probably have behaved ethically, even though the situation may be unpleasant for both parties to the transaction.

The implication here is that unfortunate things do happen to people in society through no fault of their own. Sometimes such things are caused by the unethical acts of others, but many times they result from unforseen circumstances that arise and are not due to anybody's fault but just the passage of time and events. If we compassionately witness such things and lack the resources to be of assistance, most people probably don't consider their inability to be of assistance as being unethical. In situations where one does have the resources to be of assistance to people caught in unfortunate circumstances, does it become an ethical issue?

I personally believe that possession of the resources or ability to relieve someone else's misfortune does not make a person unethical for inaction in the situation. However, such inaction does miss an opportunity to promote trust, confidence, and efficient communication in a business relationship or transaction. The following section of this chapter makes a case for the value of listening to one's spiritual intuition *beyond* ethical considerations where reputation influences how others deal with you—and that doing so in situations where the opportunity exists for repeat transactions will contribute to furthering both your and the other party's financial, mental, and physical well being.

Role of Trust and Compassion

Is what constitutes good business practice limited to what is considered to be ethical in the marketplace? In a number of real estate marketplaces, my experience suggests that good business practice encourages buyers and sellers to do more than merely conform to what has been discussed above as ethical. For example, whenever market participants become known by their actions and behavior, and such reputations are deserved as well as impact future market transactions, these participants are probably constrained by more in their dealings with each other than just ethical considerations. Many times this occurs where one party does repeat market transactions with another party and the actual experience of the parties involved replaces their need to rely on hearsay reputation of the other party.

Such a marketplace situation, where mutual trust between marketplace participants is highly valued, was described to me by a Trammel Crow executive (the developer-owner) in the presence of the senior corporate real estate executive at Grumman Corporation (the tenant). Grumman was seeking to move one of their operations to a new facility and the executive with Trammel Crow was hoping to be awarded the development contract and become Grumman's landlord on a long term lease. As common in many lessee-lessor marketplace transactions, Trammel Crow (as prospective landlord) wished to charge as much rent as possible, while Grumman wished to pay as little rent as possible. Each party's considerations in this transaction were highly complex and required each participant to think long term about a complex set of risks and rewards that would result from Grumman signing a long-term lease agreement for a yet-to-be-built facility. Since the facility Grumman was committing to lease was not yet built, significant trust on Grumman's part was required in regard to completion date of the facility, adherence to agreed on architectural plans, quality of construction, and so on in order to plan ahead with more certainty. At the same time, Trammel Crow needed a lease agreement from a reliable company to obtain first the construction financing and ultimately the take-out permanent mortgage financing. Before an appropriate lease rate, lease term, and allocation of equity ownership benefits could be agreed on, a tremendous amount of research needed to be done. This research involved gathering accurate data and doing financial modeling to adequately understand the ramifications of lease agreement terms that had yet to be negotiated.

With the Grumman and Trammel Crow executives working closely together in an atmosphere of openness and trust, the burden of data gathering and financial modeling was shared by both executives. Financial modeling assumptions—about forecast construction costs, future growth rates in property operating expenses and market area rents, how long Grumman would need the facility, and what the property could be sold for in ten to fifty years into the future—were agreed on in advance of the actual lease negotiations. This open and honest negotiation process reduced both parties transaction costs by shortening negotiations, eliminating the need for additional developer bids, eliminating much uncertainty for both parties, and eliminating unnecessary complexity from the lease agreement itself. In this environment, both executives were able to better understand each other's position and to more creatively craft an ownership structure around a sharing of the facility's development risks and economic value, such that both parties were better off.

This Grumman-Trammel Crow negotiation illustrates a marketplace situation where behavior promoting trust and cooperation between the buyer and seller of this real estate interest was needed to adequately compete for the business and get it. Compassion, openness, and understanding went beyond ethical considerations, thereby empowering the creativity of each executive to jointly arrive at an improved sharing of risk and cash flow that would not have been possible otherwise.

How often and where do these win-win marketplace situations arise? I believe that they arise frequently in marketplaces where buyers and sellers, or their representatives, negotiate directly with each other and the terms of the transaction are both complex and customized. It is not uncommon for this to be the case in real estate transactions that involve large sums of money, pools of investors, institutions, or large corporate space users. These larger transactions usually afford participants the opportunity to make bigger amounts of money for both themselves and the organizations they represent. Can we conclude from this that honest and compassionate business behavior that surpasses ethical standards, will be financially rewarding? I believe the answer to this question is yes—but not in all cases.

The theory of the firm literature (Weston, Chung, and Hoag, 1990) provides indirect support for this position. This literature discusses how some marketplace transactions for goods and services have been brought inhouse within a single firm in order to take advantage of the greater inherent trust and cooperation among negotiating parties when they are also employees within a single corporate family. This literature indicates that the more complex, customized, uncertain, and long term a marketplace contract is, the more likely these transactions will be brought within a single firm in order to (1) reduce transactions costs (negotiating, contracting, supervising compliance, remedies upon default, and so on) and (2) eliminate opportunistic behavior where marketplace competition is small or nonexistent.

The theory of the firm literature (Weston, Chung, and Hoag, 1990) supports the reasons given above for expecting honesty, openness, and compassion among marketplace participants to be financially rewarding when transactions are complex, customized, and filled with uncertainty. First, it is easier to think clearly, be more understanding of the other party's needs and concerns, and creatively come up with better transaction solutions, when both the buyer and seller are negotiating in a climate of compassion and mutual trust. Second, the other party's reputation for ethical dealings and compassion often results in shorter and simpler purchase agreements, with lower costs incurred (such as attorney fees) by both parties. Third, it is very helpful (less expensive) when complying with an agreement over time if both parties have confidence in the other's motivations and intentions when unpleasant circumstances arise. Funds and time would then not need to be wasted on unfounded concerns about the other party's seemingly inexplicable behavior, and honest answers can be expected in response to direct questions.

Furthermore, larger, more sophisticated buyers of real estate space are more likely to take the time to investigate a real estate investment situation when the seller has the reputation of going beyond ethical standards to ensure that their transactions work out well for both parties. While it is not possible to always prevent unforseen circumstances from arising that damage the other party, it is possible for buyers and sellers to work through problems more creatively and compassionately with each other.

Conclusion and Summary

This chapter attempts to initiate a dialogue on the appropriate framework from which to gauge whether specific real estate marketplace behavior is ethical. Ideally, this dialogue will be among buyers and sellers of real estate interests, service firms supporting real estate transactions, and real estate educators who train future real estate market participants. While illustrations of specific unethical behavior have been presented in this chapter, it is far more important at this stage to discuss and ultimately arrive at consensus for a framework from which to distinguish unethical marketplace behavior.

Three ideas pertaining to a possible framework have been discussed in this paper. First, it is suggested that increasing restrictions on social behavior lie along a continuum that has the laws of the land at one extreme of that continuum (that is, minimum restriction on social behavior), with the teachings of world religions, which encourage honesty and compassion, at the opposite end of the same continuum, the end that inspires people to treat each other even better than mere compliance with ethical standards.

Second, it is suggested that ethical behavior is distinguishable with an enlightened conscience that people can develop within themselves if they chose to do so. And finally, it is suggested that there are both health and financial payoffs for behaving honestly and compassionately in the marketplace, in addition to ethical considerations.

Additional ideas on the appropriate theoretical framework with which to distinguish ethical from unethical real estate marketplace behavior are needed. Once researchers begin agreeing on the characteristics of an appropriate framework to distinguish ethical behavior, then specific marketplace behaviors can be evaluated and measured against it. As more ideas are put forth on how to judge whether behavior is ethical, and as specific marketplace behavior is appropriately labeled ethical or unethical, researchers then will be able to discuss the internal consistency of the characteristics of such an evolving ethical framework. Eventually, researchers will be able to perform empirical survey research on the appeal of the various characteristics of an evolving ethical framework and check marketplace behavior against evolving ethical standards.

Acknowledgments

This study was supported in part by a research grant from the Homer Hoyt Institute, a nonprofit foundation that promotes research in real estate and land economics.

Notes

1. *Spiritual intuition*, as used in this chapter, refers to a strongly felt way of knowing the true value and measure of ideas, events, actions, and other things through the direct personal experience of profound joy and inner peacefulness, that accompanies a person's profound understanding of the truths that lie beneath. This is to say that through quieting our bodies and minds (taking a break from our overstimulated emotions and thoughts that accompany the pressures of daily living), we are able to concentrate better on present events and instinctively know things more accurately and that there is also a profound joy associated with this kind of peaceful knowing. This type of joy is not unlike the thrill of discovering an answer to a troublesome problem after concentrating long and hard on it. The field of transpersonal psychology (Walsh and Vaughan, 1993; Washburn, 1988), as well as many religious beliefs, teach that meditation and prayer facilitate spiritual intuition by disciplining focus of one's attention and awareness on singular things. Often a feeling of brotherhood with all people is present at times of true spiritual intuition.

Virtually all bonafide religions teach that (what I am calling) spiritual intuition is facilitated by practicing selfless acts toward other people and contributing to their well being. The Christian ethics of "do unto others as you would have them do unto you" and "know the truth, and the truth shall set you free" are time-tested guidelines for assisting people develop their spiritual intuition.

Development of a person's spiritual intuition is a natural result of their normal everyday life experiences and reflection. Yet most people usually spend little time and energy developing this valuable faculty of perception. This is because most people's time is usually spent securing material comfort and safety, performing obligations, seeking society's approval, or being distracted otherwise. The profound understanding and intense joy that occurs when spiritual intuition is accelerated in a person usually requires much motivation, honest inquiry, discipline, and hard work integrated with some proper education and training.

Recent research in the field of neuropsychology (Hutchinson, 1986; Kornfield, 1993) discusses this greater mental clarity achieved through harmonizing the left and right brain hemispheres. In addition, new discoveries and thinking in quantum physics, psychology (Peck, 1978; Walsh and Vaughan, 1993; Washburn, 1988), and medicine now offers support for what the original teachings of major world religions have said about human nature for centuries.

Where spiritual intuition as used here refers to the deeply felt joy associated with people knowing something without the burden of substantial data or extensive related life experiences, enlightened conscience does require a person to also digest (reconcile and integrate) a substantial amount of initially confusing everyday life experiences related to the specific ethical issue being considered.

References

Hutchinson, Michael. (1986). *Megabrain*. New York: Ballentine Books.
Kornfield, Jack. (1993). *A Path with Heart*. New York: Bantam Doubleday Dell.
Peck, Scott. (1978). *The Road Less Traveled*. New York: Simon & Schuster.
Walsh, Roger, and Frances Vaughan. (1993). *Paths Beyond Ego: The Transpersonal Vision*. New York: Putnam's.

Washburn, Michael. (1988). *The Ego and the Dynamic Ground.* Albany State University of New York Press.

Wallace, Robert Keith. (1991). *The Neurophysiology of Enlightenment.* Fairfield, IO: Marharishi International University Press.

Weston, Fred, Kwang Chung, and Susan Hoag. (1990). *Mergers, Restructuring, and Corporate Control* (pp. 26–53). Englewood Cliffs, NJ: Prentice-Hall.

Wofford, Larry E. (1983). "Ethics in the Real Estate Business." *Real Estate* (rev. ed.) (pp. 155–173). New York: Wiley.

12 ETHICAL CODES OF CONDUCT FOR BUSINESS SIMPLIFIED

The Case of the National Association of Realtors

Norman G. Miller

College of Business Administration
University of Cincinnati

Abstract

Business ethics serve to provide guidelines for behaviors toward colleagues or the publics served by the affected industry. While sometimes cumbersome and often lengthy, business codes of conduct can generally be simplified to their core essence and intentions with little difficulty. Providing such interpretations aids greatly in the teaching or understanding of such codes of conduct. The National Association of Realtors is used as a base case to illustrate the process of simplification, after a review of typical ethical concerns in the real estate industry.

Introduction to Ethics: What Is Appropriate Behavior?

Any dictionary will define *ethics* as "proper or appropriate behavior," but then what is proper or appropriate? *Ethics* comes from the Greek word *ethos*, meaning "character or custom." Some of the earliest writings on ethics are attributed to Cicero, Socrates, Plato, and Aristotle all over 2,000 years ago. Aristotle wrote *Nicomachean Ethics*, Plato wrote *Republic*, and Cicero wrote *O. Duties*, all providing some early guidelines on appropriate behaviors. In these and other writings it is clear that *a custom is a behavior that individuals can expect from other individuals in specific circumstances.* Indeed, the English might suggest that customs are the very heart of what makes society "civilized." Customs include such simple behaviors as saying *please* when making requests and *thank you* when these requests are fulfilled. Other customs are to wait in line without cutting in front of others and giving priority to filling requests based on sequence of arrival. People know that this prioritization method is the custom in most countries. Expected behaviors might also be referred to as *etiquette* when they relate to voluntary courtesies. But for more complicated interactions, such as those involved in business communications, appropriate behaviors are not always clear or universally adopted. For this reason, most professional trade associations have developed a set of expected behaviors defined over a range of interactions and encoded these in set of standards known as *professional codes of conduct* or more generally as *business ethics*.

Many professional codes of conduct are merely extensions of courtesies. Others are based on prevalent standards of morality. These would include, for example, professional codes of conduct, which admonish stealing, cheating, lying, and physically or mentally hurting others. But business ethics generally go far beyond obvious moral standards and culturally influenced standards of etiquette. Most business ethics deal with a prescribed set of typical business decisions and problems and give guidelines for appropriate methods to deal with such issues.

It is interesting to note that some people believe that ethical behaviors are obvious and absolute, and therefore the case for imposing a professional code of conduct is less relevant to a professional with good moral character. Such arguments dismiss the reality that many ethical issues are not black and white but gray, often involving mixed loyalties. It is possible to have rights and wrongs on both sides of a decision.[1]

It is idealistic to believe that we always will know what to do as espoused by movie director Spike Lee in *Do the Right Thing!* Cicero, born in 106 B.C., wrote *On Duties* and tried to provide guidance on doing the right thing when he discussed questions such as "How honest must a businessman be? How should one respond to unjust demands? Is it all right to be silent when observing an injustice against someone else?" Cicero's solution was simple, "Always do the right thing," but how do you know what is the right thing? Cicero's formula was first, do what is legal, second, do what's honest, open, and fair, and last, always keep our word no matter what the consequences. Honor, above all else, describes Cicero's view.

Cicero and Spike Lee are typical of many ethical writers who occupy a rarefied high moral ground, removed from the real concerns and real-world problems of the vast majority of business people. It is easy for those who don't make their living logging near spotted owls to ignore short-run costs in favor of long-run social responsibility. Is doing the right thing preserving the spotted owl or preserving a logger's ability to pay for his child's education or put food on the table? Real estate, like all businesses, has many such ethical dilemmas. Appropriate behaviors might be dictated not by morally prescribed views but rather prevailing customs. Andrew Stark (1993, p. 38) notes that "the fact that using inside information is considered more acceptable in real estate than in the securities business does not mean that real estate people somehow are less moral." Absent a fundamental moral principle against using nonpublic information, the ethics of doing so in any given case will depend on the goals, beliefs, and attitudes of the relevant business community. There is no single standard that will apply to all industries at all times.[2]

From an economic point of view, business ethics allow members of society and within a given industry to work together and communicate more efficiently. Trade associations like the National Association of Realtors develop ethical standards as embodied in their codes of conduct to help members deal with avoiding potential conflicts, protect the association members, protect society in general, and enhance public image. Trade associations, precisely with the objective of avoiding increased government regulation, often vigorously enforce codes of conduct.

The remainder of this brief discussion on business ethics will focus, first, on the typical ethical concerns of the real estate and, second, on the professional code of conduct espoused by the largest real estate trade association in the world, the National Association of Realtors (NAR). It is argued here that most codes of conduct can be greatly simplified into fundamental intentions. The codes of conduct of NAR are described with a focus on their basic intentions. It is hoped that this illustration assists the teacher and student of business ethics to focus less on memorizing fine print codes and more on the intentions and purpose of such codes.

Typical Agency Violations and Acts of Dishonesty in Real Estate

In representing buyers and sellers and in dealing with purchase and sale contracts, there are several common complaints against agents.[3] These include the following:

1. Acts of dishonesty, such as
    *   An agent claiming to be the procuring cause of a sale when in fact he or she was incidental to the transaction, at best,
    *   Exaggerating the market value of a property to a potential seller

in order to gain control of the property through an exclusive right to sell listing contract and soon thereafter working on the seller to lower its price aspirations,

- Suggesting to an owner that the agent is working with a prospective buyer who would find the property perfect for its tastes and needs, when in fact no such buyer exists and the claim was made simply to get an exclusive listing contract, and
- Keeping an expired listing contract in the multiple listing service in order to attract new potential buyers.

2. Acts of agency and fiduciary violations, such as
   - Revealing confidential information from the seller or buyer with respect to the lowest or highest acceptable price in the process of single-agency negotiations,
   - Avoiding phone messages, faxes, or e-mail messages from other agents with prospects for a listing in order to try and complete a current transaction with an internal prospect that would mean a higher net commission, and
   - Showing a buyer only the firm's listings while more appropriate listings are available from other firms in order to try and keep more commission fee revenue within the firm or directed toward friends.

True professionals will not act dishonestly or violate agency obligations, but when markets are soft and few transactions are being completed, hungry and anxious agents might find it more difficult to stay on the professional high road. Busier agents in active markets will find it much easier to maintain professional and honest behavior in all business dealings.

Typical Unethical Acts by Buyers and Sellers in the Real Estate Market

There are also a number of typical ethical violations by buyers and sellers in the real estate market that make it more difficult for real estate agents to act professionally.[4] Examples include:

- A buyer providing misleading information to a seller in order to induce a more favorable selling price,
- A buyer using vaguely written purchase contract contingencies as an excuse for not moving forward on an offer,
- A buyer overrepresenting its ability to pay,

- Intentional stalling of a pending deal in order to compromise the situation for the other party and force a renegotiation, and
- A seller providing misleading information about market rents, values, expenses, material facts, or other problems.

Chris Manning, in a 1995 ARES presentation, asked whether it is the responsibility of an agent in a negotiation to protect the other party from its own ignorance or from misleading facts assumed to be true and unverified. His answer in the case of material facts is generally yes.

Benefits of Codes of Conduct to Trade Association Members

There are four benefits that trade association members derive from adherence to a set of ethical standards. One potential benefit in *an improved public image*. If the trade association is diligent in enforcing the ethical standards among members, and if membership in the trade association has public recognition as an indication of quality in training, service, or professionalism, then the public image can be enhanced. Effective self-regulation and enforcement of professional codes of conduct enhance the chances that members of an organization or association will be viewed as professional. A second potential benefit is the *avoidance of government regulation*.[5] Licensing, certification, and government regulation tends to be lower the higher are the industry standards of quality and the better the self-regulatory system of the industry. Some areas, like appraisal, are now more regulated as a result of history, while others, like mortgage brokerage, real estate counselors, and real estate educators (all of which have trade associations and professional codes of conduct) are generally unregulated. A third potential benefit of a professional code of conduct is *protection of members from lawsuits*, civil and criminal, that might arise from violations of the standards by training the members on avoidance of conflicts of interests and situations likely to cause an ethical dilemma. The fourth and final benefit of ethical standards is *protection of the general public* by encouraging behavior felt to be in the public interest.

A close examination of most professional codes of conduct reveals that the vast majority deals with standards of behavior required by the fiduciary requirements of agency law, the avoidance of conflicts of interest, full disclosure to principals, and competency or experience disclosure to the client. In this regard, many of the standards within a professional code of conduct are requirements of law. However, through the enforcement of an explicit set of guidelines of a trade association like the National Association of Realtors via peer review boards and arbitrators, legal disputes are often avoided or settled much more efficiently than through formal and expensive litigation.

An Examination of the Professional Code of Conduct of the National Association of Realtors

The National Association of Realtors (NAR) is a large trade association for real estate brokers and agents with a professional code of conduct including twenty-three articles in a fine print and lengthy document. These articles can be described in ways that simplify and amplify our understanding of the intentions of such codes (see Table 12.1). That is, the articles are intended to assist the trade members dealing ethically with each

Table 12.1. Analysis of the Professional Code of Conduct of the National Association of Realtors

Article	Brief Description	Intention	Internal Orientation	External Orientation
1	Stay informed about community and citizenship issues.	Professionalism		Yes
2	Don't needlessly criticize other Realtors.	Professional etiquette	Yes	
3	Assist the government in protecting the public.	Professionalism		Yes
4	Urge use of the exclusive listing contract.	Avoidance of conflicts of interest that arise with a net listing; avoidance of conflicts with other agents, which arise with an open listing	Yes	Yes
5	Share knowledge with other Realtors, and remain loyal to the community Realtor Board.	Professional etiquette; increase of local board control over industry practices	Yes	

Table 12.1. (continued)

Article	Brief Description	Intention	Internal Orientation	External Orientation
6	Seek no unfair advantage over other Realtors.	Professional etiquette	Yes	
7	Promote the interests of the client and be honest in all dealings.	Fiduciary requirement of agency and moral obligation		Yes
8	Dual agency without full disclosure is not permitted.	Compliance with agency laws in most states		Yes
9	Don't conceal material facts, exaggerate, misrepresent facts, or reveal confidential information provided by a client (except where state law requires such disclosure).	Avoidance of fraud; revealing of material facts is a legal requirement in most states		Yes
10	Don't discriminate in the provision of services to anyone based on race, color, religion, sex, familiar status, handicap, or national origin.	Paralleling of the fair housing laws and encourages nondiscrimination		Yes
11	Remain informed and educated on trends and skills affecting area of specialization. Do not undertake the provision of services beyond the scope of competency and experience level disclosed to the client.	Professionalism encouraged through skill maintenance; disclosure of actual competency and experience a fiduciary obligation, which indicates the ability to provide the expected services		Yes
12	Don't provide opinions on value when a present or future personal interest might arise.	Avoidance of agency conflicts of interest		Yes

Table 12.1. (continued)

Article	Brief Description	Intention	Internal Orientation	External Orientation
13	In buying or selling real estate, disclose personal interests, even if the interest is minor.	Avoidance of agency conflicts of interest		Yes
14	Submit disputes between Realtors to the board for arbitration to avoid litigation.	Preservation of public image; saving legal costs	Yes	Yes
15	Cooperate with board inquiries on disputes.	Professional etiquette	Yes	
16	Disclose all affiliated business relationships, which are suggested to or used by clients along with reasonable alternatives that serve the clients needs. Don't take rebates or referral fees without disclosing this to the client.	Avoidance of and disclosure of conflicts of interest		Yes
17	Do not practice law.	Limiting of services to areas of competency		Yes
18	Don't mix client moneys with personal moneys.	Fiduciary requirement of agency and legal requirement in most states		Yes
19	Don't lie or misrepresent in marketing materials or ads. Always promote the Realtor affiliation.	Avoidance of fraud, promote better public recognition of the trade association		Yes
20	Keep all contracts in writing and with appropriate signatures and copies to all interested parties.	Consistency with common law on enforceable real estate contracts		Yes

Table 12.1.   (continued)

Article	Brief Description	Intention	Internal Orientation	External Orientation
21	Don't solicit clients in exclusive listing contracts with other Realtors. Disclose all personal agency contract relationships openly to other agents. Don't solicit other firms agents without first telling the principals of such firms.	Professional etiquette	Yes	
22	Cooperate with other Realtors to the extent the cooperation serves the interest of the client.	Professional etiquette and agency obligations	Yes	Yes
23	Don't lie or make misleading statements about competitors.	Professional etiquette, same intention as article 2.	Yes	

other or deal ethically with the public. These articles might also be requirements of law or simply requirements in the sense of professional etiquette. For example, at one time NAR members could not recruit agents from other firms, as it was a violation of the professional code of conduct. This would be an example of a professional courtesy that is not a requirement of law. Once a reader understands the intentions of these codes of conduct, along with the fiduciary rules of agency, then most codes of conduct merely serve to provide more explicit interpretations for expected ethical standards of behavior. Entire seminars and courses have become federally legislated as required in some specializations, such as appraisal with the *Uniform Standards of Professional Conduct* with a myriad of case illustrations. For the most part such cases and seminars simply reiterate the importance of following agency obligations, disclosure obligations, or avoiding conflicts of interest. There is really very little fundamental material in such courses beyond understanding the types of intentions discussed here in the preceding table, and most ethics-oriented seminar instruction must become an exercise in empathetic story telling.

Note that internally oriented articles within the code of conduct are less likely to be violations of law, while most externally oriented articles are in fact violations of federal or state law. Six of the articles of NAR are oriented solely toward internal industry behaviors, fourteen are oriented toward the general public, and three are oriented toward both.

Conclusion

Ethics are based on cultural and business practices of the day and as such are always evolving over time. Ethics serve to allow for more efficient business dealings by allowing parties to rely on expected behaviors. Ethics are also not very complicated. Most codes of conduct can be filtered down to a fraction of their original verbiage while losing very little of the intentional essence. Violations of most of the externally oriented codes of conduct, at least in the case of NAR, would in fact be violations of agency or state laws. The reduced form of the NAR code provided here illustrates to educators a new approach to teaching ethics with focus on intention and orientation.

Notes

1. For example, those who support the right of a fatally ill person to ask for assistance in dying sympathize with the patient, while those who are against such assistance sympathize with the ones who are asked to do the assisting, and neither sympathies are misplaced.

2. Within another paper within this issue "Ethics as Economically Influenced: A Preliminary Test," the reader will find more discussion on ethical standards and origins.

3. Extracted from an informal survey by the Ohio Association of Realtors in 1994 and from an informal survey by the author of real estate agents in 1995.

4. These examples are from Chris Manning from a 1995 ARES presentation.

5. This is clearly the objective of recently enacted television content rating systems.

References

Stark, Andrew. (1993). "What's the Matter with Business Ethics?" *Harvard Business Review* (May): 38–48.

13 AN EMPIRICAL ANALYSIS OF REAL ESTATE BROKERAGE ETHICS

A. Ason Okoruwa

Bedrock Valuation & Realty Services
Council Bluffs, Iowa 51502-1946

A. Frank Thompson

Department of Finance
College of Business Administration
The University of Northern Iowa

Abstract

The purpose of this chapter is to provide analysis of real estate brokerage practices in relation to the National Association of Realtors' Code of Ethics and Standards of Practice and legislated standards of practice in the state of Iowa. This study investigates the relationship between real estate brokerage practices in Iowa and demographic factors such as age, income, and educational background. It utilizes data gathered from a survey questionnaire administered to a random sample of 300 real estate agents and brokers who are members of the Greater Des Moines Board of Realtors. The results of this investigation show that ethical judgment by real estate brokers may vary according to level of education, income, and sex of the selling agent. Age and whether part-time or full-time real estate brokerage work status did not appear to be significant in terms of altering ethical decisions.

Introduction

For many families, a home is the largest single purchase they will ever make (see Robins and Frankel, 1984). The *Statistical Abstract of the United States: 1993* (U.S. Bureau of the Census, 1993) shows that in 1992, 3,520,000 existing and 610,000 new one-family homes were sold in the United States. The median prices for these existing and new one-family units are $103,700 and $121,500, respectively. The National Association of Realtor (NAR), the dominant real estate industry trade association, has 727,435 registered real estate agents and a code of ethics first adopted in 1913. The NAR's Code of Ethics and Standards of Practice (1995) contains seventeen articles pertaining to the Realtor's dealings with clients, customers, other agents, and the general public. In addition, there are sixty-three published Standards of Practice, which provide interpretation of particular articles in the Code of Ethics.

In general, a real estate agent's income is based wholly on the agent's share of a commission generated through the sale of property. This compensation structure could be a major source of pressure to be less than ethical in the selling of properties. Compensation and legal liability issues make the study of agent compliance with the code of conduct and legislative standards an important area for real estate research.

Two definitions of ethics in the second college edition of *Webster's New World Dictionary* are (1) the study of the standards of conduct and moral judgment and (2) the system or code of morals of a particular person, religion, group, or profession. In relation to a specific profession, a conduct or practice is characterized as ethical if it conforms to that profession's standards of conduct. According to Ferrell, Greham, and Fraedrich (1989, p. 56), ethics is "the study and philosophy of human conduct with an emphasis on the determination of right and wrong." The study by Bartels (1967) provides a clear explanation of the concept of marketing ethics. He specifies five basic assumptions in his development of an ethics model in marketing:

1. That ethics is a standard by which business action may be judged right or wrong,
2. That ethics is a standard for judging the rightness not of action per se but of action of one person relative to another,
3. That business is primarily a social process, within which it is an economic process, and that, within the latter, marketing is a specialized process involving role relationship and interactions,
4. That the expectations of the participants in the respective marketing roles are known, and
5. That ethics is a matter of social sanction, not a mere technical appraisal.

Assumptions 2 and 5 indicate that marketing ethics could best be understood in relation to the fulfillment or violation of expectations sanctioned by society. Marketing is a function in the social institution called economy. Bartels (1967, pp. 20–26) stated that

As a social institution consists of relationships among participants in roles essential to the performance of the needed function, each institution has myriad sets of expectations and obligations among these participants. Thus, in each institution are evolved ethics peculiar to the relationships and activities involved. In turn, the norms of behavior in each or all institutions are the product of the general cultural characteristics of the society, which differ among societies, producing dissimilar standards, codes, and patterns of behavior among men in their role relationships.

The present study is an endeavor to examine real estate brokerage practices in relation to the social standards set by National Association of Realtors' Code of Ethics and state-legislated standards of practice. After a brief review of literature related to ethics and real estate codes of conduct, the chapter reports on data collected from a survey of 300 agents and brokers in Des Moines area conducted in 1993 and 1994. The methodology and empirical results of this investigation are followed by a conclusion and suggested implications of the findings of survey analysis.

Literature Review

Real estate brokerage is a specialized marketing function related to the transfer of physical and legal interests associated with real estate purchase and ownership. There are numerous studies dealing with ethics and marketing. For example, Murphy and Laczniak (1981) cite more than 100 articles on the subject of ethics, and in a followup study, Murphy and Pridgen (1987) examine additional studies on ethical issues in marketing. However, few studies address real estate brokerage ethical practices as a separate area of study.

The study by Sturdivant and Cocanougher (1973) looks at how executives, students, workers, and housewives viewed differently the ethics of five marketing situations, real estate brokerage included. Sturdivant and Cocanougher find that ethical judgment varies in relation to the occupations of those interviewed. Allmon and Grant (1990) focus on using voice stress analysis in examining real estate sales agents' responses to ethically based questions. They show that the presence of formal ethical guidelines does not guarantee adherence to ethical codes.

The literature on research that directly relates to real estate brokerage and ethical decision making is very thin. Most studies tend to lump real estate ethics in with other ethical issues in marketing. This study endeavors to expand the literature on real estate brokerage ethics by examining decision making in relation to demographic variables that characterize real estate agents themselves. Specifically, the two main objectives of this study are (1) to examine the relationship between real estate brokerage practices and demographic characteristics, such as age, income, gender, and level of education and (2) to examine demographic and ethical decision making within real estate brokerage practices in the State of Iowa.

Data

The data for this study come from a survey of members of the Greater Des Moines Board of Realtors (GDMBR), Des Moines, Iowa. The data represent information from a self-administered questionnaire sent to a simple random sample of 300 agents and brokers who were members of the GDMBR. The data consist of data taken from fifty-five completed questionnaires returned in 1994. This represents a response rate of 18 percent. This response rate compares favorably to the response rates for two other published real estate surveys. Ball and Nourse (1988) reports a response rate of 17 percent, and a study by Glower and Hendershott (1988) shows a 33 percent response rate for surveys of real estate brokers and agents. Some of the respondents marked two responses to a question or failed to respond on some questions. In the analysis of specific questions, we dropped those cases with multiple responses. Table 13.1 shows the description of the variables included in the study, and Table 13.2 presents descriptive statistics of the data. In Table 13.3 the means and percent responses to the practice questions are presented.

Methodology

Articles 1 and 2 of the NAR's Code of Ethics, which regulate the dealings of Realtors with buyers or customers, provide the basis for some of the practice questions contained in the questionnaire used to collect the data. The responses to these practice questions are analyzed in relation to demographic characteristics, such as age, gender, level of education, and income. Specifically, Articles 1 and 2 of the NAR's Code of Ethics, respectively, state that.

> When representing a buyer, seller, landlord, tenant, or other client as an agent, Realtors® pledge themselves to protect and promote the interests of their client. This obligation of absolute fidelity to the client's interests is primary, but it does not relieve Realtors® of their obligation to treat all parties honestly. When

Table 13.1.   Description of Variables

Seller disclosure	Time when property disclosure form is given the seller to complete
Disclosure to buyer	Time when buyer is given completed property disclosure form
Duty to disclose	Extent the disclosures in the property form relieves the agent's duty to disclose personally observed property defects
Agent's listings	Number of properties sold that were also listed by the selling agent
Firm's listings	Number of properties sold that were listed by the selling agent's employing firm
Other's listings	Number of properties sold that were listed by other brokerage firms
Age of listing	Whether the length of time property has been on the market should be disclosed to the buyer
Compensation	Whether strict commission compensation have on some occasions compelled the agent's to bend the rules
Complete listings	Whether the buyer should be provided during the first meeting a complete list of all available properties that satisfy his requirements
Presenting offers	Whether the agent should wait to receive multiple offers expected within two days to make a combined presentation to the seller
Employment	Whether agent is employed full-time or part-time
Experience	Number of years the agent has been selling properties full-time or part-time
Income	Total income from real estate brokerage last year
Position in firm	Position held in the firm
Specialty	Real estate brokerage specialty
Education	Level of education
Age	Age of the agent
Sex	Sex of the agent
Household	Composition of agent's household

serving a buyer, seller, landlord, tenant or other party in a nonagency capacity, Realtors® remain obligated to treat all parties honestly. (Amended 1/93)

Realtors® shall avoid exaggeration, misrepresentation, or concealment of pertinent facts relating to the property or the transaction. Realtors® shall not, however, be obligated to discover latent defects in the property, to advice on matters outside the scope of their real estate license, or to disclose facts which are confidential under the scope of agency duties owed to their clients. (Amended 1/93)

Table 13.2. Descriptive statistics

Variable	Mean	Standard Deviation	Minimum	Maximum	Number of Cases
Agent's listings	6.77	8.84	0	50	47
Firm's listings	6.97	5.96	0	30	48
Others' listings	5.05	5.46	0	27	48
Experience	8.48	5.98	0.5	21	53
Age	48.72	9.89	25	68	54

Variable	Frequency	Proportion
Employment		
Full-time	48	91
Part-time	5	9
Experience		
0 to 5 years	20	38
5.1 to 10 years	16	30
10.1 to 15 years	7	13
15.1 to 20 years	9	17
Above 20 years	1	2
Income		
Below $15,000	12	23
$15,000 to $24,999	7	13
$25,000 to $34,999	12	23
$35,000 to $44,999	5	9
$45,000 to $54,999	3	6
$55,000 to $64,999	6	11
$65,000 to $74,999	2	4
$75,000 to $84,999	3	6
$85,000 to $100,000	1	2
Above $100,000	2	4
Position in firm		
Sales associate	42	79
Broker associate	9	17
Broker-in-charge	1	2
Owner/broker	1	2
Education		
Some college	30	57
College degree	16	30
Masters degree	7	13
Age		
Under 30 years	1	2
30 to 39 years	8	15
40 to 49 years	24	44
50 to 59 years	11	20
60 and above	10	19
Sex		
Female	31	57
Male	23	43
Household		
Married couple with dependents	22	42
Married couple without dependents	20	38
Single female with dependents	3	6
Single female without dependents	5	9
Single male without dependents	3	6

Table 13.3.   Mean and percent responses to practice statements

Variable: Time when property disclosure statement is given to the seller
      to complete
Number of cases: 49

Before the listing contract is signed	39%
When the listing contract is signed	61%

Variable: Time when buyer is given seller completed property disclosure
      statement
Number of cases: 47

At the showing of the property	77%
Before an offer is made	23%

Variable: The extent a seller completed disclosure statement relieves
      agent's duty to disclose observed property defects
Number of cases: 54

Relieves me completely	46%
Relieves me somewhat	52%
Does not relieve me at all	2%

Variable: Should age of a listing be disclosed to buyers?
Number of cases: 52

Yes	67%
No	25%
Don't know/not sure	8%

Variable	Number	Mean	Strongly Agree	Agree	Don't know/ Not sure	Disagree	Strongly Disagree
Compensation	54	4.46	2%	4%	0%	35%	59%
Complete listings	53	2.57	26%	34%	4%	28%	4%
Presenting offers	51	3.72	4%	18%	6%	47%	25%

There are eight demographic questions in the survey. The age and experience of the agent are measured on a ratio scale; level of education and income on an interval scale; and type of employment, position in the firm, sex, and household composition on a nominal scale. This study created class intervals for agents' ages and experience variables before their use in the analysis. In order to measure the association between the eight demographic variables and the seven practice questions, we apply two different

Goodman and Kruskal's proportional reduction in error measures. For the nominally scaled real estate practice variables—seller disclosure, disclosure to buyer, duty to disclose, and age of listing, the Kruskal's lambdas were computed. For the ordinal scaled variables—compensation, complete listings, and presenting offers—the Goodman and Kruskal's gammas were calculated (see SPSS/PC+ 1988, pp. B-100 to B-103).

One-way analysis of variance (ANOVA) was used to examine demographic variations in the responses to the real estate practice questions that are related to compensation, complete listings, and presenting offers variables. In analyzing differences in the means of more than two classes of a variable, we use the Duncan's multiple-range test, a multiple comparison procedure of one-way ANOVA. This enables us to tell which pairs of classes have means statistically different from one another. Additionally, the utilization of multiple comparison procedures helps us to avoid the problem of finding that the means of one or more pairs are significantly different, when, in fact, they are not. In general, the probability increases that the means of a pair will turn out to be different when the same means are used for multiple comparisons, as would be the case with t-tests for pairs of means.

Analysis of Results

Responses to Practice Statements

Table 13.3 presents the mean and percentage responses to the practice statements included in the study. Thirty-nine percent of the respondents indicated that they gave the blank property disclosure statement to the seller to complete before the listing contract was signed; while 61 percent of the agents gave the statement after the listing contract had been signed by the seller. It would be helpful to the listing agent to be aware of defects in the property before the listing agreement is signed by the seller. In the listing contract document, the agent indicates the asking price for the property. To establish a reliable and supportable asking price, the agent needs to consider all defects and determine their impacts on the value of the property being listed, if any. A significant percentage (61 percent) of the agents are not considering pertinent information about property defects before establishing an asking price for a property. The relevant administrative rule of the Iowa Real Estate Commission states that "At the time a licensee obtains a listing, the listing licensee shall obtain a completed disclosure signed and dated by each seller represented by the licensee." The preceding rule does not specifically state that a seller signed disclosure statement should be obtained by the agent before entering into a listing agreement. However, having information about the defects in a property will be extremely useful to the agent in establishing the asking price and, more important, in complying with the duty to disclose ascertainable adverse facts relating to a property.

With respect to the time the completed property disclosure statement is given to the buyer, 77 percent of the respondents indicated that they gave the statement at the showing of the property, and 23 percent of the agents gave the statement before a prospective buyer makes an offer to purchase the property. Largely, agents are complying with the pertinent administrative rule of the Iowa Real Estate Commission. The pertinent administrative rule stipulates that the disclosure statement should be delivered to a potential buyer prior to the seller's making a written offer to sell or the seller's accepting a written offer to buy. Ideally, the property disclosure statement should be given to the prospective buyer at the showing of the property. This would enable the prospective buyer to make an informed decision after considering relevant facts about the property of interest.

The responses to the question "To what extent do you think that the completion of the property disclosure form by the seller completely relieves you of the duty to disclose any property defects you personally noticed?" are quite revealing of the attitude toward duties to third parties. Forty-six percent of the respondents indicate that it relieves them completely, 52 percent, indicate that it relieves them somewhat, and 2 percent state that it did not relieve them at all. The pertinent section of Iowa Real Estate Commission's administrative rules states that "A licensee acting as an exclusive seller's or exclusive landlord's agent shall disclose to any customer material adverse facts actually known by the licensee pursuant to Iowa Code Supplement section 543B.56." A great majority (98 percent) of the agents would have failed to disclosure adverse facts about the property to buyers. Nondisclosure is clearly a violation of Iowa Real Estate Commission's rule. This result may indicate a cavalier attitude to the disclosure of material facts about the property that may also violate Article 2 of the Code of Ethics of the National Association of Realtors and real estate laws of many states.

In relation to the statement dealing with the disclosure to buyers of the total numbers of days a property has been on the market, 67 percent of the respondents indicated that it is pertinent information to be disclosed, 25 percent responded in the negative, and 8 percent responded "don't know/not sure." Again, this information is related to the property and agents are duty bound to disclose it. Knowing the length of time a property has been on the market could enhance the bargaining position of the buyer.

With respect to the statement "Because my earnings are based strictly on the commissions that I generate, I have, on occasions, 'bent the rules' in order to close a sale," 6 percent of the respondents agreed, and 94 percent of the agents disagreed with the statement. From the responses to the preceding question, it appears that a majority of the agents do adhere to a strict code of ethics. However, it is quite likely that the responses would have been different if the question was framed differently—for example, "How many times did you observe another agent bending the rules in order to sell a house in the last one year?" Sixty percent of the respondents agreed that a prospective buyer should be given a full list of all available properties that satisfy his or her requirements during the first meeting with the agent, 32 percent disagreed, and 4 percent responded "don't know/not sure." The more properties the prospective buyer inspects, the more likely he or she is going to gain a better understanding of the functioning of a real estate market and form an educated opinion of market values of properties. In addition, this would enhance the ability of the house hunter to find the property that best meets his or her requirements.

Finally, with respect to the statement concerning not immediately presenting an offer to the seller because multiple offers are expected within a two-day period, 22 percent of the respondents agreed that it is appropriate, 72 percent disagreed, and 6 percent indicated "don't know/not sure." However, according to the rules and regulations of the Iowa Real Estate Commission, "failing to immediately present offer" is one of the violations for which civil penalties may be imposed.

Relationships Between Variables

It is important to know if two variables are related and the strength of the relationship, if any. For example, it is relevant to know if the level of experience of agents is related to affirmative disclosure of adverse facts observed in a property to prospective buyers. If experience is related to the disclosure of adverse property facts, knowing the level of an agent's experience, one could reliably predict whether disclosure of property defects would likely be made to buyers. Table 13.4 shows the association matrix for the demographic and practice questions. The entries in Table 13.4 are Goodman and Kruskal's lambda and gamma statistics. The lambda measure indicates the reduction in error that occurs when the additional information provided by a variable is used to predict another variable. The lambda is used to measure the association for nominal and ordinal scaled variables. Its value range is between 0 and 1. A value of 0 indicates that a specific independent

Table 13.4. Association of practice statements with demographic variables

Variable	Employment	Position	Education	Sex	Household	Experience	Income	Age
Seller disclosure[a]	.2222	.0556	.0000	.0000	.0000	.0000	.3333	.1053
Disclosure to buyer[a]	.0000	.2727	.0000	.0000	.1818	.0909	.0909	.0000
Duty to disclose[a]	.0400	.0400	.0385	.0000	.1154	.2000	.1600	.1923
Age of listing[a]	.0000	.0000	.0000	.0000	.0588	.0000	.1177	.0000
Compensation[b]	.0820	-.3141	-.1732	-.5000	.1103	-.0148	.0853	.0866
Complete listings[b]	-.1807	.5054	.4144	.6664	-.0682	-.0501	.0459	.2720
Presenting offers[b]	-.2340	.1096	-.0427	-.0111	.0429	-.0181	.0400	-.0111

a. Lambda: Seller disclosure, disclosure to buyer, duty to disclose, and age of listing are the dependent variables.
b. Goodman and Kruskal's gamma: No variable is identified as the dependent or independent variable.

Table 13.5. Mean response to practice statements by agent's real estate brokerage income

Practice Statement	Below $15	$15 to $24.9	$25 to $34.9	$35 to $44.9	$45 to $54.9	$55 to $64.9	$65 to $74.9	$75 to $84.9	$85 to $100	Over $100	F Ratio	F Probability
Compensation[a]	4.5000	4.4286	4.2500	4.6000	4.6667	5.0000	3.0000	4.6667	5.0000	4.0000	1.2366	.2989
Complete listings	2.5000	3.1429	2.2727	1.8000	2.3333	2.6667	4.5000	2.3333	2.0000	3.5000	0.9622	.4841
Presenting offers[b]	3.5833	3.5714	4.1000	3.8000	4.3333	4.2000	4.0000	2.6667	4.0000	2.0000	1.1534	.3501

a. Mean for income level $65 to $74.9 is different from the means of below $15, $35 to $44.9, and $55 to $64.9 at the .05 level of significance.
b. The means for income levels $25 to $34.9 and over $100 are different at the .05 level of significance.

variable is not useful in predicting the dependent variable, while a value of 1 means that the categories of the dependent variable are perfectly specified by the independent variable.

For ordinal scaled variables, association measures are based on the difference between the number of concordant (like) pairs and discordant (unlike) pairs, for all distinct pairs of observations. Goodman and Kruskal's gammas, which are computed in this study, are one way that the difference is standardized. If the value of a gamma is positive, this indicates that there are more concordant cases than are disconcordant cases. The absolute value of a gamma is interpreted as the proportional reduction in error. Therefore, in addition to measuring the strength of association between two variables, the gamma measure uses the order characteristic of ordinal variables to indicate the direction of association between them.

The variables that help explain when the property disclosure statement is given to the seller to complete are type of employment, position in the firm, income, and agent's age. In the prediction when the completed property disclosure statement is given to the buyer, position in the firm, household composition, experience, and income are important variables. The variables important in explaining the perceptions of agents of their duty to disclose property defects they personally observed to prospective buyers are employment type, position in the firm, level of education, household composition, experience, income, and age. Household composition and income are relevant variables in predicting the disclosure of the length of time a property has been on the market.

The relation between bending rules to close a deal variable and employment type, household composition, income, and age is positive, while the relation is negative with respect to position in the firm, level of education, sex, and experience variables. With respect to providing a complete list of qualified properties to the prospective buyer, position in the firm, education level, sex, income, and age are positively related, while employment type, household composition, and experience are negatively related. Finally, in relation to delaying presenting offers to sellers, employment type, education level, sex, experience, and age are negatively related, while the relation is positive for the position in the firm, household composition, and income variables.

Demographic Variations in Practices[1]

In this section, we examine variations across demographic classifications of agents with respect to three practice questions. The three practice questions are (1) whether strict commission compensation has on some occasions compelled the agent to "bend the rules," (2) whether the buyer should be provided a complete list of all available properties that satisfy his or her requirements, and (3) whether the agent should wait to receive multiple offers, expected within two days, to make a combined presentation to the seller. To test whether the population means for the different groups are the same, F statistics are computed. At a significance level of 5 percent we tested the null hypotheses that the means for various variables, for different groups, are the same. If the level of significance is 5 percent or less, the interpretation is that the computed F statistic is unlikely to be seen if the means of the groups were indeed equal in the population.

There were no significant differences, at the 5 percent level of significance, in the means of the different classes of employment, years of experience, age, and household composition. In Table 13.5, the mean scores for the ten income classes are presented. The mean score for income level $65,000 to $74,999 is different for the mean scores for income levels below $15,000, $35,000 to $44,999, and $55,000 to $64,999 with respect to the question of bending rules in order to effect a sale. It appears that the higher the income level, the more likely it is an agent will bend rules to close a deal. Also, Table 13.5 shows that agents making more than $100,000 a year differ from agents making between $25,000 and $34,999 with regards to waiting for all anticipated offers within a two-day period to make a joint presentation to the seller. It appears that agents making more than $100,000 annually favor waiting for all anticipated offers rather than presenting a prospective buyer's offer to the seller immediately, when received.

Table 13.6 shows the means for the four different positions held in the brokerage firm. The mean score for the owner-broker is different from the mean scores for other positions in the firm with respect to bending rules to effect a transaction. It appears that an owner-broker is more likely to bend rules to close a deal. However, this interpretation should not be given too much weight given that there was only one broker-owner in the observations. In Table 13.7 one could see that there was a significant difference between agents with master's degrees and agents with just some college education in relation to providing a prospective buyer a full list of properties meeting her or his requirements. The lower the education level, the more likely a complete list of qualified properties is given to the prospective buyer during the first meeting.

In Table 13.8 the mean scores by sex are presented. The table shows that—with regard to the questions related to the time the completed property form is given to the buyer, bending rules to effect a sale, and providing a complete list of qualified properties to a prospective buyer—there

Table 13.6.   Mean response to practice statements by position held in the firm

Practice Statement	Sales Associate	Broker Associate	Broker-in-Charge	Owner/ Broker	F Ratio	F Probability
Compensation	4.5238[a]	4.4444[a]	5.0000[a]	1.0000[a]	8.2225	.0002
Complete listings	2.3659	3.2222	4.0000	4.0000	1.8102	.1579
Presenting offers	3.7250	3.5000	5.0000	4.0000	0.5045	.6811

a. Owner/broker mean is different from the means for the sales associate, broker associate, and broker-in-charge at the .05 level of significance.

Table 13.7.   Mean response to practice statements by level of education

Practice Statement	Some College	College Degree	Masters Degree	F Ratio	F Probability
Compensation	4.5667	4.1875	4.5714	1.1358	.3293
Complete listings	2.2667[a]	2.8667	3.4286[a]	2.7069	.0767
Presenting offers	3.8667	3.6429	3.6667	0.2292	.7961

a. Groups different at the .05 level of significance.

Table 13.8.   Mean response to practice statements by sex

Practice Statement	Female	Male	F Ratio	F Probability
Compensation	4.6452	4.2174	3.5886	.0637
Complete listings	2.1667	3.0870	6.6950	.0126
Presenting offers	3.7500	3.6957	0.0276	.8686

were significant differences between the sexes. Male agents are more likely than female agents to bend rules to close transactions. Also, male agents are more likely to delay presenting an offer to the seller, when multiple offers are expected within a two-day period.

Conclusion

This study identifies significant demographic variables that are related to specific real estate brokerage practices and ethical decision making. In addition, one-way ANOVA analysis indicated the significant variations in practices according to demographics. Differences in ethical perspective appear to exist based on variation in income, age, position in the firm, level of education, and gender of agents and brokers in Iowa. Given the variation in responses to ethical questions concerning real estate disclosure, an educational need exists to communicate ethical standards to agents and brokers in a way that supersedes such demographic variables as income, age, educational level, and length of time as a real estate broker.

Acknowledgments

The authors are grateful to Karma Cahill of the Des Moines Area Association of Realtors and Denise Hinton of Iowa Realty for their suggestions in the design of the real estate ethics questionnaire used in this study and their help with data collection.

Note

1. All the mean differences are evaluated at the 5 percent level of significance.

References

Allmon, D. E., and J. Grant. (1990). "Real Estate Sales Agents and the Code of Ethics: A Voice Stress Analysis." *Journal of Business Ethics* 9(10) (October): 807–812.

Ball, J. N., and H. O. Nourse. (1988). "Testing the Conventional Representation Model for Residential Real Estate Brokerage." *Journal of Real Estate Research* 3(2) (Summer): 119–131.

Bartels, R. (1967). "A Model for Ethics in Marketing." *Journal of Marketing* 31 (January): 20–26.

Ferrell, O. C., L. G. Gresham, and J. Fraedrich. (1989). "A Synthesis of Ethical Decision Models for Marketing." *Journal of Macromarketing* (Fall): 55–64.

Glower, M., and P. H. Hendershott. (1988). "The Determinants of Realtor Income." *Journal of Real Estate Research* 3(2) (Summer): 53–68.

Iowa Code. (1993). Real Estate Commission [193E]. Des Moines: State of Iowa.

Murphy, P. (1981). "Marketing Ethics: a Review With Implications for Managers, Educators and Researchers." In B. Enis and K. Roering, *Review of Marketing*, American Marketing Association: 251–266.

Murphy, P., and M.D. Pridger. (1981). "Ethical and Legal Issues in Marketing." Paper presented at A.M.A. Marketing Ethics Workshop, University of Southern Mississippi.

National Association of Realtors (NAR). (1995). *Code of Ethics and Standards of Practice*. Chicago: NEA.

Norusis, M. J. (1988). *SPSS/PC+ V2.0 Base Manual*. Chicago: SPSS.

Pearl, R. B., and M. Frankel. (1984). "Composition of the Personal Wealth of American Households at the Start of the Eighties." In Seymour Sudman and Mary A. Spaeth (eds.) *The Collection and Analysis of Economic and Consumer Behavior Data*. Bureau of Economic and Business Research Laboratory, University of Illinois, Urbana-Champaign.

Sturdivant, F. D., and A. B. Cocanougher. (1973). "What Are Ethical Marketing Practices." *Harvard Business Review* 10–12 (November-December): 176.

U.S. Bureau of the Census. (1993). *Statistical Abstract of the United States: 1993* (113th ed.). Washington, DC; U.S. Government Printing Office.

V TENANTS AND ETHICS

14 SEXUAL HARASSMENT OF TENANTS IN RENTAL HOUSING
An Ethical and Leagal Debate in the Wake of the Shellhammer and Gnerre Cases

Robert J. Aalberts

Lied Institute of Real Estate Studies
College of Business and Economics
University of Nevada–Las Vegas

Terrence M. Clauretie

Lied Institute of Real Estate Studies
College of Business and Economics
University of Nevada–Las Vegas

Abstract

Sexual harassment of tenants by landlords is a serious problem today. Although the extent of the practice is not fully known, it is likely widespread and can produce a profoundly negative effect on its victims. This chapter explores and critiques some of the important legal and ethical issues that have arisen. In particular, the article examines the seminal cases of Shellhammer v. Lewellan *and* Gnerre v. Massachusetts Commission Against Discrimination. *In presenting the current legal environment spawned by these cases, the authors offer proposals for creating a fairer and more ethical environment for both tenants and landlords in dealing with sexual harassment in housing.*

Introduction

Sexual harassment of tenants in rental housing is a serious ethical, social, economic, and legal problem today. Although commentators, scholars, and journalists have been successful in educating the public on the topic of sexual harassment in the workplace, particularly in the wake of headlines stories such as Clarence Thomas's U.S. Supreme Court hearings, the U.S. Navy's *Tailhook* scandal, and Robert Packwood's U.S. Senate its counterpart in housing has generally been given little attention (Aalberts and Clauretie, 1992; Butler, 1989; Cahan, 1987; Linn, 1989). One commentator has described the issue as "not just a problem of isolated tenants, but a systemic ill" (Butler, 1989, p. 195). Likewise, another researcher and commentator, Regina Cahan, reported that the incidence of sexual harassment in housing may be significantly greater than anyone realizes. In probably the only empirical study on the subject, 300 cases of sexual harassment, virtually all brought by women, were reported in a 1986 survey of 150 public and private fair housing centers, agencies, and organizations across the country. The author estimated from this return that there were between 6,818 and 15,000 actual cases, based on, at that time, only a 2 to 4.4 percent report rate for sexual harassment in the workplace. The author further pointed out that even the higher estimate may be disproportionately low since the report rate for workplace harassment is probably higher than it is in housing. This may be because there is less awareness of tenant sexual harassment and because the protections and enforcement mechanisms now found in most workplaces do not exist in housing situations. Moreover, tenants who are victims of sexual harassment may also not report such harassment for fear of being evicted, being blacklisted from government housing, having the rent raised in retaliation, and having requests for repairs ignored. In such a situation, both the tenant and her family may be affected detrimentally (Cahan, 1987).

Another commentator, Kathleen Butler, has observed that the impact of sexual harassment is considerably magnified by the fact that practically all the victims are women, particularly single mothers. This unfortunate victimization adds to other housing troubles. In numerous legal cases, women have been discriminated in securing housing. Men are considered to be preferable tenants by some landlords (Butler, 1989). Women have also been discriminated against in leading and insurance practices. For these and other socioeconomic reasons, women now occupy the largest subgroup of the nation's poorly housed population, with more than one-third of women bearing housing costs that are in excess of 25 percent (the traditional measure of affordable housing) of their income (Butler, 1989).

Finally, the practice is especially damaging for what it does to its victims.

In Cahan's study, it was revealed that 68 percent of the sexual harassment reported was requests for sexual intercourse. This was followed by abusive remarks and unsolicited and improper touching at 35 and 31 percent, respectively. Thus, the most common type of harassment is the most serious, with the implication that rape occurred in some cases.

In fact, female victims of sexual harassment often suffer the same traumatizing effects as rape victims. The reported effects have included a feeling of losing control of one's life, physical illness, decreased work productivity, loss of self-esteem, and depression (Cahan, 1987). When one considers that the tenant often cannot escape because of a lack of affordable housing or a reluctance to uproot children, the effects are compounded even more.

This chapter explores a number of legal and ethical issues that have arisen due to the sexual harassment of tenants. First, a history of sexual harassment in general is examined, culminating with a look at how the law developed in respect to sexual harassment of tenants. Next, two important cases are examined and assessed: *Shellhammer v. Lewellan*[1] and *Gnerre v. Massachusetts Commission Against Discrimination*.[2] Several important issues that arose in those cases are then analyzed from both legal and ethical perspectives, including a discussion of proposals for creating a fairer and more ethical environment for both tenants and landlords in dealing with sexual harassment in housing.

A Brief History of Sexual Harassment

Despite the fact that sex discrimination in employment practices was proscribed in Title VII of the Civil Rights Act of 1964,[3] sexual harassment was not interpreted to be a form of sex discrimination until 1976. Sexual harassment in housing, even more retarded in its legal development, was finally construed by a court as a form of sex discrimination under Title VIII of the Fair Housing Act in 1983. A discussion of the legal and ethical creation and evolution of both kinds of harassment will show that sexual harassment in housing was theoretically created as a direct result of its counterpart in employment.

When the Civil Rights Act of 1964 was first being debated, sex or gender discrimination was not included. However, a last-minute tactic by the Act's opposition was to incorporate it to foster more resistance to the Act's passage (Whalen and Whalen, 1985). Its late inclusion in the Act meant that there was an almost total lack of deliberation about it, which resulted in no useful legislative history for clarifying exactly what sexual discrimination was meant to encompass. It wasn't until 1976, in the ground-breaking case of *Williams v. Saxbe*,[4] that sexual harassment was recognized as a form of sex discrimination in the area of employment. In that case, the court justified its inclusion as a form of sex discrimination by emphasizing that the victim would not have been sexually harassed had she *not* been a woman. These earlier cases were referred to as *quid pro quo* ("something for something") *cases* because they were generally characterized by a supervisor who offered a promotion, a raise, or other such benefits on the condition of receiving sexual favors.

Despite the *Williams* case, many federal district courts were hesitant about recognizing this new variation of sex discrimination. This changed in 1980 when the Equal Employment Opportunity Commission (EEOC) promulgated its EEOC Guidelines on Sexual Harassment (1980).[5] In the Guidelines, the EEOC interpreted sexual harassment to be "unwelcomed sexual advances, requests for sexual favors, and other verbal or physical conduct of a sexual nature." Moreover, sexual harassment, as just described, would be actionable, according to the Guidelines, when they occur in three situations: (1) the "submission to such conduct is made either explicitly or implicitly a term or condition of an individual's employment," (2) "submission to or rejection of such conduct by an individual is used as the basis for employment decisions," or (3) such conduct has the purpose or effect of unreasonably interfering with an individual's work performance or creating an intimidating, hostile, or offensive working environment."[6] The first two types of sexual harassment, as first derived from the *Williams* case, are characterized as quid pro quo cases. The third kind, which is now referred to in employment law, as well as in housing, as a *hostile environment case*, was subsequently recognized in 1981 by the federal district court for the District of Columbia in *Bundy v. Jackson*[7] and shortly thereafter by the eleventh Circuit in *Henson v. City of Dundee*.[8] Ultimately, the hostile environment concept was sanctioned as law of the land by the U.S. Supreme Court in 1986 in the landmark case of *Meritor Bank v. Vinson*.[9]

The Legal Development of Sexual Harassment in Housing

Sexual harassment in housing developed as a legal, political, and ethical consequence of sexual harassment in employment. Its origins were in Title VIII of the Fair Housing Act of 1968 (FHA).[10] The FHA did not actually prohibit sex discrimination until the passage of the Housing and Community Act amendments in 1974. In 1983, the federal district court of the

Western District of Ohio ruled that Title VIII of the Fair Housing Act forbids both quid pro quo and hostile environment sexual harassment in the watershed case of *Shellhammer v. Lewallen*, and the case was later affirmed by the Sixth Circuit Court of Appeals.[11] In a rather curious twist, however, the opinion of the latter case was only a memorandum case, and so the text was not made available in the West Reporter system. At least one observer blames the slow spread of the concept to other jurisdictions on the opinion's relative inaccessibility (Linn, 1989). It should be noted that the *Shellhammer* court, in justifying its new ruling, relied heavily on the *Henson* case, referred to above. This relationship is discussed in detail later in the chapter.

Since the issuance of the *Shellhammer* case, a number of other jurisdictions have also proscribed sexual harassment in housing. In *Grieger v. Sheets*,[12] the federal district court for the Northern District of Illinois and the federal court for the Southern District of New York in *People of the State of New York by Abrams v. Merlino*[13] both found sexual harassment to be actionable under Title VIII of the FHA. In two 1992 cases, *Fiedler v. Dana Properties* and *United States v. Dana Properties*,[14] field in the federal Eastern District of California, a significant settlement of $1.65 million came as a result of a suit arising from a series of sexually harassing events.

There have also been legislation and cases arising out of state fair housing acts. One state, Minnesota, specifically defines *sex discrimination* to include sexual harassment.[15] In the case of *Chomicki v. Wittekind*,[16] a Wisconsin state appeals court interpreted the words *sex discrimination* to include sexual harassment. And in *Gnerre v. Massachusetts Commission Against Discrimination*,[17] a state court construed its state fair housing act in a similar fashion. The *Gnerre* case, is discussed in detail later.

Dispite the apparent frequency of sexual harassment in housing, the foregoing indicates that the amount of litigation over sexual harassment is far from reaching its potential. However, sexual harassment in employment also was not heavily litigated until it started to receive a great deal of publicity and attention by both the popular press as well as academic commentaries. The sanctification of the hostile environment approach by the Supreme Court in 1986 in the *Meritor Bank* case was a particularly significant event, both legally and in terms of raising the public's consciousness. The authors feel that a similar route is likely to transpire to raise the public's attention concerning sexual harassment in housing. The lurid details and now big awards, as exemplified by the *Dana Properties* cases, will almost certainly become the object of more press in the future. When that occurs, the lawsuits will likely be close behind.

The Legal and Ethical Parameters of Sexual Harassment:
A Discussion of *Shellhammer* and *Gnerre*

As the discussion above indicates, there has been comparatively little attention given to sexual harassment in housing. Due to this lack of scrutiny by
the courts, legislatures, and commentators, the legal and ethical status of the
issue is still in it earliest stages of thought and development. The two cases
that have been best developed from both legal and ethical perspectives are
the *Shellhammer* and *Gnerre* cases. Both of these cases, at least from the
standpoint of the authors, do have some serious shortcomings, however. The
next part of this article discusses and analyzes these cases. The focus of
the analysis is on how these courts treated the crucial issue of what standard to use in hostile environment cases to judge whether sexual harassment exists. After that discussion, the authors propose a new legal and more
ethical standard to replace those standards that were applied in those
important two cases.

The Shellhammer Case

As stated earlier, the *Shellhammer* case was the first in which a court
interpreted sex discrimination under Title VIII of the Fair Housing Act
to include sexual harassment. In *Shellhammer*, the plaintiffs, Tammy and
Thomas Shellhammer, entered into a lease with landlord-defendants
Norman Lewallen and his wife. It was alleged that Mr. Lewallen first approached Mrs. Shellhammer to pose for nude photographs for him. After
she had rebuffed him, he solicited her to have sexual intercourse with him,
which she likewise rejected. Three months later the Shellhammers were
evicted ostensibly for not paying their rent. However, they claimed they had
not paid it because of Lewallen's failure to fix a refrigerator and that his
actual motivation was to evict them for Mrs. Shellhammer's refusal to
surrender to his sexual solicitations.

The Shellhammers sued under Title VIII of the FHA, contending in this
case of first impression that sexual harassment is a form of sexual discrimination. The court agreed, stating that, in view of the "policy of broad interpretation of the Fair Housing Act, the statute's remedial purposes, and the
absence of any persuasive reason in support of the defendants' contentions
that sexual harassment is not actionable under the Act . . . it is entirely
appropriate to incorporate this doctrine [of sexual harassment] into the fair
housing area" (*Shellhammer v. Lewallen*).[18]

The *Shellhammer* court further ruled that both kinds of sexual harassment found in employment cases, quid pro quo as well as hostile environment, are actionable under Title VIII. In constructing the elements of both types (note that *all* elements of a claim must be proved by the plaintiff to win the case), the court borrowed heavily, albeit not precisely, from the *Henson* case. For quid pro quo cases, the court stated that four elements must be proved by the plaintiff—(1) membership in the protected group, (2) an unwelcome demand for sexual favors, (3) a demand based on the plaintiff's sex, and (4) a reaction by the plaintiff that affected "one or more tangible terms, conditions, or privileges of the tenancy." The court subsequently ruled that the Shellhammers had proven the four elements. The court justified its ruling by explaining that the couple's failure to pay the rent was not the real motivating factor for the eviction. Instead, the real reason was Mrs. Shellhammer's refusal to comply with Mr. Lewallen's requests for sexual favors.

The Shellhammers did not fare as well in their argument of a hostile environment claim. Again, borrowing heavily but not verbatim from *Henson*, the court laid out four elements to establish such a claim: (1) the plaintiff must be a member of the protected group, (2) the plaintiff must be subjected to unwelcome and extensive sexual favors and other such "verbal or physical conduct of a sexual nature," not sought by the plaintiff, (3) the harassment would not have occurred but for the plaintiff's sex, and (4) the harassment renders "continued tenancy burdensome and significantly less desirable than if the harassment were not occurring" (*Shellhammer v. Lewallen*).[19]

Ethical and Legal Criticisms of Shellhammer

The court's handling of the hostile environment claim raises some troubling legal and ethical problems. First, is the manner in which the court interpreted the word *extensive* in the second element. The court asserted that extensive should mean "pervasive and persistent." That is, before a plaintiff, such as Mrs. Shellhammer, proceeds to prove the other elements, she must establish, by a preponderance of the evidence, that the defendant's actions were pervasive and persistent. This essentially imposes, in the second element, a quantitative requirement to measure the *nature* of the harassment (Butler, 1989). Employment cases like *Henson*, on the other hand, require that proof that the harassment was pervasive and persistent be made instead in the fourth element. Proof of the fourth element is to show the extent at which the sexual harassment altered and impacted the victim's conditions of the employment. Put another way, under the

Shellhammer court's approach, unlike *Henson*, a numerical amount of harassment must be proved to determine the *nature* of the harassment as opposed to requiring a numerical amount to show the *impact* of the harassment of the victim. That means that only sexual harassment that occurs consistently for a long time is actionable.

As a means of contrast, in the *Gnerre* case, discussed next, the court rejected this strategy by pointing out that an approach such as in the *Shellhammer* case "does not recognize the variety of conduct that may constitute sexual harassment" (*Gnerre v. Massachusetts Commission Against Discrimination*).[20] The *Gnerre* court further explained that this condition for proving a hostile environment case, which it termed a "numerosity requirement," does not "recognize that different conduct, depending on its nature, can more or less quickly render a tenancy less desirable."[21] The significance of this difference can be seen in the differing results of the two cases. In *Gnerre*, the court found that the defendant created a hostile environment even though it amounted to only four incidents in two years. This was because the four incidents complained of were serious enough to render the plaintiff's tenancy less desirable. Clearly, if the *Gnerre* court had applied the *Shellhammer* pervasive and persistent requirement in order to prove the nature of the harassment, the plaintiff in the *Gnerre* case would not have prevailed (Butler, 1989).

There are several ethical problems with the *Shellhammer* court's approach to hostile environment cases. First, for a plaintiff to succeed, she must endure a potentially repugnant living situation for a relatively long time. The two solicitations for sex over a several-month period that Mrs. Shellhammer had to bear, for example, were apparently not pervasive and persistent enough to satisfy that court in proving the *nature* of the acts under the second element, although *impact* of the two solicitations likely created pervasive and persistent fear in the mind of Mrs. Shellhammer and consequently negatively altered her enjoyment of her tenancy. Second, under the pervasive and persistent approach, the court ignores the likely scenario of one particularly extreme episode of harassment, such as an attempted rape, as actionable sexual harassment. Put another way, if an attempted rape were the only thing that happened to the tenant and nothing more happened after that, she might not have an action under the logic of *Shellhammer*. However, the tenant would, thereafter, live under perpetual fear of the landlord. If that fear could be assessed in proving impact, as it was in the *Gnerre* rationale as discussed above, it would show that the tenant's fear of the landlord had a pervasive and persistent *impact* on her enjoyment of the tenancy but at the same time would fail in proving the *nature* of the harassment.

Another ethical criticism of the *Shellhammer* approach is the court's use of a subjective standard for ascertaining how the alleged offensive and hostile acts should be judged. As will be discussed, courts in sexual harassment cases in both employment and in housing generally use either an objective or subjective standard. To illustrate the latter, under a subjective standard in cases involving sexual harassment in housing, the court would look at how the offensive acts affected the *specific* victim's enjoyment of her tenancy as well as whether the acts in question were unwelcomed. The *Shellhammer* court chose the standard because the hostile conduct is "personal and subjective in nature." In addition the court explained that what" one person finds intolerable might be viewed as simply annoying or even amusing by another person" (*Shellhammer v. Lewallen*).[22]

At least one commentator (Butler, 1989) supports the *Shellhammer* court's use of the subjective standard. We submit that there is a major ethical problem with this approach. The concern involves how a hypersensitive tenant may react to certain acts by a landlord. In *Shellhammer*, the court stated that once a number of episodes of sexual harassment have occurred, satisfying the persistent and pervasive requirement of the second element, *whatever* a tenant personally feels to be offensive and therefore a negative alteration of her tenancy could amount to actionable sexual harassment. This would leave landlords open to costly lawsuits from such tenants.

The following is an example of how the foregoing could occur. Say that every time a landlord sees his tenant he says, "You sure look beautiful again today. You sort of remind me of Marilyn Monroe," or a similar such compliment. A hypersensitive tenant might feel that he is looking at her like a sex symbol and a sex object. Since the statement is made pervasively (almost everytime he sees her) over a period of time, all the tenant must do to win her case is prove by a preponderance of the evidence that the statements made her tenancy "burdensome" and "significantly less desirable."

This may seem improbable. However, sexual harassment cases in employment do not, in some cases, factor in the intent of the alleged harasser. For example, in the case of *Ellison v. Brady*,[23] the court explained that "well-intentioned compliments by co-workers or supervisors can form the basis of a sexual harassment cause of action if a reasonable victim of the same sex as the plaintiff would consider the comments sufficiently severe or pervasive to alter a condition of employment and create an abusive environment."[24] Indeed, because of this, some companies today do not permit workers to touch each other in any manner or fraternize after work for fear of how certain actions will be perceived. The fact remains that a landlord's open vulnerability to expensive litigation and possibly large settlements or judgments is, in the authors' view, too burdensome, unfair, and unethical of a standard to impose.

The *Shellhammer* case is indeed puzzling. In it there were legal advantages given to both the plaintiff and defendant, but the advantages to each went too far. On the one hand, the court ruled that proof of a number of abusive acts was necessary, directing that the acts must be pervasive and persistent. On the other hand, in adopting the subjective standard, the court ignored the severity and seriousness of the harassment. Put another way, by embracing the former requirement, the court created an unreasonably rigorous burden on tenants by requiring tenants to put up with a repugnant situation for a relatively long period of time in order to prevail. Then the court turned around and came down unreasonably hard on landlords by leaving the door open for a hypersensitive tenant to win her case once she had proven that the acts complained of were pervasive and persistent, even it they were perhaps quite harmless. As will be explained next, the authors support an objective standard, sometimes referred to as the *reasonable victim approach*. Neither the *Shellhammer* court, as mentioned, nor the *Gnerre* court, reviewed next, applied this standard.

The Gnerre *Case*

The *Gnerre* case arose out of a Massachusetts fair housing act. The Massachusetts law forbids an owner, lessee, sublessee, real estate broker, or other such party from discriminating against any person because of his or her race, religion, creed, color, national origin, sex, age, ancestry, or marital status in, among other situations, the "terms, conditions or privileges of such accommodations".[25] The statute also provides that its language should be "construed liberally" for the accomplishment of the policy goals.

In the 1988 case of *Gnerre v. Massachusetts Commission Against Discrimination*, the victim, Barbara Silverstein, a single mother, was subjected to unwelcomed harassment from her landlord, Antonio Gnerre. The harassment consisted of offensive speech of a sexual nature in which Gnerre made crude public comments regarding Silverstein's anatomy in front of her young son and queried her about how her sex life was. As a result, Silverstein felt "terribly embarrassed," "degraded," "cheap," and "low," following these incidents and suffered severe and prolonged stress as a result. She also testified that she became "terrified" of confronting Gnerre and changed her behavior patterns to avoid him.

The commissioner for the Massachusetts Commission Against Discrimination ruled that the facts were sufficient to prove sexual harassment under state law. The commissioner's ruling was subsequently affirmed by a state appellate court. The court held that two elements must be proved in a sexual harassment case: (1) the victim must be "subject to unsolicited harassment of a sexual nature," and (2) "the harassment was of such a nature as to make the tenancy significantly less desirable than if the harassment had not occurred" (*Gnerre v. Massachusetts Commission Against Discrimination*).[26]

As discussed, the *Gnerre* court expressly rejected what they referred to as a "numerosity requirement," contending that it fails to recognize a variety of harassment and that different conduct can swiftly render a tenancy less desirable. Earlier in this chapter, the authors lent their support for this approach, while opposing the *Shellhammer* court's reliance on a pervasive and persistent guideline.

Ethical and Legal Criticisms of the Gnerre Case

The authors do feel, however, that the *Gnerre* court's acceptance of the objective standard has notable ethical weaknesses. In the case, the court upheld the Commission's objective "reasonable person in the plaintiff's position" standard for judging whether the landlord's acts caused "a significant decline in the desirability of the tenancy" (*Gnerre v. Massachusetts Commission Against Discrimination*).[27] The average reasonable person standard has long been used in American jurisprudence and is still applicable in many situations today. The expression generally conveys two meanings. One is an ideal, although not a perfect person, on whose behavior an objective standard is used to measure and judge everyone's actions. The second is a typical or average person who has all the foibles and weaknesses that are tolerated by the community (Collins, 1987). A common application of the first meaning of the reasonable person standard had been in tort law, especially negligence. In car accidents, for example, courts look to how the average reasonable person in a similar situation would have driven and contrasts it with how the defendant actually drove. If the latter falls below the standard of how the average reasonable person would perform, the defendant would be in violation of a standard of care and so at fault for the accident. The second meaning has more application to sexual harassment in housing. Under this meaning we are looking at how a typical person in the community, with normal attributes, both strong and weak, would react in a given situation.

The problem with adopting a reasonable person standard to sexual harassment in housing is that men and women often perceive many kinds of sexual behavior differently. Clearly, certain extreme acts, such as rape, physical attacks, patently obscene language, and vulgar sexual advances would be similarly perceived. In those cases, a reasonable person standard would be sufficient. But in the so-called gray areas, the reasonable person standard would lack effectiveness.

Courts in sexual harassment employment cases have also raised this concern. In a 1990 federal Third Circuit case entitled *Drinkwater v. Union Carbide Corp.*,[28] the court ruled, among other things, that the victim must prove that the discrimination would detrimentally affect a "reasonable person of the same sex in that position." Similarly, in the 1991 case of *Ellison v. Brady*,[29] the federal Ninth Circuit rejected a reasonable person standard in favor of a reasonable victim (or reasonable women standard if the victim is a woman) standard. Since that time the federal Eighth Circuit court has likewise embraced the requirement (*Burns v. McGregor Electronic Industries*).[30]

The court, in *Ellison*, advanced several valid reasons for adopting this innovative stance. One was that a reasonable person standard tends to reinforce "stereotyped notions of acceptable behavior." Such a standard, the court explained, would allow harassers to continue to harass "merely because a particular discriminatory practice was common, and victims of harassment would have no remedy." The court justified this by arguing that the "sex-blind reasonable person standard tends to be male-biased and tends to systematically ignore the experiences of women" (*Ellison v. Brady*).[31] Put another way, in a reasonable person standard, which is dominated by how males view various acts with a sexual content, certain acts could be perceived as relatively harmless fun. However, a women evaluating the same exploits could very well be appalled. The court felt that one of the reasons for this is "because women are disproportionately victims of rape and sexual assault, women have a stronger incentive to be concerned with sexual behavior. Women who are victims of mild forms of sexual harassment may understandably worry whether a harasser's conduct is merely a prelude to violent sexual assault. Men, who are rarely victims of sexual assault, may view sexual conduct in a vacuum without a full appreciation of the social setting or the underlying threat of violence that a woman may perceive" (*Ellison v. Brady*).[32]

The adoption of the reasonable victim (or woman) standard would control the foregoing bias. At the same time, it would lessen the effects of the hypersensitive tenant that might prevail if a subjective standard is imposed, as was discussed earlier in the analysis of the *Shellhammer* case.

One strong and perhaps legitimate argument against adopting a reasonable victim standard is that legal liability could be imposed on a man for innocent, and what he would regard as, reasonable acts. This creates a virtual strict liability standard since fault or intent is not considered as a defense. We submit that, although not perfect, this standard is necessary in the area of housing. In fact, if a reasonable victim standard is considered by an increasing number of courts and commentators as applicable in employment situations, then certainly sexual harassment in housing should have at least as rigorous a standard. The reasons are self-evident. Tenants, particularly female tenants, are more vulnerable when they are harassed at home then in the workplace. They have no where to escape. Clearly, being sexually harassed in one's apartment can be far more crushing to the spirit than if it occurs in the workplace. As mentioned, the victims often are single and have children, making it difficult to leave. They frequently have to depend on the harassing landlord to repair things in their apartment, and this, plus the fear that they may be evicted for trumped up reasons, makes the victim even more exposed to harassment. If the victim is poor and has no other kind of affordable housing to go to, her choice may be between staying and being harassed or being homeless with her children. There is also little awareness of legal avenues and procedures for fighting this harassment. In the workplace, these policies are now generally well known and followed.

The reasonable victim standard also protects the landlord who does not harass his tenant. The reasonable victim or woman would likely not regard, for example, trivial kinds of flirtation, innuendo, or even certain kinds of offensive language even if the hypersensitive woman might. Also, as the *Ellison* case makes clear, there must generally be a pattern of offensive conduct unless the few incidents of harassment are truly severe. Furthermore, we agree by analogy with the EEOC in its Guidelines, which provide that the harassment must be conduct that "unreasonably interferes with an individual's work performance" or creates "an intimidating, hostile, or offensive working environment."[33] Accordingly, the average reasonable woman would have to feel that her tenancy was being unreasonably interfered with or her living environment was becoming intimidating before the harassment would be actionable.

Finally, the Supreme Court in the famous *Meritor Bank* case also stated that one must look at the "totality of the circumstances" in judging whether sexual harassment in employment exists. This can include, according to the Court, whether the victim exhibited "sexually provocative speech or dress" (*Meritor Bank v. Vinson*).[34] Although this has been criticized as tantamount to blaming the victim for the crime, we submit that a reasonable woman engaging in such speech or dress (the mythical average reasonable person isn't a saint) should be required to take into account another's reaction to her behavior.

Summary and Conclusion

Sexual harassment of tenants is indeed a serious problem that has only begun to receive attention in the popular press and in scholarly commentaries. It is very likely, however, that soon a particularly abhorrent act of sexual harassment will receive press attention sufficient to propel it into the nation's consciousness. If this occurs, the incidence of litigation will increase correspondingly.

We submit that the few cases that have addressed the issue have not approached it correctly from both legal and ethical standpoints. The *Shellhammer* failed to take into account particularly grave acts of sexual harassment and instead required a pervasive and persistent or "numerosity requirement." Its use of a subjective standard is also lacking because it could allow a hypersensitive tenant to wage a successful legal battle. The *Gnerre* case correctly, in our opinion, abandoned the quantitative requirement. However, that court failed when it adopted a reasonable person standard. Such a standard does not take into account the obvious differences between men and women. An average reasonable victim or woman standard, on the other hand, would incorporate those differences while protecting the landlord against the specious accusations of the hypersensitive tenant.

A number of other related legal and ethical issues must be further explored in the area of sexual harassment in housing. For example, might the strict and serious approach we have advocated have a deleterious effect on the parties it is meant to protect? For example, might landlords overreact and engage in a secret policy of not letting woman lease their apartments? Moreover, in this era of political correctness is a public housing supervisor's statements, albeit offensive in content, protected under the First Amendment since state action is involved? After all, the First Amendment was specifically designed to protect controversial expression from government control. Who is going to judge whether speech is simply distasteful on the one hand or obscene and pornographic in nature on the other? This in turn could create an unpleasant chilling effect on speech between landlords and tenants, perhaps worsening a relationship that needs to be congenial.

Clearly, the issue is full of intriguing and disturbing implications. In the meantime, courts and legislatures must continue to search for acceptable parameters for dealing with this vexing problem.

Notes

1. 4 Equal Opportunity Housing Reporter (P-H) sec. 15472 (W.D. Ohio Nov. 22, 1983), 770 F.2d 167 (6th Cir. 1986).
2. 524 N.E. 84 (Mass. 1988).
3. 42 U.S.C. sec. 2000(e) (1964).
4. 413 F. Supp. 654 (D.C. Cir. 1976).
5. 29 C.F.R. sec. 1604.11 (1980).
6. 29 C.F.R. sec. 1604.11 (1980).
7. 642 F.2d 934 (D.C. Cir. 1981).
8. 692 F.2d 897 (11th Cir. 1982).
9. 477 U.S. 57 (1986).
10. 42 U.S.C. sec. 3604 (1982).
11. 4 Equal Opportunity Housing Reporter (P-H) sec. 15,472 (W.D. Ohio Nov. 22, 1983), 770 F.2d 167 (6th Cir. 1986).
12. 689 F. Supp. 835 (N.D. Ill. 1988).
13. 694 F. Supp. 1101 (S.C.N.Y. 1988).
14. 7 Fair Housing Fair Lending (P-H) sec. 9.1 (E.D. Cal. Jan. 27, 1992).
15. Minnesota Statutes Annotated sec. 363.12.
16. 128 Wis. 2d 1988, 381 N.W. 561 (Ct. App. 1985).
17. 524 N.E. 84 (Mass. 1988).
18. 4 Equal Opportunity Housing Reporter (P-H) sec. 15,472 (W.D. Ohio Nov. 22, 1983).
19. 4 Equal Opportunity Housing Reporter (P-H) sec. 15,472 (W.D. Ohio Nov. 22, 1983).
20. 524 N.E. 84 (Mass. 1988).
21. 524 N.E. 84 (Mass. 1988).
22. 4 Equal Opportunity Housing Reporter (P-H) sec. 15,472 (W.D. Ohio Nov. 22, 1983).
23. 924 F.2d 872 (9th Cir. 1991).
24. 924 F.2d 872 (9th Cir. 1991).
25. Massachusetts Annotated Laws ch. 151B, sec. 1(6).
26. 524 N.E. 84 (Mass. 1988).
27. 524 N.E. 84 (Mass. 1988).
28. 904 F.2d 853 (3rd Cir. 1990).
29. 924 F.2d 872 (9th Cir. 1991).
30. No. 92-2059 (8th Cir. 1993).
31. 924 F.2d 872 (9th Cir. 1991).
32. 924 F.2d 872 (9th Cir. 1991).
33. 29 C.F.R. sec. 1604.11 (1980).
34. 477 U.S. 57 (1986).

List of Cases

Bundy v. Jackson, 642 F.2d 934 (D.C. Cir. 1981).
Burns v. McGregor Electronic Industries, No. 92-2059 (8th Cir. 1993).
Chomicki v. Wittkind, 128 Wis. 2d 188, 381 N.W. 561 (Ct. App. 1985).
Drinkwater v. Union Carbide Corp. 904 F.2d 853 (3rd Cir. 1990).
Ellison v. Brady, 924 F.2d 872 (9th Cir. 1991).
Fiedler v. Dana Properties, 7 Fair Housing-Fair Lending (P-H) sec. 9.1 (E.D. Cal. Jan. 27, 1992).

Gnerre v. Massachusetts Commission Against Discrimination, 524 N.E. 84 (Mass. 1988).

Grieger v. Sheets, 689 F. Supp. 835 (N.D. Ill. 1988).

Henson v. City of Dundee, 692 F.2d 897 (11th Cir. 1982).

Meritor Bank v. Vinson, 477 U.S. 57 (1986).

People of the State of New York by Abrams v. Merlino, 694 F. Supp. 1101 (S.D.N.Y. 1988).

Shellhammer v. Lewellan, 4 Equal Opportunity Housing Reporter (P-H) sec. 15,472 (W.D. Ohio, Nov. 22, 1983), 770 F.2d 167 (6th Cir. 1986).

United States v. Dana Properties.

Williams v. Saxbe, 413 F. Supp. 654 (D.C. Cir. 1976).

References

Aalberts, R.J., and M.T. Clauretie. (1992). "Sexual Harassment in Housing." *Journal of Property Management* 57(1): 44–47.

Butler, K. (1989). "Sexual Harassment in Rental Housing." *University of Illinois Law Review* 1989(1): 175–214.

Cahan, R. (1987). "Home Is No Haven: An Analysis of Sexual Harassment in Housing." *Wisconsin Law Review* 1987(2): 1061–1093.

Collins, R. (1987). "Language, History, and the Legal Process: A Profile of the Reasonable Man." *Rutgers-Camden Law Review* 8(2): 312–346.

Linn, D. (1989). "Sexual Harassment by Landlords." *Proof of Facts* 3: 581–622.

Whalen, C., and B. Whalen. (1985). *The Longest Debate: A Legislative History of the 1964 Civil Rights Act*. Washington, DC: Seven Locks Press.

15 THE NORMATIVE ASPECTS OF RENT CONTROL

Craig P. Dunn

Department of Management
College of Business Administration
San Diego State University

A. Quang Do

Department of Finance
College of Business Administration
San Diego State University

Abstract

Rent control occurs in various forms and is a prominent feature in many housing markets throughout the United States and in many countries around the world. In spite of an enormous literature, however, there has been very little discussion about the ethical aspects of rent regulations. This chapter uses the general ethics frameworks of concern for rights, overall welfare, and fairness to examine several of the key issues involved in rent control.

Introduction

In most major metropolitan areas, housing affordability is of great concern for policy makers. Rent control is an attempt to resolve, or at least alleviate, the high cost of rental housing. It is perhaps the most controversial governmental program to provide affordable housing to low-income families. Rent control—or more generically, rent regulation (Hanly, 1991)—occurs in various forms and is a prominent feature in housing markets throughout the United States and many other part of the world. In spite of an enormous literature, however, there has been very little discussion about the ethical aspects of rent regulation. This chapter examines the key issues involved in rent regulation from a variety of ethical points of view. The objective is to determine under what conditions a just price for rental housing might be established?

The general argument of both classical and neoclassical economists has been that to the extent a free market exists for residential rental housing stock, we need be little concerned about the ethics of rental regulation. Economists have consistently, and in many cases vociferously, argued that a *free*—and thereby *efficient*—market is an adequate mechanism for ensuring the fair price of goods and services provided under such market conditions (Friedman, 1982). To the extent that such economists have been concerned with ethics, it has been only to offer the claim that the free market is superior to other forms of resource allocation because it respects the *liberty* of both buyer and seller. However, it ought to be remembered that economists have developed special meanings for terms such as fair price that may have little to do with what constitutes a just price.[1] These terms need to be carefully distinguished. Throughout this study, the term *fair price* will be used to reference the economic understanding of a price established under the free-market conditions of unrestrained negotiation between a willing buyer and a willing seller who may or may not possess equal bargaining power. The term *just price* will refer to a price that is established through a fair process (the principle of *procedural justice*) and that results in a fair allocation of both wealth and housing (the principle of *distributive justice*).

The distinction between a just price and a fair price rests on the important differences between *allocation efficiency* and *normative value*. Notions of both efficiency and value are of central concern under conditions of resource scarcity. When such scarcity exists, as is often the case with rental housing stock, the desired outcome might be taken to be maximization of the *supply* of housing stock. Free-market transactions are well equiped to achieve the greatest number of outputs (rental housing units) relative to inputs (land, labor, and capital). What free-market transactions are not designed to do is to ensure that the resulting housing stock ends up in the right hands. Principles of procedural and distributive justice are designed to ensure such fairness in distributive allocations.

The force of the argument contained herein does not completely depend on the distinction between a fair price and a just price. Empirical, as well as logical, evidence will be offered suggesting the market for rental housing departs in significant ways from the free-market model, thus calling into question whether real-world economic conditions can be relied on to establish even a fair price (let alone a price that is just). To the extent this is the case, discussions of both ethical and social theory become relevant. Our attention will therefore turn to outlining the deontological (concern for rights), utilitarian (overall welfare), and justice (fairness) arguments that might be presented to provide an ethical justification for some form of rent regulation (see also Hanly, 1991)—and thereby lead to determination and establishment of a fair price for rental housing stock.

Historical Overview: A Brief Sketch

According to Arnott (1995), there are two generations of rent control (see Table 15.1). The first rent controls in the United States were put in place during World War I as a result of emergency shortages in the housing market. Materials and labor were in short supply when it came to building houses, since most resources were shifted to defense-related production. In order to prepare the country and its labor force for war, it was necessary for a large portion of the population to relocate, and this put many pressures on various local housing markets. State and federal rent regulations were crafted for the benefit of servicemen and their families, as well as for workers involved in manufacturing or preparing various war-related products. The primary purpose for rent control in this era was to protect these segments of the population from eviction and prevent widespread rent prof-

Table 15.1. Typology of rent regulation

	First-Generation Rent Control	Second-Generation Rent Control
Types of regulation	Freeze on nominal rent	Flexible rent control; allowable rent increases for inflation with cost pass-through provision, etc.
Purpose	To ensure affordable housing and preventing profiteering	70 assist low- and moderate-income households obtain decent housing at an affordable price with reasonable and fair rate of return to landlords
Jurisdiction	New York City (for pre-1947 housing)	Santa Monica, Los Angeles, Boston, San Francisco, etc.

iteering within the impacted areas (Keating, 1987). Many locally organized committees were formed and promoted by the U.S. Bureau of Industial Housing and Transportation to combat the profiteering.

It was at the beginning of World War II that rent freezes were put in place on a national scale. The strategy of freezing rents (initiated during wartime via the Emergency Price Control Act of 1942) originally seemed to be an acceptable idea for ensuring affordable housing. However, the subsequent shortage of rental housing and the owner-occupied housing boom resulted in the phasing out of most of the rent control programs in the United States.

Currently the city of New York is the only jurisdiction that still has many of the original rent control features. These stringent forms of rent control, however, are only for pre-1947 rental properties. While rent freezes are one obvious form of rent regulation, a more popular legislative course has been to limit the rent increase on properties. The Housing and Rent Act of 1947 began the process of eliminating federal rent controls. This Act provided prompt adjustments to property owners who were not receiving fair levels of rent. The Act was amended in 1949 in order to shift control from the federal government to individual states.

Following a period of economic stabilization, various forms of rent control measures have been implemented across the country. Approximately 200 cities and counties covering roughly 10 percent of the nation's housing stock presently have some form of rent regulation. The specific form of control varies from area to area and is generally highly flexible, having little in common with the early imposition of a ceiling rent level. By comparison with past controls, current forms of rent regulation are somewhat moderate in their restrictions (Hanly, 1991). Most rent control laws seek to ensure landowners a fair and reasonable risk-adjusted rate of return, one competitive with alternative investment opportunities. In addition, these regulations also allow landlords necessary increases to recoup operating expenses and generally exempt new rental housing stock from existing rental regulation. In Los Angeles, for example, the amount of rent increase is limited to only 7 percent per year in addition to the landlord's utility expenses. This limit is applicable only to current tenants and there are no restrictions on the amount of rent increases for new tenants.

Rent Prices and the Free Market

It is evident that the transition from rent control to alternate forms of rent regulation has largely been motivated by concern for the justice of measures that have the effect of fixing rent prices. Justice—or more particularly *distributive* justice—is an ethical concept that recognizes that "all . . . goods . . . are social goods [which] cannot be idiosyncratically valued" (Walzer, 1983, p. 7). Within a just society there need to be rational systems in place that allow for the establishment of just value for a variety of goods and services—including rents. As noted earlier, within free-market economies the actions of individual buyers and sellers are presumed to provide an adequate basis upon which fair value can be established. It ought to be here noted, however, that in addition to *free exchange, desert,* and *need* have been suggested as appropriate mechanisms for making distribution decisions that are just (Walzer, 1983, p. 21).

It is generally recognized that there are several assumptions underlying the free-market model that do not hold in the real world for rental space. Three relevant assumptions underlying the free-market model are (1) the presumption that there are a great number of buyers (renters) and sellers (landowners) in a particular market, (2) that both buyers and sellers possess roughly the same degree of bargaining power relative to one another, and (3) that the product (rental stock) is of a relatively homogeneous character. While this chapter follows a long tradition of distinguishing between what *ought* to be (the domain of *prescriptive* or *normative* inquiry) and what *is* (the domain of *descriptive* or *empirical* or *positivistic* analysis), it should be noted that the normative arguments that are presented herein rely, in part, for their theoretic force on the claim that these three market conditions are not empirically grounded. The argument here offered is not that rent control has been ineffective (a point to be discussed elsewhere) but rather that assumptions about market conditions for rental property depart in significant ways from the assumptions underlying the free-market model.

Market Failure: The Case of Monopoly

Let us critically examine each of these claims in turn. Suppose for the moment two markets, with identical rental housing stocks, that differ only in that in the first market there are an equal number of buyers (renters) and sellers (landowners) and in the second there are many buyers but only one seller. Obviously, the second case can be characterized as a classic monopoly. But what is wrong with monopolies? "Monopoly describes a way of owning or controlling social goods in order to exploit their dominance" (Walzer, 1983, p. 11). So it is not the market failure of monopoly, *per se,* that poses the problem but rather the opportunity for dominance—the ability to "command a wide range of other goods" (Walzer, 1983, p. 10)—which leads to distributions of wealth that are considered unjust on the grounds that they result in "social and economic inequalities" that cannot be "reasonably expected to be to everyone's advantage" (as cited in De George, 1986, p. 77). Of course, it might be argued that due to their supernormal profits, monopolistic markets can be expected to attract other opportunistic sellers. To the extent that the monopolistic operator has exclusive control over the rental housing stock, conjoined with the fact that urban space is by definition finite, there may be *no opportunity* for new entrants in the marketplace. At a minimum, real estate transactions may create what has been termed by James Graascamp "monopoly in an instant." With the seller bearing the ability to uniquely control the market during what for the buyer is likely to be a critically short time span of search behavior, alternatives become irrelevant. The degree of uniqueness of housing stock, with resultant lack of substitutability, intensifies the occasion for price setting. The rents that are likely to inhere in a monopolistic market—absent moral restraint on the part of the seller—are therefore likely to be *unjust*. In such hypothetical cases, some variant of rent regulation would certainly seem appropriate.

The truth is that rental markets don't mirror either one of these hypothetical cases (neither complete lack of regulation nor rent control represent the appropriate legislative stance). *To the extent* rental markets depart from an assumption of pure competition, rental regulation is more or less appropriate. Rental regulation is not justified *carte blanche*; rather, rental markets need to be assessed on a case-by-case basis to determine whether or not the assumptions of free-market capitalism are in sufficient evidence that the market can be relied on to establish a fair price for rental housing. Rental markets need to be reevaluated whenever there is the reasonable expectation that concentration of rental stock ownership has been substantially altered.

It is worth briefly noting the interdependence of fair housing costs and other social objectives. Recent reports indicate that some low-income families spend as much as 60 percent of their income on rent. Such families are unable to save sufficient funds to qualify for home ownership. DiPasquale and Glaeser note that "homeowners are 10 percent more likely than renters to work to solve local problems, or know their local congressman by name. . . . they're also more likely to vote in local elections, . . . and join nonprofessional organizations" (article is from Business Week 6/15/98, p. 30, from 'Economic Trends' column; piece is entitled 'The Rewards of Homeownership,' and begins 'Should the Federal Government . . . , 1998). Additionally, to the extent huge proportions of income are allocated to rents, families are more likely to rely on other forms of public assistance. In short, carefully crafted rent regulation bears the capacity to achieve much more than the stated objective of ensuring affordable housing.

Market Failure: The Case of Unequal Bargaining Power

The second assumption of the free-market that is under scrutiny—the claim that buyers and sellers possess roughly equal bargaining power—is clearly related to the assumption just reviewed. Resource-dependence models of human interaction (see, e.g., Pfeffer and Salancik, 1978) suggest that disparities in the wealth of two bargaining parties result in the wealthier party gaining a clear transactional advantage over the poorer party. This power disparity can occur, however, only to the extent that the resource being bargained for is of critical importance to the weaker party. Consider, for the purposes of illustration, a very wealthy person bargaining with a very poor person to establish the price for a preowned Lamborghini Countach that the rich person is offering for sale. The conditions for exploitation are not in force, for it is not likely that the monetarily challenged prospective purchaser has a strong interest in acquiring an automobile that costs thousands of dollars a year to operate. Other transportation options are available. But take this same buyer and have her negotiate a rental price for an apartment this same wealthy landowner is offering for occupancy, and the possibility for exploitation is clear. Why? We are now discussing a resource—affordable housing—on which the poorer party is dependent for her very survival. The paradox is that to the extent affordable housing is in short supply, the greater the likelihood that landowners will be able to exact rents above a fair price. The ability of the landowner to set the rental price is, of course, dependent on the availability of affordable housing from other sources. Our claim is that the market can be relied on to set a fair rent price only if the bargaining parties have roughly equal power—and that rent regulation is appropriate to the extent that bargaining power is unequal.

Market Failure: The Case of Product Heterogeneity

The third free-market assumption has to do with the relative homogeneity of the rental housing stock. The seeming conflict between endemic homelessness and high rental vacancy rates—and abundance of housing generally and scarcity of affordable housing specifically—can be better understood when variations among housing markets are considered. As Gilderbloom and Applebaum (1987) point out, arising from the heterogeneous nature of properties, as well as variations among submarkets, there are a myriad of ways in which the rental housing market departs in crucial respects from the conditions underlying the perfect competitive model. Real estate agents, after all, have been telling us for decades that location is everything. To the extent this is true, no two properties are truly identical—nor can they be. To return to an earlier example, while it might be argued that one Lamborghini Countach is the same as any other, this argument cannot be extended to rental housing. Not only is each property unique; there may be no close substitutes for the rental housing that a buyer occupies. The market for rental housing is more like the market for pets than the market for automobiles. Time, experience, and personalization tend to create heterogenous markets. Each pet is unique, with particular attributes that recommend it to its owner. Most pet owners, if asked to trade their pet for one of seemingly identical breeding, stature, marking, and temperament, would be unwilling to do so. The collective, internalized, personal experiences associated with living with a pet for an extended period of time result in uniqueness. Such experiences are clearly not objective attributes of the pet but create value nonetheless. And therefore most pet owners would place a value on their pet that is significantly higher than the value the free-market would establish for said pet. This simile is relevant to discussions concerning our reliance on the allocational efficiency of the free-market as the appropriate price-establishing mechanism for rental housing, for to the extent that goods are truly unique there does *not* exist a free market for such goods; and one might well ask whether or not there really *should* be a free market for unique goods, such as priceless art. Renters might be tied to particular locales due to job concerns (Hanly, 1991, p. 193), caring relationships with family and neighbors, educational opportunities for their children and themselves, and any number of other economic and noneconomic considerations. Houses, condominiums, and apartments become home, a place that has meaning beyond the boundaries of the physical space that such a structure occupies. To the extent this is true, and the perceived value of the home is greater than its value in the free market, the relative bargaining power of the landowner is enhanced. Implications relative to the free market's lack of ability to establish a just price under such a power imbalance should be evident.

Again, the point is not that the free market can never be relied on to establish a fair price for rental housing. It can be relied on but only to the extent that the assumptions underlying the free-market model are present in the real world. Whether these assumptions are veritable is largely an empirical question. Our claim is that we ought not paint rent regulation with a broad brush by claiming that such policies are never justified or always justified. Rather, we favor an approach that seeks justification for rent regulation on a case-by-case basis. Overall, the rental housing market seems at best to be imperfectly competitive. There are only a handful of empirical studies on the effects of rent control (see, e.g., Olsen, 1972; Hubert, 1993; Marks, 1984; Moon and Stotsky, 1993; Smith and Tomlinson,

1981; Albon and Stafford, 1990). Althought taken collectively the results of these studies (see, for example, Marks, 1986; Santerre, 1986; DeSalvo, 1971; Roistacher, 1972; Linneman, 1987; Gyourko and Linneman, 1989; Ho, 1992) seem to affirm the negative effects of rent control, they are not entirely persuasive due to shortcomings of the housing data or the econometrics and also due to the complexity in different measures of rent control (Hubert, 1993). In those instances in which the market for rental property adequately reflects the assumptions of the free market outlined above, rent regulation is not clearly justified. Under such conditions, the free-market can be relied on to establish a fair price for rental housing. Conversely, in those instances in which the free-market assumptions do not hold, resulting in market failure, an alternative mechanism for establishing just rental prices needs to be sought. In such instances legislative relief in the form of rent regulation may well be normatively justified, on the grounds that reasoned social judgment is that certain households, or classes of households, *should* have affordable housing. Such social judgment begs the question of who appropriately pays for losses associated with rent regulation, an issue that will be taken up in due course. Attention will next turn to the normative bases on which such justification might be grounded.

Rent Prices and Ethics

Normative analysis, or *ethics*, is concerned with what ought to be rather than with what is, and seeks an answer to what is good and bad, what is right and wrong, and what is just and unjust. Three general ethics frameworks guide our inquiry into the establishment of a proper rent price: (1) *deontology*, or concern for rights (De George, 1995, pp. 83–84), (2) *utilitarianism*, or concern for overall welfare (De George, 1995, p. 61), and (3) *justice*, or concern for fairness (De George, 1995, p. 72). It is our contention that none of these frameworks can be relied on exclusively as a normative option to free-market rent setting. However, collectively these ethical systems bring to the fore the relevant issues that must be considered when negotiating a fair rent. And each framework implies specific policy positions relevant to the formulation of rent regulation.

Just Rent Prices: The Rights Perspective

These ethical frameworks are examined in turn, with the twin aim of applying each system to the particular problem of establishing a fair rental price as well as outlining the policy implications that might follow from each such analysis. *Deontology* is an ethical system that suggests that actions are right or wrong independent of their consequences. Immanuel Kant has been credited with developing this view, which presupposes that moral persons can discover authentic moral truth through the exercise of their capacity for pure reason. Deontological arguments often take the form of specifying the (potentially competing) rights-claims within a particular moral dilemma—and determining which rights-claims have precedence.

Several interests are in conflict when the task is to establish a fair rental price. It can be argued landowners have rights that are grounded in our notions of property ownership. Property rights confer on the owner of property the exclusive right to the use, quiet enjoyment, and disposition of said property. While these rights can be assigned to others, they are still most fundamentally rights that attach to the ownership of property. Renting one's property to another, of course, represents one mechanism by which some of the rights attending property ownership are transferred—albeit temporarily—to another party. At issue here is how to value the right to use and quiet enjoyment of particular landholdings. But this is not the most fundamental issue, for rental landowners are not merely property owners. They are capitalists as well. As such, they have a right to a fair return on their investment in rental property. So it would seem that landowners are entitled to a rent that represents a fair compensation for the value of the use and quiet enjoyment privileges that the tenant experiences, plus a fair return commensurate with their financial and marketplace risk.[2]

Rights-claims are seldom, if ever, absolute. They are most often tempered by the rights-claims of other affected parties. The general principle is that one is free to pursue one's interests so long as in the pursuit of such interests one does not infringe on the equal or greater rights of others. In the current context the other is, of course, the tenant. Tenants have rights of specific contract, which usually include the transfer of the use and quiet enjoyment privileges of the owner to the tenant in return for rent paid. Beyond this, renters benefit from a social contract that seeks to ensure that rents not be usuriously established by monopolistic owners. Tenants also are entitled to some minimum level of maintenance of the property that they occupy—a privilege derived from a more fundamental right to their health and safety. Any other specific rights that inhere within any particular landowner and tenant contract are a matter of negotiated agreement.

Deontological rights-claims are directly relevant to the establishment of rent regulation. In the absence of competitive market forces serving to reliably establish a fair rent price, and even under such conditions when the establishment of a just price is clearly called into question, such prices need to be legislatively influenced. Under such conditions policy makers ought to take care to arrive at a price that appropriately balances the competing interests of landowners and tenants. These interests, or rights-claims, will not only vary from geographic locale to geographic locale but also from individual transaction to individual transaction. The challenge for regulators under such conditions is to craft policy that is just across the board but that respects the individual differences of particular rental agreements.

Just Rent Prices: The Greatest-Good Perspective

One common criticism of the deontological focus on rights-claims is that within this framework the *outcomes* of particular courses of action are taken to be altogether *irrelevant*. Consequentialist ethical frameworks seek to remedy this oversight by specifying the particular results that are of essential importance in moral decision making and then suggesting the right action is the one that achieves this desired outcome. *Utilitarianism* is one form of consequentialism. First proposed by Jeremy Bentham (1823/1970) and John Stuart Mill (1863/1962), utilitarian moral systems specify that right action is action that achieves the *greatest amount of good* for the *greatest number of persons*. Utilitarian analysis asks us to weigh the benefits and costs of alternative courses of action—in our general case, rent regulation versus no rent regulation—and then select that alternative that maximizes good consequences over bad consequences. In focusing on maximizing net benefits the utilitarian model allows no place for second- or third-best alternatives in the proper resolution of the moral problem. More sophisticated versions of utilitarianism would require assessing the impacts of a variety of rent regulations relative to one another.

Utilitarianism has the effect of translating ethical concerns into empirical questions relating to the benefits and costs associated with alternative courses of action. Regardless of the specific form, rent regulation usually achieves its intended aim of rent reduction—an immediate benefit for renters. This savings is the difference between rents under rent control conditions and the rent landowners would extract in the absence of such limits. But rent reduction is not a free good. This benefit comes at a cost. One common criticism of rent regulation is that if rents are legislatively controlled, landowners can be expected to reduce their commitment to property maintenance in order to offset the decrease in gross income attending regulation. Such neglect leads to housing stock deterioration and a commensurate reduction in the quality—and ultimately the quantity—of housing services available to tenants. An alternative response to restrictions on rental unit profitability may be for landowners to abandon the rental business altogether by either boarding up properties or converting properties to alternative uses such as condominiums—again resulting in a reduction of affordable rental housing stock. Unless specifically excluded from regulation, limitations on the amount of rent charge reduce the financial feasibility of proposed projects and thereby retard new rental property development—ultimately leading to disequilibrium in the rental segment of the housing market as more tenants seek scarcer rental housing (Smith and Tomlinson, 1981; Downs, 1983). All these actions represent the costs of achieving the benefit of affordable housing—and indeed occur in the market for controlled properties.

Utilitarian concerns, however, are not limited to economic considerations. It has been argued that there are specific social costs associated with rent regulation. Tenants' mobility is restricted to the extent they become dependent on artificially low rents that may not be readily available in alternative communities. There is some evidence that a black market for affordable housing develops in those municipalities that have adopted strict rent control measures (Goetze, 1983; Hubert, 1993). The normative prescription of utilitarianism requires quantification of all of the benefits and costs associated with alternative forms of rent regulation—the *benefits* of affordable housing and the enhanced standard of living of tenants, the *benefits* of unemployment reductions as government agencies hire bureaucrats to staff rent-control housing offices, the *costs* of decreases in landowner profit, the *costs* of degradation in both the quality and quantity of rental housing stock, as well as the *costs* of restricted mobility and black-market payments—and selection of that policy prescription that maximizes good consequences over bad consequences. There are less tangible benefits and costs to be considered as well, such as those associated with social control *vs* individual choice.[3]

The local character of such benefits and costs has been overlooked in the majority of discussions of rent regulation as social commentators have sought to prove either that rent control is good or bad. The position taken here is that such notions of good or bad can be understood only in the context of that *specific local housing market* under *current consideration*. All rent regulation should not be dismissed merely because it can be demonstrated that in one municipality strict uncompromising rent control has led to deterioration in available affordable housing. Admittedly this is an undesirable outcome, but perhaps a more moderate form of rent regulation would have worked in this same community. Or perhaps this cost was more than offset by the benefit of a higher level of owner-occupied housing as apartments were converted to condominiums and subsequently purchased by former tenants.[4] A normative analysis of the appropriateness of rent regulation requires that policy be grounded in a true assessment of local housing conditions and in the projected overall impact of alternative policy prescriptions on this specific community.

Nor are we ready to rely *exclusively* on utilitarian arguments. It is evident that even if it could be conclusively demonstrated that the costs of rent regulation outweighed the benefits—or *vice versa*—issues of rights cannot be easily overlooked. Consider this classic formulation of the potential conflict between rights and outcomes: "Would you be willing to murder an innocent person if it would end hunger in the world?" For most of us, the mere fact that a good outcome would be achieved by the murder of the innocent would not fully justify the act. We might *nonetheless* be willing to take this action but only after carefully considering that this act would violate the victim's right to live. The rights of landowners and tenants, as described earlier, cannot be fully discounted in favor of utilitarian concerns. Rather, *both* rights *as well as* outcomes need to be taken seriously as public policy relating to rent regulation is designed. And both the quest to balance potentially competing rights claims, as well as the search for the greatest good, need to be tempered with concern for the *justice* of the rent regulation under consideration if we are to arrive at a more completely satisfactory ethical outcome (Brady and Dunn, 1995).

Just Rent Prices: The Distributive-Justice Perspective

"The idea of distributive justice presupposes a bounded world within which distributions take place: a group of people committed to dividing, exchanging, and sharing social goods, first of all among themselves" (Walzer, 1983, p. 31). Considerations of justice seek to remedy one of the failings of utilitarianism, which is that the least advantaged members of society can continue to be made worse off within the utilitarian logic, as long as the greatest good for the greatest number is achieved. This outcome is also consistent with the logic of the free market. Moral intuition suggests a lack of justice in such a conception of ethics.

One useful mechanism for deciding on the just course of action is offered by Rawls (1971). Rawls introduces the notion of the "veil of ignorance," asking us to consider what societal rules we would agree to if we had no idea what our station in life within a particular society would be. Suppose for the moment two societies, each with 100 members and each with equal aggregate wealth. In the first society, all wealth is held by a single individual. In the second, wealth is equally distributed among all 100 citizens. In which society would you prefer to live? While our answer to this question is to some extent influenced by our risk tolerance, as a general principle Rawls argues our choices are strongly influenced by our knowledge of *who we are* within the society: I am more likely to opt for the first society if I know I will be the one landowner. In order to avoid the moral failure of making decisions that are primarily influenced by our self-interest, consideration needs to be given to what policies would be supported if we had *no knowledge* of how such regulations would affect us personally.

Rawls's principle of the "veil of ignorance" has clear implications for rent regulation. Again suppose two societies, each with 100 members and each with equal aggregate wealth—but in this case in *each* society one person both owns and controls all the landholdings of the community. In the first society, rent regulations place a cap on allowable housing charges. In the second, the single landowner is free to set rent prices at whatever level she sees fit.[5] Again the question is, in which society would you prefer to live? Having no knowledge of our position in society, one would likely opt to live in the regulated society. Why? Because there is a high likelihood that one would end up with the status of a tenant, rather than that of the landowner, and under monopolistic conditions would see the merit in resorting to non-market pricing mechanisms in order to establish a just price for rental housing.

The decision to impose rent regulation under conditions of market failure admittedly does not present us with a thorny moral dilemma.[6] Nor would we encounter a severe ethical challenge if considering the appropriateness of rent regulation under conditions of perfect comptetition because absent an empirical justification for rent control, we would choose to live free from such unnecessary mandates. What Rawls adds to our understanding of the complexities associated with moral choice is the role of *self-interest* (or *moral failure*) in making decisions related to the allocation of scarce resources. We *are* less likely to support rent regulation if such restrictions have a deleterious effect on us personally—even if such measures are empirically justified. However, we *ought not* to be less likely to support rent regulation if such restrictions have a deleterious effect on us personally—if such measures are empirically justified. The present concern is with this latter statement, for we are developing principles of *prescriptive* rather than *descriptive* ethical theory.

Rawls makes another contribution relevant to our understanding of the ethical justification for rent regulation. Again consider two societies, each of which has 100 members, and in each of which five persons both own and control all the landholdings of the community. In both societies, rent regulations currently place a cap on the allowable housing charges. However, in the second society the resolve to continue rent control has weakened, and a revocation of rent controls is imminent. Again the question is, in which society would you prefer to live? Having no knowledge of our position in society, one would likely opt to live in the regulated society recognizing the occasion for price gouging under oligopolistic market conditions. But suppose it could be empirically demonstrated that the greatest good for the greatest number could be achieved through a revocation of rent regulation? Does achievement of this utilitarian objective bear sufficient force to support abandonment of rent regulation? Rawls's answer is no and for a very specific reason. There seems something fundamentally wrong, says Rawls, with making even the majority better off if this improvement comes at the expense of the *least advantaged members of society*. The free market cannot be relied on to achieve a just price for rental housing, even if market forces achieve good utilitarian outcomes. Beyond concern for rights and outcomes, Rawls would have policy makers consider the impact of their decisions on those members of society who are already the least fortunate. If proposed policy changes negatively impact these citizens, the action is morally unacceptable—in spite of its consistency with important rules or its ability to benefit even a supermajority. For the least advantaged of our society, the interests of the beneficiaries of rent regulation deserve special consideration as public policy relating to rent control is drafted.

Conclusion

This essay has discussed the development of a normative grounding for rent regulation. The conclusion has been that the free-market bears the *potential* to provide such a grounding in that perfectly competitive markets can achieve a fair price, but that in many specific instances rental market conditions depart in potentially important respects from the assumptions of free-market capitalism, calling into question whether the action of a free market necessarily results in a just price. Under such conditions of market failure, rent regulation may be justified. However, such regulation needs to fully reflect the extent to which the local rental market violates free-market conditions. The general principle is that regulation is only *empirically* justified to the extent that there is hard evidence of market failure. In order to be *normatively* or *ethically* justified, the specific form such regulation takes ought to demonstrate (1) respect for the rights of all affected parties (the *deontological* condition), (2) achievement of the greatest good for the greatest number (the *utilitarian* condition), and (3) preference for the interests of the least advantaged members of society (the *justice* condition) (Rawls, 1971).[7]

Adequate housing[8] is necessary for the life and well-being of our citizenry. As with all vital societal resources, our governmental representatives hold a legitimate interest in ensuring reasonable access to housing for all our citizens. There are a full range of options available to achieve the goal of reasonable access to housing, ranging from government ownership of public housing stock to *laissez faire* free-market capitalism. Assuring a just price for rental housing represents a justified intrusion of government into the free-market when market failure can be empirically verified or when the operation of a free market erodes the interests of the least-advantaged members of our society. The normative guidelines outlined in this chapter should serve policy makers well as they seek a just substitute for a market pricing mechanism.[9]

Market failure *per se* is not as problematic as those cases in which monopolistic conditions exist *and* monopolists behave in a self-interested manner insensitive to the rights and welfare of tenants. Our assumption throughout has been that individuals will secure positions of economic advantage wherever possible. However, it is worth noting that *moral restraint* on the part of ologopolist landowners would resolve the harmful consequences of opportunistic marketplace behavior. Such restraint would be a useful substitute for governmental regulation. The economic assumption of self-interested buyers and sellers, however, precludes taking this possibility seriously. This is true even if landowners were subject to a unified set of professional standards in the same way that, say, physicians and attorneys are. Currently, the best that can be offered are several specific ethical frameworks that bear some potential for the crafting of rent regulation.

Notes

1. Consider, for example, the economists use of the term *rational man*. This concept has nothing to do with acting consistently with reasoned principles; rather, to the economist a rational man is one who acts according to the dictates of self-interest.

2. The measurement complexities associated with establishing alternative rates of return only ameliorate the difficulty of establishing a fair return on investment.

3. Perhaps the thorniest issue has to do with costing *efficiency* (or the lack thereof).

4. The quasi-speculative nature of the preceding two hypotheticals is here acknowledged.

5. Of course, one might reject the premise of this construction and argue that the monopolist is at risk from both within as from outside the existing market. To this end, one can choose to accept rent as imposed, to move to a new community, or to overthrow the rulers of the

existing power structure. While these possibilities are here acknowledged, they have little to do with the force of Rawls argument in favor of making decisions from behind a "veil of ignorance."

6. Unless, of course, we take the libertarian position that we should *maximize* the capacity for free, informed personal choice—and that property rights are critical to the preservation of such liberty. In this case property rights are trump, and no amount of benefit can justify the erosion of liberty attending regulation.

7. It could be argued such provisions have provided the justification for current legislation, such as the 1949 Housing Act.

8. Admittedly a difficult term to define precisely.

9. The process used to arrive at rent regulation is as important as its content. Systems that are procedurally just are recommended (Rawls, 1971).

References

Albon, R., and D. Stafford. (1990). "Rent Control and Housing Maintenance." *Urban Studies* 27(2) (April): 233–240.

Arnott, R. (1995). "Time for Revisionism on Rent Control?" *Journal of Economic Perspectives* 9(1): 99–120.

Bentham, J. (1823/1970). *An Introduction to the Principles of Morals and Legislation*. Oxford.

Brady, N., and C. Dunn. (1995). "Business Meta-Ethics: An Analysis of Two Theories." *Business Ethics Quarterly* 5(3): 385–398.

De George, R. (1986). *Business Ethics*. Englewood Cliffs, NJ: p. 77 ff.

De George, R. (1995). *Business Ethics*. Englewood Cliffs, NJ. pp. 61–84.

DeSalvo, J. (1971). "Reforming Rent Control in New York City: An Analysis of Housing Expenditures and Market Rentals." *Regional Science Association Papers and Proceedings* 27 (December): 195–227.

Downs, A. (1983). *Rental Housing in the 1980s*. Washington, DC: Brookings Institution.

Friedman, M. (1982). *Capitalism and Freedom*. Chicago: University of Chicago Press.

Gilderbloom, J., and R. Appelbaum. (1987). "Toward a Sociology of Rent: Are Rental Housing Markets Competitive?" *Social Problems* (June): 261–276.

Goetze, R. (1983). *Rescuing the American Dream: Public Policy and the Crisis in Housing*. New York: Holmes and Meier.

Gyourko, J., and P. Linneman. (1989). "Equity and Efficiency Aspects of Rent Control: An Empirical Study of New York City." *Journal of Urban Economics* 26 (July): 54–74.

Hanly, K. (1991). "The Ethics of Rent Control." *Journal of Business Ethics* 10: 189–200.

Ho, L. (1992). "Rent Control: Its Rationale and Effects." *Urban Studies* 29(7): 1183–1190.

Hubert, F. (1993). "The Impact of Rent Control on Rents in the Free Sector." *Urban Studies* 30(1): 51–61.

Keating, D. (1987). "Landlord Self-Regulation: New York City's Rent Stabilization System 1969–85." *Journal of Urban and Contemporary Law* 31 (Winter): 77–134.

Lett, M. (1976). *Rent Control: Concepts, Realities, and Mechanisms.* New Brunswick: Center for Urban Policy Research.

Linneman, P. (1987). "The Effect of Rent Control on the Distribution of Income Among New York City Renters." *Journal of Urban Economics* 22 (July): 14–34.

Marks, D. (1984). "The Effect of Rent Control on the Price of Rental Housing: An Hedonic Approach." *Land Economics* 60(1) (February): 81–94.

Marks, D. (1986). "The Effect of Rent Control on the Price of Rental Housing: A Reply." *Land Economics* 62(1) (February): 106–108.

Mill, J. (1863/1962). "On Liberty." In M. Cohen (ed.), *The Philosophy of John Stuart Mill.* New York.

Moon, C., and J. Stotsky. (1993). "The Effect of Rent Control on Housing Quality Change: A Longitudinal Analysis." *Journal of Political Economy* 101(6): 1114–1148.

Olsen, E. (1972). "An Econometric Analysis of Rent Control." *Journal of Political Economy* 80 (November-December): 1081–1100.

Pfeffer, J., and G. Salancik. (1978). *The External Control of Organizations: A Resource-Dependence Perspective.* New York.

Rawls, J. (1971). *A Theory of Justice.* Cambridge, MA.

Roistacher, E. (1972). "The Distribution of Tenant Benefits Under Rent Control." Ph.D. dissertaion, University of Pennsylvania.

Santerre, R. (1986). "The Effect of Rent Control on the Price of Rental Housing: A Reply." *Land Economics* 62(1) (February): 104–105.

Smith, L., and P. Tomlinson. (1981). "Rent Control in Ontario: Roofs or Ceilings?" *AREUEA Journal* (Summer): 93–114.

Walzer, M. (1983). *Spheres of Justice.* New York: 31.

Index